A very happy Christmas
to my old drama teacher
and dear friend.
Sincerely,
Bill

Mary McCarthy's Theatre Chronicles

1937–1962

Mary McCarthy's
Theatre Chronicles 1937–1962

BY MARY McCARTHY

FARRAR, STRAUS AND COMPANY
New York

The major part of this book was originally published in 1956 as *Sights and Spectacles*.

Library of Congress catalog card number 63–18449
First Printing, 1963

Published simultaneously in Canada by
Ambassador Books, Ltd., Toronto
Manufactured in the U.S.A.

CONTENTS

Introduction   vii

TWO BAD CASES OF SOCIAL CONSCIENCE   3

ODETS DEPLORED   9

ELIZABETHAN REVIVALS   13

CLASS ANGLES AND A WILDER CLASSIC   21

THE FEDERAL THEATRE   30

SHAW AND CHEKHOV   39

SAROYAN, AN INNOCENT ON BROADWAY   46

THE SKIN OF OUR TEETH   53

THE RUSSIAN SOUL IN WARTIME   57

BROADWAY'S SPRING OFFENSIVE   63

WARTIME OMNIBUS   67

WE MUST HAVE FAITH   76

EUGENE O'NEILL—DRY ICE   81

FIVE CURIOS   89

GEORGE KELLY   97

THE UNIMPORTANCE OF BEING OSCAR   106

THREE PLAYS WITH MUSIC   111

WHAT A PIECE OF WORK IS MAN!   116

FOUR "WELL-MADE" PLAYS   121

A STREETCAR CALLED SUCCESS   131

LITTLE THEATRE   136

A PRINCE OF SHREDS AND PATCHES   141

THE LITTLE GATE   146

SHAW OFF BROADWAY   151

THE FAMILY TEA PARTY   163

THE WILL AND TESTAMENT OF IBSEN   168

SHEEP IN WOLVES' CLOTHING   179

A NEW WORD   186

ODD MAN IN   199

THE AMERICAN REALIST PLAYWRIGHTS   209

DRAPES   230

GENERAL MACBETH   235

INTRODUCTION

For the current reader, the point of view of this book may be hard to locate; where is this criticism coming from? "It is to be hoped that Mr. Young will devote himself to one of Chekhov's more mature plays." So *The Seagull* in a distinguished dramatic critic's adaptation was dismissed by an insufferable little-magazine reviewer— myself, twenty years ago. This probably could not have happened in England, or France or Italy, even during the thirties; only in America, or rather in a tiny section of New York, could an air of supreme authority be assumed with so few credentials.

In the first fourth of the book the reader will find quite a few such sentences, which make me wince with pain to read over but which I have let stand, in the interests of the record and because I think anyone who could write so foolishly owes a debt to society that cannot be cancelled out by the mere process of getting older. But it is not usually the opinions I aired (as in this case) that give me such pain to hear again; it is the tone of voice in which they are pronounced—the voice of a young, earnest, pedantic, pontificating critic, being cocksure and condescending.

"The playwright assumes that his hero's irresolution is

of a tragic order, while, as a matter of fact, it is comico-pathetic." It is the voice of a period as well as that of a person. The period was 1937—the time of the Spanish Civil War and the Moscow Trials. The place was Union Square, New York, where radical demonstrations were always held and which was surrounded by cheap dress shops, cafeterias, subway kiosks and run-down office build-ings, like the one at 22 East 17 Street, a tall, skinny, grey building at the northern end, the first address of the new *Partisan Review*, a magazine that had been "stolen" from the Communists by a group of young people, including me, who were supposed to be Trotskyites. This whole region was Communist territory; "they" were everywhere—in the streets, in the cafeterias; nearly every derelict build-ing contained at least one of their front-groups or schools or publications. Later, when the magazine moved to the old Bible House on Astor Place, *The New Masses* had offices on the same floor, and meeting *"them"* in the elevator, riding down in silence, enduring their cold scrutiny, was a prospect often joked about but dreaded. The fact of being surrounded physically, of running a gamut, was a concrete illustration of their power in New York at that time, a power that spread uptown to pub-lishers' offices and to the Broadway theatre and to various cultural agencies of the Government, like the W.P.A. Writers Project and the Federal Theatre. They were strong, and we were weak, and the note of haughty disdain found in the early pieces of this book was, in part, a girl's way of meeting this unequal situation.

The story that we on *Partisan Review* were Trotskyists was an exaggeration. The boys, as we used to call the prin-cipal editors because they were always in the back room, powwowing, had been through the Communist discipline, which made them wary of direct political ties. We wanted to be wholly independent in artistic matters, and the daring of our attitude was summed up in the statement that we would print a poem by T. S. Eliot if we could get one (later we did). The "boys" were still committed to Marxism, and so were the other young men who figured on the masthead as editors, except one—the backer. The backer, a young abstract painter from a good old New York family, was so "confused" politically that one day he went into the Workers' Bookshop (Stalinist) and asked for a copy of Trotsky's *The Revolution Betrayed;* he was wearing spats that day, too, and carrying a cane, and the thought of the figure he must have cut made the rest of us blanch. "Did anyone recognize you? Do you think they knew who you were?" we all immediately demanded.

My position was something like the backer's; that is, I was a source of uneasiness and potential embarrassment to the magazine, which had accepted me, unwillingly, as an editor because I had a minute "name" and was the girl friend of one of the "boys," who had issued a ukase on my behalf. I was not a Marxist; I should have liked, rather, to be one, but I did not know the language, which seemed really like a foreign tongue. At college I had majored in Elizabethan literature and studied the Roman classics, Renaissance and medieval Latin, and Renaissance and medieval French; in contemporary literature I had not got much beyond *The Counterfeiters,* in English, and Aldous Huxley. All my habits of mind were bourgeois, my fellow editors used to tell me. They were always afraid that I was going to do something, in real life or in print, that would "disgrace *Partisan Review*"; this was a fear that worried me even more than it did them. I used to come down to the office on Saturdays (I worked for a publisher during the week) and listen to the men argue, in the inner room, beyond the partition, pounding the table and waving their arms in the air. Once a month, late at night, after the dishes were done, I would write my "Theatre Chronicle," hoping not to sound bourgeois and give the Communists ammunition.

The field assigned me was the theatre, because, just before this, I had been married to an actor. It was often debated whether we should have a theatre column at all. Some of the editors felt that the theatre was not worth bothering with, because it was neither a high art, like Art, nor a mass art, like the movies. But this was also an argument for letting me do it. If I made mistakes, who cared? This argument won out. Being an editor, at least in name, I had to be allowed to do *something*, and the "Theatre Chronicle" (we spelled it "theater") was "made work," like the W.P.A. jobs of the period. I could not fail to see this or to be aware that nobody had much confidence in my powers as a critic. Nevertheless, I was determined to make good. And the column was successful. People liked it, the editors decided. It was "something a little different." A university professor who was also a leading Marxist said that it was "the best theatre criticism he had read since Georg Brandes." Probably the professor had not read any theatre criticism since Georg Brandes, whom, incidentally, I had never heard of, or just barely, but we did not stop to examine the compliment too closely.

At that time (and this is doubtless still the case), *Partisan Review* was unknown to press agents and to theatre people generally; we *paid* for my balcony tickets. Most of our readers never went to the theatre. Out of these two circumstances arose some of the peculiarities of the column. Since we were not on the free list, we did not have to worry about coverage, about reviews coming out on time, or about what anybody in the theatre thought of my judgments, which were mostly unfavorable. In the same

way, our readers did not look to my column as a guide or
wait to hear from me whether or not to line up for tickets.
Consequently, reviews often came out after a play had
closed, and nobody minded; there were long hiatuses too
during which I lived in the country and did not review at
all. That is why this collection has nothing on *The
Cocktail Party* or Arthur Miller or William Inge. It was
not a check list but a chronicle, and, like some old
chronicle, full of lacunæ.

Our readers were young people, college and high-school
teachers, radicals, and bohemians. Many of them, even if
they lived in New York, were too poor to buy theatre
tickets. They went to the movies instead. As movie-goers,
they had their own æsthetic and were prone to suspect that
the theatre was no good; yet they liked to read about it,
from a distance, and see it taken to pieces (i.e., analyzed).
This accounts for the fact that, though the column was
always popular, I almost never received a letter taking
issue with my judgments; once, when I reviewed Tennessee Williams, two or three letters did come in, disagree-
ing, but this was unique. Our readers, an intellectual
minority, were ready to take it on assurance that the
American theatre was not only bad, but very bad.

This was and remains a closely held national secret.
Foreign readers and critics would be astonished to learn
that there was, to say the least, a difference of opinion
among American intellectuals about the worth of such
writers as Clifford Odets, Tennessee Williams, Arthur
Miller, or of the Actors' Studio style of playing just as the
Nobel Prize Committee was probably astonished to learn
that in American Literary circles Steinbeck was not regarded as a great writer.

The agreement, passive or active, of a group of readers
does not, of course, prove anything about the theatre,

except that it had failed, as a whole, to interest these people enough to make them go see for themselves. Recently this has changed, owing partly to prosperity, partly to the off-Broadway theatre, with its foreign and *avant-garde* plays, and partly to the movies themselves, which have made Tennessee Williams and the others available to anyone to judge; today most intellectuals have seen at least one play by Williams, Inge, and Miller, and at least one movie directed by Kazan. Their opinion, so far as I can tell, remains about the same as when they did not have the price of a ticket: they think this theatre is corn, and they are glad when someone says so.

None of the regular critics do, and this, in itself, provides grounds for suspicion. Any concert of opinion, in America, on official levels, creates automatically a swell of discord from below, and it was the function of *Partisan Review* for many years, in all its departments, to express this discord as loudly as possible. We on *Partisan Review* were continually attacking something or somebody—the Right, the Middle, and the so-called Left, which in the thirties was hardly distinguishable from the Middle ("Communism is twentieth-century Americanism" was one of the great slogans of the period). The novels of John Steinbeck, the plays of Clifford Odets, the criticism of Van Wyck Brooks, the philosophy of Jacques Maritain, the poetry of Archibald MacLeish (to name some of the main enemies) were all very successful commercially or very much *à la mode*.

To be continually on the attack is to run the risk of monotony, an effect we tried to counteract by a lively style. A greater risk is that of mechanical intolerance. Aesthetic puritanism, of which we were rampant examples and which, I believe, is absolutely necessary in America, has, like all puritanism, a tendency to hypocrisy—based on a denial of one's own natural tastes and instincts. I remember how uneasy I felt when I found myself liking Thornton Wilder's *Our Town;* I was almost afraid to praise it in the magazine, lest the boys conclude that I was starting to sell out. I am still surprised to discover that a commercial success, like *Come Back, Little Sheba,* is really quite good, even though this no longer makes me wonder, as it once would have, whether my standards are slipping. . . . The American fear of failure, about which so much has been written, has its logical counterpart: the fear of success—of becoming one oneself or of admiring it in others. This was our (or my) besetting phobia, a product of the time, the place, and perhaps the person.

Yet in all honesty it must be said that it was not a question of *looking* for flaws in most of the plays here discussed ("You people are looking for pimples on the great smiling face of the Soviet Union," somebody charged at a meeting of the League of American Writers, the year *Partisan Review* was founded). The flaws, to me, were so evident that I found it hard to believe that others did not notice them. I really hated the kind of theatre the regular critics liked or at any rate treated respectfully. And, going rather frequently to the theatre, in the course of time I learned that many members of the audience and many actors felt the same way; it was an almost invariable law, for instance, that the most glaringly bad performer in any given cast would be the one who "got the notices" in the newspaper criticisms. This strange situation has not changed in twenty years. "America's Greatest Actress," the "First Lady of our Theatre," etc., who is still going strong, is our worst actress, famous as such in the profession. It is as though Toscanini had really been a terrible conductor. These "secrets" of the theatre make it appear, sometimes, as a fantastic conspiracy which can be talked about quite openly without ever reaching the ears of the critics or of the ordinary ticket-buyer. The commonest explanation offered is that the critics are stupid, but they are not more stupid, probably, on the average, than critics of music and books or than the theatre critics of other countries. I have been speaking, just now, about acting, where the mystery is deepest, but the same queer blindness or deafness extends to plays. How often, for example, one reads in the paper or in a weekly magazine that a "dull" play—let us say *Measure for Measure*—has been redeemed (or failed to be redeemed) by a valiant performance. That the exact opposite will prove to be the case can be predicted with certainty without moving from the breakfast table. (All this is only true, by the way, of the "legitimate" theatre; with revues and musical comedies there is a common standard, at least about performers: Ethel Merman, Bobby Clark, Bert Lahr, Mary Martin, Pinza, Fred Astaire, Beatrice Lillie, have been liked by nearly everyone.)

My early reviews lisp the Marxist language; I was trying to tell the reader, in his own words, why he would agree with me. Maxwell Anderson has "no system of intellectual values"; in the thirties that was the worst thing, short of "fascist," you could say about a person, and not only in left-wing circles—had not T. S. Eliot rated Shakespeare lower than Dante for lack of a "system of thought"? It was a doctrinaire time, and everybody was engaged in "smoking out" the latent tendencies in works of art, like F.B.I. investigators. On *Partisan Review* we did not call innocent people fascists; that was a Communist trick. But we, or at least I, did use labels and cant-terms to beat poor mediocrities like Maxwell Anderson over the head. This begins to disappear from the chronicles toward the end of the war. By that time I had become more skillful at obliging a play to "tell something," but no longer for the sake of incriminating the author; now the play was telling something about the society that was paying to see it.

I had begun to treat Broadway plays as commodities, which is what they are, and to ask what they were being used for, what needs, wishes, and transient moods they satisfied. And here is the interest of the more journalistic part of this collection: it is a kind of social history seen through the theatre of the last two decades. Most of the plays discussed were trivial and have long been forgotten, but in these *ephemeridæ*, studied with such care, the America of that time is, for me at any rate, recaptured: the New Deal years, the war years, the years of Truman. The theatre, being sociable by nature, is a more sensitive register of time and its fleeting humors than the movies, which address themselves to the solitary mass man. The difference between the theatre and the movies is illustrated by the intermission and the coming-up of the house lights; the intermission and the discussions that take place during it, the moving about and watching other members of the audience, are a real part of the play. Few people remember the circumstances under which they saw a movie, while most people do with a play; going to the movies alone is a common habit or vice, but going to the theatre alone is a practice, chiefly, of dramatic critics.

Looking through these chronicles, I see that time itself, the lost dimension, figures again and again as the playwright's toy. Fantasies of going backward in time seem to have been popular from *Berkeley Square* to *Brigadoon,* as though a sigh rose from these decades: "If we had it to do over. . . ." There is a great deal, too, about money, always to the same sad tune: money does not bring happiness. Love, as a theme, is scarcely present; it has retreated to the dark temples of the movie houses. But politics and military affairs—"current events"—play a bigger part than I would have thought, which means that the theatre is still close to the newspaper and the pamphlet, a medium for rational discussion, as it was for Beaumarchais and Shaw.

In the early reviews there is evident a naïve belief that artistic judgments can be enforced on the reader by a battery of argument. This, I think, is again a mixture of period and person. The notion that abstract reasoning can crush a fact (e.g., a successful play, a political phenomenon), a wholly un-Marxist notion, was nonetheless the principle on which most of our criticism was practiced. I "proved" that the public was being taken in by Playwright X, just as *Partisan Review*'s political analyses proved, issue after issue, that Stalin was bamboozling the working class. Such irrefutable proofs had no power, I fear, to alter a single opinion. Those who were taken in by Stalin or by Playwright X, as I have already suggested, were unlikely to read *Partisan Review* in any case.

What I did not realize was that my own judgments had not been reached by relentless logic and lawyer's points— the methods by which I sought to convince the reader. It was not logic but my ears that told me that most American plays were horribly badly written. This is either heard or it isn't. The false notes continually struck by American playwrights either offend or they don't—you cannot *argue* that a singer is off pitch. The desire to argue dies hard, however, especially in a woman, and I cannot drop the subject of bad writing, here, without trying to get in a last word. "Yes," some people will agree, of a play by Tennessee Williams, "it *is* badly written, but it's good theatre." I have never been able to make out what this expression means, exactly. "Strong" situations? Masochistic grovelling? Sexual torture? Is Sophocles "good theatre"? Is Shakespeare? Apparently not, for the term is always used

defensively, to justify a kind of shoddiness, which is held
to be excusable for the stage. Indeed, the American playwright is always being "excused," as though he were some
wretched pupil bringing a note from his parent: "Please
excuse Tennessee or Arthur or Clifford; he has a writing
difficulty." This started with O'Neill, whose lack of verbal
gift was a genuine affliction, from which he suffered just
as a stammerer does; he speaks of it in *A Long Day's
Journey into Night.* "I couldn't touch what I tried to tell
you just now," says Edmund, who is the young O'Neill.
"I just stammered. That's the best I'll ever do. . . . Well,
it will be faithful realism, at least. Stammering is the
native eloquence of us fog people." O'Neill's handicap,
however, which made it painful for him to articulate his
thoughts, was quite another thing from the bad writing of
his successors, which is unconscious and serene and often
takes the form of pretentious "fine writing," as in the
choruses of Arthur Miller's *A View from a Bridge.* Miller
is not just lame; he is what textbooks and grammars call
hazy; that is, he does not seem to know what he wants to
express.

But what is the use of saying this? It is either well
known to the reader or so unsuspected by him that a
genuine revelation, an opening of the eyes and ears, as in
some Biblical miracle, would be required to bring it home
to him. A comparison will sometimes do this; the appearance of John Gielgud beside Marlon Brando in the film of
Julius Caesar made many people, and particularly actors,
aware for the first time of something wrong in the very
rudiments of American acting. Recently the off-Broadway
theatre, with its productions of Molière, Shaw, Chekhov,
Turgenev, Ibsen, Montherlant, Strindberg, O'Casey,
Hauptmann, Brecht, Genet, at least offers an idea, even
though the playing is very amateurish, of what a real artic-

ulate theatre can be. It does suggest a standard. And the public has responded by deciding that the off-Broadway theatre is "fun," an adventure to go to, like the speakeasies of the old days.

No wonder there is a general sense of blinking surprise. This lively, witty theatre found in downtown basements and converted lofts is a different world altogether from the Broadway cave-world of the American School playwrights, who have accustomed us to a stage inhabited by apes with complexes. The typical character of the so-called American realist school is a sub-human member of the lower urban middle class. This creature is housed in a living room filled with instalment-plan furniture, some of which will be broken before the play is over. The sound of breakage and the sound of heavy breathing will signify "theatre." As directed by Elia Kazan, whip-cracking ringmaster of this school of brutes, the hero is found standing with clenched fists, stage left, yelling at some member of his family, stage right, until one of them breaks into hysterical weeping and collapses on to a chair by the stage-center table, his great head buried in his hands. The weeping character is confessing to being alcoholic, homosexual, a failure.

The sight of a strong man or, even better, of two strong men crying uncontrollably is one of the commonest sights on the American stage, uptown, today. I have never seen such a spectacle in real life; perhaps my experience is too limited. I have seen men cry when somebody died and I have seen drunken tears, but I have never seen two men sobbing loudly together—over something one of them has said to the other. Whittaker Chambers said that he and Alger Hiss cried together when he decided to leave the Party. Even if this is true (and Chambers was not very reliable), at least one of these two men was exceptionally histrionic, while the characters who behave this way on the stage are supposed to be average Americans. The characters of Tennessee Williams are supposed to be average *southern* Americans, fruitier, that is, than the northern kind.

One thing, however, must be said for Tennessee Williams: his characters do sometimes talk with a local, recognizable accent. They come from a definite place, and their speech shows it. A disturbing aspect of *Death of a Salesman* was that Willy Loman seemed to be Jewish, to judge by his speech-cadences, but there was no mention of this on the stage. He could not be Jewish because he had to be "America." All the living rooms, backyards, stoops, and fire escapes of the American School claim to be "America," which is not so much a setting as a big, amorphous idea; the puzzle for the audience, except with Tennessee Williams, is to guess where these living rooms, roughly, are and who is living in them, which might make it possible to measure the plausibility of the action. "Those old Irish actors were exactly like that," the man next to me said of Frederic March's performance in *A Long Day's Journey into Night;* this was a real testimonial to the performer and to the (now old-fashioned) solidity of O'Neill's play. On the contrary, the man who was quoted by the *New Yorker* as saying, after *Death of a Salesman,* "That damned New England territory never was any good" had committed a boner; he had missed the play's "profundity" by trying to localize the trouble.

Still, *Death of a Salesman* is the only play of the new American School that can be said to touch home; *Come Back, Little Sheba,* by William Inge, though good, does not attempt to be more than a *genre* study of an alcoholic and his wife, which is watched with that same detached fascination exercised by a pair of quarreling neighbors

seen through a window or heard in an adjoining flat:
"Look! He's beating her up again!" The Salesman, as
Arthur Miller calls him, signaling with the capital *S* in the
stage directions, is meant to be someone we all know, if
not Ourselves. What is the matter with Willy Loman?
Why is he so unhappy and why do we feel for him with a
pang of recognition? "America" is what is wrong with
him, Arthur Miller would answer, and to some extent this
is true. The conception of the salesman's home with its
instalment-plan furniture as a house of shabby lies and
competitive boasts is sadly close to our national life; it is
in fact precisely a close-up of the "home" depicted in full
color by advertisers in the national magazines, with Father,
Mother, two fine Kids, and the Product. But the play is
wholly conceptualized, like the ads to which it gives a
bitter retort. Parents, children, and neighbors are cut-out
figures, types, in both the advertised dream and the nightmare that closes in on Willy Loman like a mortgage fore-
closing. Ideally, the play would be a kind of grim satire,
the negative of the positive. *This is the way your pretty
picture looks from the inside,* the playwright would be
saying to the advertising men. In so far as the play does
this, it is arresting and moving in a sardonic way. "He's
liked but not *well* liked," Willy keeps insisting, of a neighbor, and the shrewdness that persists in making this distinction is both funny and horrible. The problem is to convert this into tragedy; that is, to make genuine Universals
out of these prefab types, which Arthur Miller can only do
by having someone preach about them.

   "Attention must be paid," intones the shrill, singsong
voice of the mother, ordering her sons to take notice of
their father's plight. "Attention, attention, must finally be
paid to such a person." She is really admonishing the
audience that Willy is, as she says, "a human being." But

that is just it; he is a Human Being without being anyone, a sort of suffering Statistic. The mother's voice raised in the old melancholy Jewish rhythms ("Attention must be paid" is not a normal American locution; nor is "finally," placed where it is; nor is "such a person," used as she uses it) seems to have been summoned from some other play that was about particular people. Yet poor Willy is only a composite, like one of those faces in magazine guessing-games with the eyes and forehead of one film star, the nose of another, the mouth and chin of a third; as a composite, he is a subject for the editorial page, which could take note of his working conditions, ask for unemployment benefits and old-age care for him, call "attention," in short, to the problem of the salesman in the Welfare State. No one could write an editorial calling attention to the case of King Lear. Yet some of the same elements are present; there is an old man with thankless children and a grandiose dream of being "well liked"—i.e., of being shown the proofs of love—that ends in isolation, ignominy, and lunacy. Lear, however, has the gift of language, which is not just a class-endowment, for the Fool has it too. This gift of language is what makes him human and not just "a human being."

Mary McCarthy's Theatre Chronicles

1937–1962

TWO BAD CASES
OF SOCIAL CONSCIENCE

MR. BEN HECHT at the opening of *To Quito and Back* at the Guild Theatre the other night must have felt like a man in a new suit of clothes which nobody notices. I am not sure whether Mr. Hecht was wearing a transformation or had actually undergone one, but indubitably the play at the Guild was intended to reveal its author in a New Phase. The creator of *Erik Dorn* and *The Front Page,* the Hollywood scenario writer and Paramount film producer, has gone Left. That the full effect of this dramatic quick-change was lost on audiences and critics is in part attributable to Mr. Hecht's own confusion but in the main to the blundering production of the Theatre Guild. I happened to see in manuscript the play Mr. Hecht wrote. It was infinitely more interesting, more playable, and even commercially more valuable than the play the Guild produced. Indeed, the staging of this play is proof conclusive that the Theatre Guild, whatever its history and pretensions, is indistinguishable from the Shuberts in the bright glare of the footlights.

In its handling of *To Quito and Back* the Guild went in for the kind of tinkering that has made the more groundling managers the laughing-stock of serious theatre people;

and, as is usually the case with the Shuberts when they attempt a non-musical attraction, the Guild directors, between them, carved the play into a turkey. Mr. Hecht gave the Guild a play that was in essence autobiographical, a play about an articulate, clever man who talked himself to a standstill. But the producers, apparently still under the spell of the old superstition that a play cannot be "talky," proceeded to excise almost all of the hero's connected conversation and to substitute scenes of action and love interest. What talk of a semi-intellectual nature was left the hero they camouflaged as best they could. All the antique conventions of drawing-room comedy were invoked: the characters in the midst of whatever they were saying were bounding about the stage, jumping up and sitting down, climbing over furniture and pacing the floor, going through all the dreary, monkey tricks of what is known as "stage business." When everything else failed, the actors were made to deliver their "difficult" lines in as hasty and apologetic a manner as possible, while every wisecrack was handled as slowly and reverently as a soliloquy by Shakespeare. The ironic boomerang came, of course, with the morning papers, where the critics dismissed the play as talky. Paradoxically, the remnants of talk in the produced play were just sufficient to make it appear over-talkative, and the patent embarrassment of director and actors only underlined the fact.

In another notable way the producers obstructed the author's communication with his audience. The hero of the play is an American novelist, whose mixed sincerity and attitudinizing, vulgarity and pathos, are peculiarly indigenous to the America of the twenties whose mood Mr. Hecht helped to set. The awkward, asymmetrical contours of this American type were quite flattened out by Mr. Leslie Banks, an actor of rigid and shiny technique,

who has been for too many years in harness to the role
of the English Gentleman to deviate from his eternal and
international character.

The mistaken commercialism of the Guild has not
deprived the theatre of a good play. *To Quito and Back*
was never that. What has been lost, or at least obscured,
is a kind of curious case-history written by the patient
himself. Mr. Hecht is a veteran exhibitionist, and this is
perhaps his fullest confession. Here he states his symptoms often and earnestly. The weakness of the play is that
it cries for diagnosis. The plot has to do with Alexander
Sterns, who arrives in Ecuador on a rather dismal elope-
ment, and gets embroiled in a revolution for which he
eventually dies. Thematically, it is a study in irresolution.
The hero, who describes himself as "a second-hand Hamlet with a hollow heart and a woodpecker mind," for two
acts engages in vacillation, amorous and political. He can
love neither a woman nor a cause truly, no matter how
desperately he desires to do so. In all branches of experience he is irrevocably a tourist, and his most poignant cry
is "If I could only care!" His heroic death, which (to Mr.
Hecht's mind) is his final salvation, is admittedly the product of a mood, whose impermanency he recognizes even
while yielding to it.

The melodramatic absurdity of the play lies in the
Hamlet comparison and its implications. The playwright
assumes that his hero's irresolution is of a tragic order,
while, as a matter of fact, it is comico-pathetic. It is not,
as Mr. Hecht believes, the irresolution of a man who is
able to see all sides of a question; it is the impotence of a
man who is afraid of making a fool of himself. The play,
indeed, is a small, undignified monument of social and
intellectual terror. The seesawings of the hero are a mere
objectification of the nervousness of the author. Mr.

Hecht, it would appear, has been converted, or frightened by intellectual fashion into giving lip-service to radicalism. Yet this radicalism he does not dare face squarely in the drawing-rooms of New York or the studios of Hollywood. He must transport it and himself (in a somewhat flattering disguise) to a comic-opera Ecuador, where revolutionary generals are just-too-pricelessly-funny, Emperor Jones Negroes are commissars, and the working class is represented by a sentimental servant girl who sympathizes with the communists but knows her place just the same. Only in a baroque and slightly goofy setting is communism accessible to Mr. Hecht. Even there humor must be regularly applied as an antiseptic to idealism. Throughout the play, Mr. Hecht's Sense of Humor keeps popping up like a grisly jack-in-the-box whenever he feels that eloquence may have betrayed him into *gaucherie*. Even his relentless self-revelation shows itself to be a form of insurance, a peace offering to the perspicacious; and his agonized sincerity must be rated as the final, most vulgar sham.

The temperament of Mr. Maxwell Anderson is antipodal to Mr. Hecht's. If Mr. Hecht has converted face-saving into a minor literary art, Mr. Anderson has built a career on incaution. *The Star-Wagon* at the Empire, while not one of Mr. Anderson's major efforts, is nevertheless very characteristic of him. Once again he has been inspired by a lofty theme, and once again the mediocrity of his talent has reduced it to inconsequentiality. Here the theme is quite as ambitious as ever, but the play is more homespun, more trivial. There were forebodings of *The Star-Wagon* in *Winterset,* in the philosophical musings of the rabbi: "They say there is no time but we grow old. . . ." Now Mr. Anderson takes the theory of the

simultaneity, the presentness of time, and fashions a period comedy-drama out of it. Two old inventors, who have
made millions of dollars for capitalists at a combined
salary of $27.50 a week, build a machine which will take
them back to any given moment in history. After a short
scientific explanation of the machine and the theory behind it, and a good deal of exposition about the characters, the inventors throw the switch and the play is off.
They elect to return to their youth in an American village
at the turn of the century. For some reason, not explained
by the dramatist, they have the power of intervention in
the action of the past. They therefore attempt to rectify
their errors, and they wind up rich but very unhappy. The
moral is that everything is for the best, and if one
wouldn't make the same mistakes a second time, one
ought to. Charmingly produced by Guthrie McClintic,
the play is richer in period comedy than in metaphysics.
It is entertaining and quite harmless. To the critic it is
interesting only because it seems to demonstrate certain
facts about the nature of Mr. Anderson's work.

Though Mr. Anderson has lately been hailed as America's first dramatist, it has long been obvious that he was
essentially a popular playwright, distinguished from his
fellows only by his ambition. Yet ambition alone would
hardly account for his enormous commercial success, for
many of Mr. Anderson's subjects, no matter how sugar-
coated, must have been at least partially indigestible to
the public. Neither *Winterset* nor *High Tor* were "easy"
plays; the turgidity of Mr. Anderson's verse made it ardu-
ous going. The answer, I think, lies in Mr. Anderson's
attitude toward his material. Mr. Anderson is a genuine
naif, a rustic, a Mr. Deeds. He has no discrimination, no
system of intellectual values; he is moved solely by his own
fancy. In the present play, a joke about bloomers and a

metaphysical speculation are on a par; the playwright is not aware of a difference between them. Unconscious of categories, he makes himself at home in the Infinite, because he has no sense of not-belonging. It is his sublime unself-consciousness which endears him to his public. The spectacle of Mr. Anderson relaxing in the Forbidden Places of the intellect induces a corresponding feeling of comfort in the spectator: whether or not he understands exactly what Mr. Anderson is doing, he is put at ease by the utter homeyness of Mr. Anderson's manner. The familiar jokes about Irish policemen, horseless cars, and gangsters heighten the illusion of security.

To this gift, Mr. Anderson, a native Middle Westerner, adds a real sense of old-fashioned American symbols. In *The Star-Wagon* there is the inventor; in *High Tor,* the American Indian; in *Winterset,* the senile, learned judge; in *Valley Forge,* George Washington; and everywhere there is the passion for social justice, which is visualized in terms of the square deal. In a more subtle way, the blank verse is itself a symbol of an obsolescent American taste. Mr. Anderson's mind is like a musty, Middle Western law office of thirty years ago, full of heterogeneous books on the law, on American history, on philosophy, and the morocco-bound complete works of William Shakespeare.

ODETS DEPLORED

As SHAKESPEARE has been said to have populated all corners of history and legend with "deathless Englishmen," so Clifford Odets seems to have resettled America and even China *(The General Died at Dawn)* with citizens of the Bronx. The salient feature of *Golden Boy* (Belasco Theatre), which is supposed to be a play about an Italian boy named Bonaparte who wanted to be a violinist but became a prizefighter instead, is that it is not at all about an Italian boy but about that same talkative, histrionic Jewish family to which Mr. Odets has introduced us before. *Golden Boy* again demonstrates the lesson of the Odets' *Paradise Lost:* that this author appears to be psychically glued to the material of his first play. He cannot advance beyond *Awake and Sing:* he can only revive it with different costumes, scenery, and (sometimes) accents. That the refurbishing of the material implies its adulteration seems not to concern Mr. Odets, who perhaps imagines that he is exploring genuinely new horizons; but to those who have admired *Awake and Sing,* each new play seems a more shocking caricature of the first.

It is well known that actors who have been playing for a long time in the same play will, unless disciplined by a vigilant stage manager, "hoke" their performances more and more. A giggle becomes a laugh; a catch in the throat, a sob; a tremor, a spasm. This is a form of auto-intoxication which is psychologically necessary for the type of player who must "feel" his performance. He must behave more and more violently in order to be aware that he is acting. This law of diminishing returns from a given stimulus is, of course, observable in every field of sensibility, and its workings are particularly striking in the case of Mr. Odets. The narrowness of his invention, the monotony of his subject matter have anaesthetized him to a point where he must wade in blood and tears in order to feel that he is writing a play; he must turn the Belasco Theatre into a Grand Guignol to believe it a playhouse.

Thus the simple Bronx apartment dwellers of *Awake and Sing* appear in *Golden Boy* dressed up as gangsters, prizefighters, and tarts. Mr. Odets has taken a collection of types out of any underworld film, and on them he has grafted the half-ludicrous, half-touching cultural aspirations, the malapropisms, the pride in material possessions, the inarticulate longing for a sunny life, that make up the Odets formula of frustration. The Chekhovian baggage of middle-class futility with which Mr. Odets equips these low-life stereotypes is, of course, fearfully inappropriate to the milieu of lust, murder, crime and perversion in which they must travel. The voices are the dreamy, ineffectual voices of the little people of the world; the deeds are the deeds of the headliners. This contradiction between form and substance gives the play the aspect of a fancy-dress ball; there is the same grotesquerie, the same stridency, the same laughable yet indecent incongruity.

Golden Boy is a much more popular play than *Awake and Sing*. The melodramatic nature of the characters and events would alone guarantee its success at the box office.

But Mr. Odets has taken out double insurance against the failure of his work by stuffing it with familiar Jewish low-comedy jokes and ancient wheezes out of vaudeville. Yet, though the stale luridity of characters and plot and the stale gag-comedy of the lines have been sufficient to keep audiences in the alternate shivers and stitches to which the underworld films have habituated them, it is not these qualities which have commanded the deferential attention of both critics and playgoers. Serious people have sat unflinchingly through this play, because they knew or thought they knew that Mr. Odets had Something To Say, that somewhere in this theatrical grab bag there lay a treasure.

Mr. Odets has a theme which in the last century would have been stated as Money Does Not Bring Happiness. But Mr. Odets conceives of it in more modern terms. He would summarize it, I suppose, by saying that the struggle for financial success which the capitalist system tends to impose on the individual is detrimental to personal happiness and to culture. Stated thus abstractly, the theme does Mr. Odets credit. Concretely visualized as a choice between playing the violin and fighting in the prize ring, it already becomes a little ridiculous. But, granting Mr. Odets the virtue of this rather simple-minded antithesis, one finds that here it has been distorted out of all truth and vulgarized out of all nobility. In the selection of a superman for a hero lies the essential hollowness of the play, for the choice between culture and money cannot be valid for a character who possesses two such remarkable gifts. If Mr. Odets' hero were a potentially great violinist, he could have become rich or at least prosperous via the concert stage, and he need never have considered prize-fighting as an alternative career. If he were not, then his abandonment of the violin was surely no tragedy. But

Mr. Odets' juggling of his theme does not stop with this original false alternative; it eats deeper into the plot. What is the cause of Bonaparte's downfall and death? His greed for money, his selection of prizefighting as a life work? Not at all. A purely *accidental,* non-social circumstance: the fact that the girl he loved felt pity, loyalty, and tenderness for another man. One assumes that, were it not for the girl, Mr. Odets' hero would have been as successful and as long-lived as Jack Dempsey, Mickey Walker, Gene Tunney, or any other well-known fighter. He might have even become a restaurant-owner and had some very satisfying musical conversations with Yehudi Menuhin. Mr. Odets' social theme, like his formula for the manufacture of characters, is a carry-over from his first and most sincere play. It is clearly inoperative in the world of macabre melodrama into which he has imported it. That he was forced to use a fortuitous, melodramatic device to dissolve the elements of his play and bring it to its falsely tragic curtain is itself an exposé of the play's "serious" pretensions.

ELIZABETHAN REVIVALS

THE AMERICAN THEATRE, unable to produce a renaissance of its own, has imported an old one. With the withering away of the American playwright, the Elizabethan playwright has been called in to understudy. During the nineteen twenties, the most energetic years of the American theatre, a few old stagers with repertory companies of confirmed Shakespearean hams were, as if by common consent, appointed official caretakers of the Bard, and an occasional revival of *Hamlet* or *Romeo and Juliet* on the part of a recognized star was no more than a duty call paid to the grave of an honored but distant relative. Today the best and liveliest young talent has been turned full blast on Shakespeare and his colleagues. The last two seasons have seen nine high-powered Elizabethan revivals, with three more promised before the season's end. Since both American and British acting seem to be temporarily in crescendo, and the Elizabethan plays are admittedly good, the result has been two quite stimulating theatrical seasons.

The current phenomenon of a theatre without playwrights suggests that classic plays have an additional function beyond those generally assigned to them. Classics, in general, are supposed (a) to please readers and (b) to instruct writers. The present Elizabethan façade of

Broadway makes one think that classics, by their very nature, are also meant to fill a cultural interregnum, to tide over an art medium which, without them, would collapse. In a literal sense, this can only be true of the interpretative arts—music, stage production and criticism— and, obviously, such use of the classics is most observable in these fields. I am totally ignorant of music, so of that I cannot speak, but it is painfully clear that in American literary criticism the tendency is to re-examine the great works of the past, since practically no creative literary work is being done in the present. However, in a more obscure and less explicable manner, the classics can, it seems to me, act as a life line to the primary arts themselves. This is because the relationship between the primary and the interpretative arts is not one-sided but reciprocal, and the classics, by keeping the interpretative arts alive and perhaps even fermenting them a little, can vicariously succor the primary arts. Thus the interest in problems of acting and production which this régime of revivals has imposed upon theatre people can hardly fail, if properly handled, to introduce new techniques, which will evoke new playwrights who will be anxious to use them. So simplified, this sounds a bit too much like the-house-that-Jack-built to have any but a fairy-tale truth, and, of course, an art so carefully inbred would become too attenuated to be worth preserving. This recipe for the fertilization of the arts is but one of several with which it must be applied jointly; it cannot be taken as a panacea.

At any rate, on Broadway today the process is only in its foetal stage. No serious new techniques are yet being evolved from Shakespearean productions; rather, tricks are being played on them. A spirit of carnival excitement possesses these revivals, and an annual Shakespearean

World Series seems to have been written into the rules of the game. Last year it was John Gielgud versus Leslie Howard with *Hamlet* as the ball park; this year it will be Orson Welles versus Maurice Evans with *Henry IV, Part I.* (Mr. Evans on tour is doing an occasional matinee with himself as Falstaff, and expects to bring the play into town in the fall. Mr. Welles anticipates a spring production with himself in the same role.) In these ostentatious rivalries one can see the exploitation of Elizabethan plays in its most blatant and harmless form. In the actual productions of Gielgud's *Hamlet* and Welles's *Caesar,* the exploiter, that is, the stunt artist, wears a more successful disguise.

The two productions were poles apart in theory and in performance, but they met on common ground in their attitude toward the material. In both cases there was a preoccupation with the forms of the play at the expense, of course, of its meanings. Mr. Gielgud was obsessed with the acting traditions of *Hamlet,* and a book recently published by the Oxford University Press, *John Gielgud's Hamlet,* by Rosamond Gilder, makes this very clear. Mr. Gielgud himself has a chapter on "Costumes, Scenery, and Stage Business," in which he appears to have set up a virtual barricade of stage props between himself and the lines of the play. He seems always more interested in his differences or agreements with, say, Sir Henry Irving, as to whether or not a sword should be worn at a certain point, than in any less conspicuously physical feature of the production. His connoisseurship of the fine points of past productions of *Hamlet* seduced him also into a rather desperate hunt for new readings, new inflections in familiar speeches. These were sometimes illuminating, more often tortured and distracting. I do not mean to imply that Mr. Gielgud had no conception of Hamlet. He

did, but it was muffled by his precious, strained, almost
dandified manipulation of the baggage of the production.
His own performance was so decorated, so crammed with
minutiae of gesture, pause, and movement that its general outline was imperceptible to an audience.

The rococo style is of all styles probably the most inappropriate to a production of Shakespeare, and Mr. Gielgud's *Hamlet,* with all its refinements, was a kind of
climax of the rococo. Indeed, I think it impossible to do
a good production of Shakespeare in terms of the tradition of the eighteenth and nineteenth centuries. Whether
actor and producer swallow that tradition whole, or
whether they deviate from it in much or in little, as long
as their thinking is bounded by that tradition the result
will be a more or less competent theatrical barbarism. It
is strange that Mr. Gielgud's interest in the stage history
of Shakespeare should not have carried him back to
Shakespeare's own day. If any style of presentation is rele-
vant to Shakespeare's plays it is surely the style of Shakespeare's period, the style to whose terms he adapted those
plays. Yet Mr. Gielgud, speaking of the first scene of
Hamlet, where the Ghost appears on the sentinel's platform, is full of pity and condescension for the Elizabethans. "One wonders," he says, "how this scene can have
been played effectively when it was originally written. A
noisy, fidgeting, mostly standing audience, no darkness,
afternoon sunshine streaming on to a tidy little platform."
The point is that the plays were written with these conditions, consciously or unconsciously, in mind. There being
no stage paraphernalia to create the "illusion," the lines
themselves had to do the work of scenery, careful costum-
ing and props. It is therefore a tautology to add exter-
nally to Shakespeare what exists already in the very fiber
of his plays, and the heaviness one feels in most tradi-

tional presentations of Shakespeare is the heaviness of repetition, of underscoring. Moreover, it seems as if Shakespeare were intended to be played fast; in fact, I can think of no other way in which blank verse can be read effectively. The caressive attention Mr. Gielgud gave his lines, the pregnant pauses, the judiciously interlarded stage business, all interfered with the sweep of the verse, and the dramatic sweep of the play. This kind of acting (which is and has been, by the way, the prevailing style for Shakespeare) tends to atomize the plays, to reduce them to collections of small and (again) quite heavy nuggets.

If Mr. Gielgud's production was a sort of ornamental appliqué imposed on the original, Mr. Welles's *Caesar* was a piece of plastic surgery. Mr. Welles, to judge from his interpretations of *Macbeth, Dr. Faustus,* and *Caesar,* has the idea an Elizabethan play is a liability which only by the most strenuous showmanship, by cutting, doctoring, and modernizing, can be converted into an asset. Mr. Welles's method is to find a modern formula into which a classic can somehow be squeezed. In the case of *Macbeth,* the formula was *The Emperor Jones*; for *Dr. Faustus* it was a Punch and Judy show; for *Caesar* it was the proletarian play. Now of these three it seems to me only *Dr. Faustus* was truly successful, for here the formula actually corresponded in a way to the spirit and construction of the original, and one saw a play that was modern and that was, at the same time, *Dr. Faustus.* The other two have been what people call "interesting"; they have not been good.

The Harlem *Macbeth* is now far enough in the past so that even those who enjoyed it can see that it was at best a pleasant bit of legerdemain. *Caesar,* however, is still thought of as an important production. This is not the first play of Shakespeare's to have been done in modern dress, and superficially, therefore, Mr. Welles's stunt of taking the Romans out of their togas does not sound as novel as on the stage it seems. What is novel about the production is Mr. Welles's motive for putting it in modern dress. In the past, when *Hamlet,* for example, was done by Basil Sydney in a dinner jacket, the motive was, apparently, to say something about Hamlet, to show how modern a character he is. The purpose of the Mercury Theatre *Caesar,* on the contrary, was to say something about the modern world, to use Shakespeare's characters to drive home the horrors and inanities of present-day fascism. *Caesar,* in fact, was Mr. Welles's personal acknowledgment of the bankruptcy of contemporary playwriting, for in *Caesar* Mr. Welles as director tried to construct a modern play of his own: an anti-fascist melodrama in which Caesar figures as a proto-Mussolini and Brutus as a fighting Progressive.

Only a very superficial understanding of Shakespeare's play could have permitted Mr. Welles to entertain this notion for long. *Julius Caesar* is about the tragic consequences that befall idealism when it attempts to enter the sphere of action. It is perhaps also a comment on the futility and dangerousness of action in general. In a non-political sense it is a "liberal" play, for it has three heroes, Caesar, Antony, and Brutus, of whom Brutus is the most large-souled and sympathetic. Shakespeare's "liberal" formula, which insists on playing fair with all its characters, is obviously in fearful discord with Mr. Welles's anti-fascist formula, which must have heroes and villains at all costs. The production of *Caesar,* consequently, turns into a battleground between Mr. Welles's play and Shakespeare's play. Mr. Welles has cut the play to pieces; he has very nearly eliminated the whole sordid tragic business of the degeneration and impotence of the republican forces; he has turned the rather shady Cassius into a shrewd and jovial comedian whose heart is in the right place; he has made Caesar, whose political stature gave the play dignity and significance, into a mechanical, expressionless robot; he has transformed the showy, romantic, buccaneering Antony into a repulsive and sinister demagogue. If he could do all this and still come out with a play that was consistent and uniformly forceful, the experiment might be forgivable. There were some things, however, which could not be cut or distorted, and these by their very incongruous presence, destroyed the totality of the play's effect. The most prominent of these unassimilated chunks of Shakespeare was Antony's final speech ("This was the noblest Roman of them all"—too famous, doubtless, to be cut), which in the mouth of the blackshirt monster of the Welles production seemed an unconvincing and even tasteless tribute to the memory of Brutus.

The Mercury Theatre *Caesar,* it goes without saying, had virtues that are lacking in the ordinary Shakespearean revival. The simplicity of the mounting, the calm, conversational tone of the players, an excellent if wrongheaded performance by George Coulouris as Antony, were all new and commendable. There were, on the other hand, certain vulgarities of playing that arose from the oversimplification of a complex work. Orson Welles's Brutus was cloying and monotonous: his performance seemed to be based on the single theory that if you drop your voice two registers below the voices of the other actors you will give an impression of innocent saintliness.

Yet whatever the technical virtues or faults of the Mercury Theatre company, its energies, like the energies of

Mr. Gielgud, seem to me to be misapplied. If the classics are to play any important role in the American theatre, their contents ought at least to be examined. To encrust them with traditional ornament or chop them into newspaper headlines is to shut them off from the world and the theatre. Acting as an art cannot exist by itself; it must feed on the material of plays. Both Mr. Welles and Mr. Gielgud, who in a peculiar way are trying "to lead their own lives," to make themselves independent of plays, are the potential victims of a sterile cleverness, which can readily lead them to a very dead end.

Mr. Gielgud and Mr. Welles, unfortunately, represent the dominant trends in the production of revivals. Only Maurice Evans, who stands outside both the old school and the new, has given a Shakespearean performance in which the actor was in harmonious relation with the play. Yet Mr. Evans has so carefully eschewed eccentricities and mannerisms of style that he will not easily attract imitators. Mr. Welles's forthcoming Falstaff will probably create a greater stir; my money is on Mr. Evans.

Footnote, 1956. I was wrong, I now see, in overestimating Mr. Evans. It is Mr. Gielgud who has become a fine Shakespearean—witness his performance of Cassius in the James Mason-Marlon Brando film. But I was right, I think, about Orson Welles, who is still up to his old tricks, in his London *Moby Dick,* another "adaptation" of a classic that is not unlike the comic-book version. In seventeen years, Mr. Evans has faded. Mr. Welles has remained the same, and Mr. Gielgud has grown, partly, I suppose, because of that attention to detail, to the physical aspect of the production, which I mistakenly reprehended in this review.

CLASS ANGLES AND
A WILDER CLASSIC

Pins and Needles at Labor Stage is like a New Deal parade, a union picnic, a college play, a Gilbert and Sullivan operetta, a smart, up-to-date Broadway revue. "It illustrates," the program says, "the concept of working class drama which has guided Labor Stage, Inc. from the beginning: that plays for workers must be entertaining and alive." If Labor Stage, Inc., which is sponsored by the International Ladies Garment Workers Union, is any barometer of the state of mind of the working class, then America must already have achieved a classless society. For what *Pins and Needles* least resembles is the proletarian theatre. Only its actors—cutters, pressers, cloakmakers and dressmakers of the I.L.G.W.U.—are proletarian. Its themes, its techniques, its perspectives are bourgeois-Democratic.

In *Pins and Needles* there are, to be sure, certain nostalgic whiffs of revolutionary theatre, certain misleading family likenesses to the old Theatre Union Sunday night potpourris. The ancient enemies, Hitler, Mussolini, the Mikado, are once again summoned up—but with a difference. They have lost the aura of menace that used to attend them, and now appear merely as clowns. The metamorphosis of the dictators, as a matter of fact, gives the key to what estranges *Pins and Needles* from Fourteenth Street and unites it to Broadway. It is simply a question of intention. *Pins and Needles* is designed to divert. All the didactic and hortatory elements of the proletarian drama have been shed, and in their place we get high spirits, merriment, and bounce. Good nature has superseded bitterness. The dictators have turned comedians, and the indictment of capitalism is subdued to a genial spoofing of Macy's, militarism, Americanism (100 per cent, not twentieth-century), popular love songs, high-pressure advertising, social snobbery, and etiquette books. Ingratiation is the keynote of the performance. The presence of amateur actors on the stage is in itself disarming, and nothing that might disturb the good feeling between the actors and an ordinary middle-class New York audience has been allowed to creep into the production.

This bonhomie toward capitalism and the world at large is easily explained. Where the revolutionary theatre represented (by proxy) a working class which was irreconcilably hostile to society, the I.L.G.W.U. players represent (directly) a section of the working class which has made peace with society under the aegis of the New Deal. *Pins and Needles* is the group expression of a large, well-run, relatively contented labor union whose union contracts are signed without much trouble and whose demands on the system do not exceed decent minimum wages, decent maximum hours, the closed shop, and the right to picket. You cannot produce trenchant political satire—at least not in America in this period—if your political horizon is the Wagner Act, and *Pins and Needles* is at its best and most characteristic in the song numbers, where the political satire, such as it is, melts into irresponsible good humor, polysyllabic playfulness, and musical wit. "Sing Me a

Song with Social Significance," "Dear Beatrice Fairfax,"
and "Four Little Angels of Peace," all good, all by Harold
J. Rome, are in the pert, worldly, staccato tradition that
runs from Gilbert and Sullivan through Cole Porter. The
theatregoer, whatever his class allegiance, is likely to go
home humming them.

It is interesting that the one jarring note in this symphony of good cheer is struck by Mr. Marc Blitzstein,
author of *The Cradle Will Rock*. In an hysterical sketch
called "F.T.P. Plowed Under," Mr. Blitzstein belabors
the Federal Theatre, which last June abandoned his play
to the mercies of individual enterprise. The sketch is
strained and unconvincing even as burlesque: a personal
injury has been generalized into a national calamity, and
the spleen displayed by the author is manifestly in excess
of its cause. Yet it is Mr. Blitzstein's stridency—in *Pins and
Needles* so misdirected, so malapropos—that is the special,
quintessential quality of *The Cradle Will Rock*. If the
function of *Pins and Needles* is to ingratiate, the mission
of *The Cradle Will Rock* is to antagonize.

A curious feature of Mr. Blitzstein's play is that, though
it has for its subject the class war as exemplified in the
steel industry, it is almost totally lacking in internal conflict. The conflict which one ordinarily finds within or
between the characters of the drama has been moved out
past the proscenium arch into the theatre itself. *The
Cradle Will Rock* is a kind of well-drilled assault on the
feelings and nerves of its audience. What is presented is
not so much the workers versus the bosses in Steeltown,
U.S.A., as Mr. Blitzstein versus the ticket-holders in the
Mercury Theatre. The prominence of the author in the
production—he is actor, commentator, and pianist—gives
focus to the sadistic impulses of the script. Mr. Blitzstein's

acrid personality is, in fact, the whole show. He, as inso-
lent and sardonic entrepreneur, sits downstage center at
the piano; the actors behind him are his marionettes. The
timing and precision of the cast's performance have the
cold, military perfection of the dance routines of the
Radio City Rockettes. *The Cradle Will Rock* is a triumph
of theatrical goose-stepping. The drama has become de-
humanized; it has been made into a marvelous mechanical
monster which begins to operate with great efficiency
whenever Mr. Blitzstein pulls the switch.

Mr. Blitzstein's creatures are, of course, abstractions, as
their names indicate. That is why they are so easily
manipulated. Mr. Mister, the steel magnate, is the biggest
abstraction of them all, and his sycophants, Editor Daily,
President Prexy, Doctor Specialist, Reverend Salvation,
and the rest, are presented solely in terms of their occupa-
tions. This is as true of the proletarians as it is of the
bosses, shopkeepers, and petty bourgeois intellectuals, for
Mr. Blitzstein's work has a wonderful uniformity. All of
the characters are exhibited as specimens of class behavior, and the result is a series of satirical and sentimental grotesques. There is an element of horror in the
perfect predictability of these unicellular creations, and
the little, white-faced, class-conscious Columbine of a
prostitute is nearly as repellent, consequently, as the over-
sexed, over-dressed, over-effusive Mrs. Mister. Larry Foreman, strike leader and hero, is meant, I suppose, to
represent the spirit of joy in the insurgent working class,
but he, too, has been stepped up into caricature until he
resembles a madcap master of ceremonies in a Broadway
night club, and his ultimate song of triumph carries an
overtone of savage hotcha which considerably detracts
from the high seriousness of the play's finale.

It is clear that Mr. Blitzstein's deterministic formula for

playwriting rules out the possibility of moral struggle within his characters. What is at first sight more puzzling is that the class struggle itself is barely dramatized. The two groups, workers and bosses, never clash, never indeed really touch each other, until the very end of the play. Then Mr. Mister tries to bribe Larry Foreman to sell out the strike; Larry reaffirms his allegiance to labor; everybody sings a song; and the house lights go up. It is as if two solar systems had been functioning separately on the stage, and their meeting, which one might have expected to be a major collision, turned out to be a passing and inconclusive contact. Perhaps Mr. Blitzstein was too well aware of the brittleness of his puppet-people to risk them in any head-on encounter. His caution, whether deliberate or accidental, was undoubtedly justified.

The abstract and heartless nature of Mr. Blitzstein's work will, I think, set up an instinctive resistance in any normal American spectator. The pleasure one takes in *The Cradle Will Rock* is the pleasure of feeling one's native sensibilities violated. This play is having much the same kind of vogue, and producing much the same response as the surrealist and abstract art shows did at the Modern Museum. Though its setting and subject matter are American, it is essentially a non-indigenous plant. Musically, it is very much indebted to the German, Kurt Weill. Dramatically, it shares a certain neo-primitivism with Auden and Isherwood, but it lacks the free play of public-school-boy fancy that one finds in *The Ascent of F. 6* and *The Dog Beneath the Skin*. Its real kinship is with post-war German expressionism, which, except for Elmer Rice's *The Adding Machine*, never managed to take root in America.

The fact is that the tendency of American playwrights has always been to particularize rather than to generalize.

Even in the revolutionary theatre where the emphasis theoretically should have been on the mass, not the individual, the American playwright's impulse was to write a "problem drama" with proletarian characters, and leave the mass recitatives to the Europeans. The Federal Theatre in its Living Newspaper productions has been working with groups, but these groups have been visibly atomized, each individual being endowed with such little eccentricities as would make him "recognizable" in a sort of neighborly fashion to the audience. That this American method of seeing and translating experience has its dangers and limitations, that it readily drops into mere homeliness and triviality, the present state of the commercial theatre testifies. This method, however, has within itself the power of expansion; Mr. Blitzstein's method can only contract.

Mr. Thornton Wilder's play, *Our Town,* at the Morosco, is the inverse of *The Cradle Will Rock.* Both plays are done without settings or props; both employ a commentator who serves as intermediary between actors and audience; both deal with an American town. But while Mr. Blitzstein is a sort of public prosecutor of Steeltown of 1937, Mr. Frank Craven, stage manager and spokesman for Mr. Wilder, appears as a kind of indulgent defense attorney for a certain small New England town of thiry years ago. Mr. Blitzstein evokes an industrial town which is abstract and odious; Mr. Craven and Mr. Wilder, a home town which is concrete and dear. *Our Town,* like *Ah, Wilderness,* is an exercise in memory, but it differs from the O'Neill work in that it is not a play in the accepted sense of the term. It is essentially lyric, not dramatic. The tragic velocity of life, the elusive nature of experience, which can never be stopped or even truly felt at any given point, are the themes of the play—themes familiar enough in lyric poetry, but never met, except incidentally, in drama. Mr. Wilder, in attempting to give these themes theatrical form, was obliged, paradoxically, to abandon almost all the conventions of the theatre.

In the first place, he has dismissed scenery and props as irrelevant to, and, indeed, incongruous with his purpose. In the second place, he has invented the character of the stage manager, an affable, homespun conjuror who holds the power of life and death over the other characters, a local citizen who is in the town and outside of it at the same time. In the third place, he has taken what is accessory to the ordinary play, that is, exposition, and made it the main substance of his. The greater part of the first two acts is devoted to the imparting of information, to situating the town in time, space, politics, sociology, economics, and geology. But where in the conventional play, such pieces of information are insinuated into the plot or sugared over with stage business and repartee, in Mr. Wilder's play they are communicated directly; they take the place of plot, stage business, and repartee. Mr. Craven himself tells the biographies of the townspeople; he calls in an expert from the state college to give a scientific picture of the town, and the editor of the local newspaper to describe its social conditions. The action which is intermittently progressing on the stage merely illustrates Mr. Craven's talk.

Mr. Wilder's fourth innovation is the most striking. In order to dramatize his feelings about life he has literally raised the dead. At the opening of the third act a group of people are discovered sitting in rows on one side of the stage; some of the faces are familiar, some are new. They are speaking quite naturally and calmly, and it is not until one has listened to them for some minutes that one realizes that this is the cemetery and these are the dead. A young woman whom we have seen grow up and marry the boy next door has died in childbirth; a small shabby funeral procession is bringing her to join her relatives and neighbors. Only when she is actually buried does the play proper begin. She has not yet reached the serenity of the long dead, and she yearns to return to the world. With the permission of the stage manager and against the advice of the dead, she goes back—to a birthday of her childhood. Hardly a fraction of that day has passed, however, before she retreats gratefully to the cemetery, for she has perceived that the tragedy of life lies in the fragmentary and imperfect awareness of the living.

Mr. Wilder's play is, in a sense, a refutation of its own thesis. *Our Town* is purely and simply an act of awareness, a demonstration of the fact that in a work of art, at least, experience *can* be arrested, imprisoned, and preserved. The perspective of death, which Mr. Wilder has chosen, gives an extra poignancy and intensity to the small-town life whose essence he is trying so urgently to communicate. The little boy delivering papers, for example, becomes more touching, more meaningful and important, when Mr. Craven announces casually that he is going to be killed in the War. The boy's morning round, for the spectator, is transfigured into an absorbing ritual; the unconsciousness of the character has heightened the consciousness of the audience. The perspective is, to be sure, hazardous: it invites bathos and sententiousness. Yet Mr. Wilder has used it honorably. He forbids the spectator to dote on that town of the past. He is concerned only with saying: this is how it was, though then we did not know it. Once in a while, of course, his memory fails him, for young love was never so baldly and tritely gauche as his scene in the soda fountain suggests. This is, however, a deficiency of imagination, not an error of taste; and except in the third act, where the dead give some rather imprecise and inapposite definitions of the nature of the afterlife, the play keeps its balance beautifully. In this feat of equilibrium Mr. Wilder has had the complete co-operation of Mr. Craven, the serene, inexorable matter-of-factness of whose performance acts as a discipline upon the audience. Mr. Craven makes one quite definitely homesick, but pulls one up sharp if one begins to blubber about it.

May 1938

THE FEDERAL THEATRE

THE FEDERAL THEATRE is settling down. In two years it has passed from an experiment into an institution. *Prologue to Glory,* at the Maxine Elliot, is a type of "little," sentimental play that the WPA has never previously stooped to offer—at least not on Broadway, though I understand that a number of hokum, patriotic works on Jefferson and other American statesmen were sent to tour the provinces in the early days of the Project. *Haiti,* at the Lafayette, which is stunningly successful on its own terms, is yet by no means as original or as enterprising as the Negro *Macbeth,* and *One-third of a Nation,* at the Adelphi, is a retrogression from *Power.*

Prologue to Glory, Mr. E. P. Conkle's play about the young Lincoln, is the least prepossessing of the new WPA offerings. It is a trivial pastiche of Lincoln myths, moral platitudes, and dialect humor, messily stuck together with the gum arabic of a conventional love story. Like all the other plays and films which set out to show the "human side" of our national heroes, it has humanized its subject out of all heroism. The best one can say for it is that it is thoroughly democratic, since it illustrates with a vengeance the infinite possibilities for self-advancement that are supposed to lie open to every man under our system of government. If this dull-witted, tractable, comical yokel, said by the playwright to be Abraham Lincoln, could rise to be President of the United States, why so, one thinks, could you and I and the village idiot. There is no hint in Mr. Conkle's play of the almost monomaniac ambition, the driving power, the passion, the violence, the harsh intelligence of the real Lincoln. Here there is only a droll, awkward, lovesick boy, strong and stupid as his father's ox. The audience is invited to love this boy, not for his genius but for his absurdity; and, audiences being only too susceptible to such indirect flattery, a spirit of teary patronage toward the Great Emancipator is nightly wafted across the footlights.

Herndon, Lincoln's law partner, declared that Lincoln "never at any time abandoned the idea of becoming a lawyer. That was always a spirit which beckoned him on in the darkest hour of his adversity." Mr. Conkle prefers to believe that it was the spirit of Ann Rutledge that did the trick. The climax of the play shows Lincoln demoralized by her premature death, determined to abandon the law and to return to his father's farm. (He had previously thought of the law, it seems, chiefly as a means of buying Ann the "purties" her beauty and charm demanded.) Fortunately for the Union an older and wiser friend is on hand to remind the boy that Ann would have wished him to pursue his studies. Once his duty to the deceased is brought home to him, Abraham embarks, in his own lackadaisical fashion, for Springfield and the White House.

This plot, while not so good as the real one, might have served Mr. Conkle at least as well as it has served others had he been able to see in the love affair anything but a worn, genteel daguerreotype of the village queen and the bashful beau. This flabby courtship is too deficient in sinews to hold the play's sketchy scenes together, so that the work lacks in the end even the coherence of its own convictions.

Mr. William Du Bois' play, *Haiti,* though it is not in its details historically more accurate than Mr. Conkle's, has spirit, color, and, above all, focus. The difference between the two plays is well illustrated by their different treatments of the stage set. In both cases, a good deal of action takes place offstage. This offstage action is vitally important to Mr. Du Bois' play, where a revolution is going on throughout the story, and foolishly irrelevant to Mr. Conkle's play, where a stranger passing down an offstage road is of sufficient interest to distract the characters and the playwright from the boredom into which events on the stage have plunged them. But, waiving the question of relevancy, and turning to the conception and construction of the sets themselves, one sees that the set of *Haiti* has been beautifully planned to relate the stage to the imaginary world beyond it, while the set of *Prologue to Glory* has established no connection at all. The scene of *Haiti* is a room in a country house which is used as a headquarters first by the Negro officials of the island, then by the French. Directly across from the house are the mountains in which the insurgent Negro army is hiding, and to the audience's left is the harbor. A relation between the house, the mountains, and the harbor, has been created, very simply, by the use of a balcony, upstage center, which becomes the focal point of the play, the point at which the inside and outside worlds converge and communicate. There is no such point in *Prologue to Glory.* Papier mâché trees fade into a backdrop of fields and hills: the stage is wide open; the characters, rubber-necking toward the wings, dangle aimlessly in space.

As the diffuseness of Mr. Conkle's play manifests itself

even in the stage set, so the tightness of Mr. Du Bois' tri-
angular setting reinforces the wedge-like concentration of
his script. The play is merely a glorified melodrama, but
it has Liberty for its theme, and it is acted with superb
and consistent style. It tells of Toussaint L'Ouverture and
Jean Christophe, who wrested Haiti from Napoleon; but
this is only half its story. The drunken, brutal French
commandant of the island garrison has for his wife a
lovely Frenchwoman, who is, unknown to herself, the
daughter of the Negro butler who serves her. The butler,
also, is not what he seems, but is actually one of Christophe's officers, set to spy on his employers. Signals flash
out at night to the rebel army in the mountains; the mistress abets her father-servant; a correct and sympathetic
young French officer woos the mulatto lady; Jean Christophe pops out of a secret panel; and the island is won
from the French. This is not a very likely tale, but it is a
rousing one, and Mr. Du Bois demonstrates his superiority
to Mr. Conkle by his discretion in handling it.

In the first place it is written and played with an unabashed bravura which forces temporary conviction upon
the audience. In the second place, Mr. Du Bois, unlike
Mr. Conkle, seems to be conscious of both the uses and
the dangers of falsification in an historical drama. Mr.
Conkle's falsifications, except for a few minor perversions
and transpositions of fact, begin and end with the character of Lincoln. Mr. Du Bois' falsifications embrace all
his run-of-the-mill characters, but never touch his heroes,
Toussaint and Christophe. Toussaint and Christophe
move in and out of the intrigue plot, but they are not
governed by its laws. Mr. Du Bois, in fact, treats his intrigue plot in the same way that he treats his secret panel,
in the same way that other writers have treated the aside
or the trap-door. It is a simple mechanical device, a short

cut. Just as the secret panel makes it easier for Christophe to enter the house, so the sensational imbroglio in the commandant's household makes it easier for Christophe to make his revolution and for the audience to watch it. Christophe is the beneficiary of the melodrama, not its creature. It is true that Christophe belongs to the melodrama to the extent that his character can, under the circumstances given, never be deeply searched or roundly sculptured. Yet his prime attributes *can* be clearly seen—the primitive courage and sweetness linked to libertarian idealism, the Emperor Jones uniform symbolically topped by the Phrygian cap. In the floridity and fervor of this vision lie the play's strength and its weakness.

The remote, operatic past of Mr. Du Bois' setting allows him to employ a shamelessly antiquated dramatic technique. *One-third of a Nation* faces an exigent contemporary problem—housing—and one would expect this fifth production of the Living Newspaper to use all the innovations of the modern theatre. A great many new devices do in fact appear, and, had this production not been preceded by *Power,* one might think it the last word in experimental stagecraft. As compared to *Power,* however, *One-third of a Nation* shows the Living Newspaper on the road back to Belasco realism.

This technical reversion is partly conditioned by the current play's subject matter. A play about housing is necessarily more concerned with people, with the single human atom, than a play about power, which interests itself in atoms of another sort. There will, consequently, be less stylization and more realism in the housing play. The set of *One-third of a Nation* is a four-story, old-law tenement house, with the front wall partly torn away to afford both an inside and an outside view of tenement accommodations. It is a masterpiece of grisly realism, and, as such, completely defensible, for what stylization of a tenement could demonstrate the horrors of modern housing as well as a tenement itself? Likewise, it is natural and right that this Living Newspaper should tell the stories of some of the people who lived in the tenement, should make plain how these cramped, dark, unhygienic, inflammable quarters affected the lives of those who occupied them. The two tenement fires, which begin and end the play, the cholera epidemic, the premature enlightenment of the little boy who watches a prostitute in her room across the areaway—all these episodes, all realistically presented, are the high spots of the play.

Yet these scenes, however affecting, seem like excerpts from a conventional play. They are, in fact, like excerpts from *Dead End,* which, with more sensationalism and less social and economic awareness, was saying the same thing. What is there in *One-third of a Nation,* then, to justify its not being written and staged in the traditional manner? Why that movie screen, that amplified Voice of the Living Newspaper, that ubiquitous, intrusive figure of the Consumer, the Little Man Who Wants to Be Housed? The answer is plain. Each Living Newspaper is intended to be a large, socio-economic document which has the power of summary and generalization to go behind case histories to origins, and beyond case histories to cures. The originality of *Power* came from its fusion of the abstract and the particular. A high school lesson in economics, which dramatized the monopoly in terms of colored blocks of wood, was shortly succeeded by a "human spectacle" in which a crowd of individualized Tennesseans danced to the coming of the TVA. In *One-third of a Nation* there is still an attempt at historical survey and economic analysis, but the human "realistic" element has eaten into the textbook side of the play with confusing and disastrous results.

Everything that in *Power* was abstract has here become personalized. An anthropomorphizing mania has pervaded the script. In the study of the development of land values, instead of the blocks of wood which so well demonstrated their efficiency in the earlier play, the lesson is acted out by people with well-marked characteristics, in full period dress. The Consumer appears again, but now he is outfitted with a great many more homely crotchets of behavior, and, as if he were not human enough by himself, he has been endowed with a wife. Even the tenement house has a personality and a voice. Where the play should be at its most businesslike, most informative, it is actually at its most whimsical. The characters assigned to forces and tendencies blur, by their concrete and untimely humanity, the perception of the forces themselves. Representationalism and pedestrian fantasy, replacing the clean, geometric didacticism of *Power,* have muddied and elongated the play's exposition. The result is that the peripheral story-telling sections of the play, to which verisimilitude of characterization is appropriate, quite overshadow the central expository sections, to which it is not. We remember the example and forget the theorem.

It is possible that the shyness with which *One-third of a Nation* expresses its theorem is deliberate. It is possible that the walking portraits, the speaking likenesses that crowd the stage are there to create a diversion. For the play's theorem is certainly faulty. The housing problem is far knottier than the power problem. It is, in fact, impossible of solution under capitalism, even the liberal capitalism of the New Deal. The government can expropriate the power plants without upsetting the system; and, as was pointed out in *Power,* many municipalities have al-

ready done so. It cannot, however, take over housing, for
to do that would be to expropriate the land. *One-third of
a Nation,* as a WPA play, is therefore in no position to
offer the one effectual remedy for the evil it pictures. It
can demonstrate, with many playful and distracting flour-
ishes, that the origin of the housing problem lay in the
private ownership and exploitation of the land; it dare
not suggest that the cure lies in public ownership and
public planning. It must plead, instead, for palliative
legislation. The spectator, having been intermittently
harrowed by scenes of slum life, scenes which cry for revolutionary action, is blandly invited to write to his congressman. The triumphal march of state-owned power
into the Tennessee Valley, which was the grand climatic
moment of the last Living Newspaper, has its tragi-comic
parallel in *One-third of a Nation*—the passage of the miserably inadequate Wagner-Stekel Housing Act.

One-third of a Nation, outwardly the most showy of Living Newspaper productions, is inwardly the least ambitious. The Living Newspaper, being the adjunct of an Administration which has exhausted its political resources,
is itself becoming superannuated. It has already chronicled
the victories of the New Deal; it can hardly go on to im-
mortalize the omissions and failures.

The Living Newspaper, because of its subject matter,
would, of all the branches of the Federal Theatre, be naturally the most sensitive to the Administration's fatigue.
But the relative tameness of all the new WPA plays suggests that the Federal Theatre as a whole is running dry.
This is a disappointment, but not exactly a surprise.

In the first place, one might have expected that the impulse that set the Project going would, when it met the
combined resistance of congressional interference, bureau-
cratic red tape, and reduced appropriations, lose a certain

amount of its force. Something that is felt as a new idea
is inevitably a little dimmed by being managed as a business. More significant, however, is the fact that the Federal Theatre, like all the New Deal ventures, is a half-
measure. It is a work-relief project which aspires to be a
National Theatre, and its ambition, unfortunately, is incompatible with its economic base. Its initial success was
due partly to the intelligence and energy of its director,
Mrs. Flanagan, and partly to the fact that it was launched
at a time when the commercial theatre was still in the grip
of the depression. Producers were unusually cautious, and
a great deal of adventurous young talent was unemployed.
The Federal Theatre offered that talent the security of a
minimum wage and endless opportunities for experimenta-
tion. With the revival of the commercial theatre, the best
of the WPA's writers, composers, actors, and directors were
quickly absorbed into private industry. The Federal Theatre, in short, had acted merely as an incubator, and now it
must await a new theatrical depression and a new crop
of talent before it can recover its original élan. The moral
is that a government which dares not pay the prevailing
wage, which dares not, in other words, compete economi-
cally with private industry, cannot in the long run compete with it artistically.

SHAW AND CHEKHOV

IF YOU WANT to make a rational structure of *Heartbreak House* you can say that it is a sort of layer cake of meanings. The top layer is a play about a houseful of unhappy, articulate, rudderless English people of the upper middle class who, while attempting to straighten out their sex relations, are surprised by the air raid of a foreign power. The second layer is an allegory of the moral and political bankruptcy of the European leisure class. The mad but profound old sea captain signifies the spirit of Old England. The captain's two daughters exemplify the class that was born to govern but that abdicated its responsibility in favor of the new forces of finance capitalism, represented by the practical business man. In the one daughter we see the upper-class escape into the strong-arm philistinism of colonial government; in the other, the retreat into the dream world of dilettante cultivation. The air raid is the war which that class has unwittingly prepared for its own destruction. The third layer is a dramatic exposition of the protean character of human nature. It is this third layer on which the play rests; yet it is a foundation neither fixed nor solid, and it keeps the other elements, superimposed upon it, in a kind of dizzying perpetual motion.

None of the characters can keep his shape; none is consistent. The captain is wise, but he is also crazy; he is the only strong person on the stage, but he gets his strength from rum. The powerful capitalist has no capital; he lives on traveling expenses and commissions. He is a hard bargainer, but his heart is pitifully vulnerable. The braggart and liar is a courageous man. The worldly diplomat is a lady's lapdog. The ingenue is a materialistic schemer. The burglar is no burglar. The churchy old reformer is a shrewd observer. The conventional snob is a troubled and intelligent woman. The great beauty has no power over her husband. These contradictory traits of character, revealed one by one as the play goes on, succeed but do not permanently displace one another. They ebb and flow through the characters, and it is no accident, I think, that *Heartbreak House* is a ship, its owner and philosopher a captain, and the play's most poetic imagery predominantly marine.

The nightmarish fluidity of the characters inundates the play's schematism. Since the people will not stay put, since good people will not be good or bad people bad, the plot misses a point and the allegory a moral. Yet the failure of the plot, the blurring of the allegory, introduce into *Heartbreak House* the extra dimension which is so often lacking in Shaw's work. The third element, by unsettling the other two—the comedy of morals, and the political allegory—has given the drama an interior tension, a sense of dubiety and disquietude. The brightness of the comedy and the grandeur of the allegory intensify this final, anxious uncertainty and raise it to the level of tragic doubt. To the pathos of the play's lost people is added the terror of the play's lost author, who could not, in conscience, make his story come out right, or, indeed, come out at all. For the author as well as for the characters the apocalyptic air raid that finishes the play appears to come as a merciful release from striving. Like a nervous and abstracted conversationalist, he had already begun to repeat himself before it happened.

Of the three elements discussed, the first is most conspicuously present in Orson Welles's production. The Mercury Theatre company act out *Heartbreak House* as if it were one of those weekend comedies by Rachel Crothers or Frederick Lonsdale. Mady Christians, as the captain's emancipated daughter, gives a fair imitation of Ina Claire. With the exception of George Coulouris, whose Boss Mangan is a genuinely strident, strangled, unhappy, self-made man, the captain's guests appear to be the poised, self-confident, ineffably impertinent loungers that we meet so often at theatrical house parties, though they lack a good deal of the style and speed to which we are accustomed. So far as possible, neuroticism and anxiety have been banished from the stage. The set, as well as the characters, has been brightened up into cheerful conventionality: the captain's psychically malodorous house seems to have been carefully air-conditioned. Since this is a play which, as Shaw himself said, "began with an atmosphere and does not contain one word that was foreseen before it was written," a play which draws its life from the ominous thickness of its atmosphere, the effect of Mr. Welles's housecleaning is obvious. Under such circumstances, the serious parts of the play lose almost all meaning, and *Heartbreak House* seems a sentimental misnomer for the gay if languid world in which the Mercury Theatre Shavians dwell.

The failure of Mr. Welles's production to expose the contradictions that corrode Shaw's people is most damaging in the key cases of Hector Hushabye, played by Vincent Price, and Captain Shotover, played by Mr. Welles.

Hector Hushabye, as written, is a real fantastico, a *commedia dell'arte* clown with a touch of nobility, an extravagant rhetorician who can be a poet, a ham actor who is tortured by sincerity. Mr. Price, who was Prince Albert in *Victoria Regina,* plays Hector as if the two characters had a good deal in common. This erratic personage, who is of all the captain's relatives his most sympathetic listener, is bleached into a good-looking, wooden Englishman with a stolid interest in routine infidelity.

The captain undergoes an even more startling transformation. Mr. Welles as an actor has always seemed to secrete a kind of viscous holy oil with which he sprays the rough surfaces of his roles. He has this time applied so thick a coat that the real Captain Shotover, is practically invisible. Where the real captain is brisk and peppery, Mr. Welles is slow and sibylline. The real captain is a retired man of action; Mr. Welles is a retired armchair prophet. The funereal deliberation of Mr. Welles's performance obliterates the distinction made by the playwright between the vigor and enterprise of the old England and the decadent lassitude of the new, a distinction which is the mainspring of the play's political allegory. The contradictions within the captain himself, the drunkenness and madness that deflect the old man's will and discolor his vision, are likewise suppressed. Mr. Welles's captain exudes an odor of unmitigated sanctity, and the play's ultimate and most grotesque irony, which reveals its wise man as a besotted crank, goes by unperceived.

The sentimentality of Mr. Welles's acting, the nervelessness of his direction, the bare, mechanical competence of the majority of his supporting cast combine to act as a steam roller on Shaw's *Heartbreak House.* The density of the original structure is lost; the play is flattened out until it looks like a sketchy blueprint of itself. Mr. Welles's production can only serve to remind the public that the original still exists in the library.

Shaw described his own play as a "Fantasia in the Russian manner on English themes," and in his preface to the published version, he notes that Chekhov "had produced four fascinating dramatic studies of *Heartbreak House*." One of these was *The Sea Gull,* which has recently been done by the Theatre Guild in association with the Lunts. The resemblances between the two plays are only superficial. They have in common the "futility" which is supposed to be Chekhov's special property. Both show the disintegration of a cultured, leisured class. Both emphasize the perverse contradictions of human nature. Both use the "confession" as a method of revealing character. Shaw's play, however, deals in generalizations; Chekhov's in particularities. Shaw's people are thought of as symbols of abstract social ideas; Chekhov's people are observed concretely, and only in the aggregate become symbolic of a social order. Shaw's conception of character is inorganic; Chekhov's organic. The dramatic quick-changes to which the characters of *Heartbreak House* are subjected proceed not from the characters themselves but from a generalization about human beings in the mind of the playwright. Even the most complex of the *Heartbreak House* people are literary fabrications, wound together skein by skein. The antithetical traits of Chekhov's people, on the contrary, have grown together in such a way that it is often impossible to disentangle a single strand. Even in the treatment of the "confession" one sees the artificiality of Shaw and the simple naturalness of Chekhov. Chekhov's confession seems to arise from an artless preoccupation with the self which runs throughout Russian life and literature. Shaw's confessions are displays of an impudent and self-conscious exhibitionism which is certainly characteristic of the playwright but can hardly be said to be typical of the class and nation he writes about.

There is a certain coldness and poverty—witness the last act of *Heartbreak House*—even in Shaw's best work which prevent him from equalling the best of Chekhov. Yet *Heartbreak House,* one of his greatest plays, compares very well, I think, with *The Sea Gull,* one of Chekhov's worst. In *Heartbreak House* the vastness and nobility of the conception, the eloquence of the style, redeem the occasional thinness of the characterization, while the sentimental triviality of Chekhov's theme tends to debase the value of his most acute and poignant observations. The older people in *The Sea Gull,* the successful writer, the actress, the unhappy spinster who drinks, the invalid landowner are among the best shabby-genteel portraits in Chekhov's gallery, but the young people, with whom the plot is really concerned, are melodramatic figures seen at a distance through a mist of tears. The commonplace character of the plot, which tells of a young girl's "ruin" at the hands of a vain and selfish older man, and of her young lover's consequent suicide, is not improved by the "poetic" analogy drawn between the girl and a sea gull shot by a bored sportsman. The difficulty is that the girl's degradation is not directly observed but summed up in its tritest outlines by one of the characters, and the inner motivation for the boy's collapse is never given. The real story takes place offstage. It is not properly incorporated in the play, and the playwright, consequently, is demanding sympathy for his characters on what are artistically false pretenses. The final irony by which Chekhov makes the novelist forget both the significance he himself had attributed to the sea gull and the fact that he had ordered it to be stuffed, is an extremely vulgar concession to the conventional demands for neatness in play-writing, a concession which Chekhov in his later plays would never have made.

The acting of the Guild company was such as to draw a clean line between what is meretricious and what is good in the play. Both of the young people were bad. The girl was merely pallid, but Richard Whorf's Constantine was a kind of museum of horrors, containing all the clichés and curiosities of juvenile acting. The older people were, on the whole, good, ranging from the excellence of Margaret Webster as the ironic Masha, through the skill and frequent insight of Alfred Lunt's Trigorin, the solidity of Sydney Greenstreet's Peter Sorin, down to the slick overacting of Lynn Fontanne's Arkadina.

Stark Young's sharp and unaffected translation cleared away a great many of the cobwebs which one had previously thought to be part of Chekhov, but which prove merely to have clung to the styles of his earlier translators. It is to be hoped that Mr. Young will next devote himself to one of Chekhov's more mature plays.

Footnote, 1956. It was Lunt's performance, actually, that made the play seem "meretricious." He played the novelist as an aging roué who seduced the young girl out of sheer idle depravity. But the novelist in Chekhov is a decent enough fellow in his late thirties (sometimes thought to be a self-portrait) who reluctantly lets himself be seduced by the young girl. The reason he forgets the seagull is that he is preoccupied with his writing; he is a vocational study of the literary man—that is why he is defenseless against a fresh young admirer.

March–April 1940

SAROYAN, AN INNOCENT
ON BROADWAY

Wᴵᴸᴸᴵᴬᴹ ꜱᴬʀᴏʏᴬɴ has been in the writing busi-
ness for eight years. He still retains his innocence. It is as
valuable to him as an artist as virginity to Deanna Durbin.
To keep it, he has, of course, had to follow a strict regi-
men—no late hours, no worries, and only a limited responsibility. That is, he has had to fight off Ideas, Movements, Sex, and Commercialism. Some of the benefits have
been remarkable. He has stayed out of the literary rackets
—the Hollywood racket, the New York cocktail-party
racket, and the Stalinist racket, which became practically
indistinguishable from both the others. What is more important, the well of inspiration, located somewhere in his
early adolescence, has never run dry. He is still able to
look at the world with the eyes of a sensitive newsboy,
and to see it eternally brand-new and touched with wonder. The price is that the boundaries of this world are the
boundaries of the newsboy's field of vision.

Saroyan is genuine, Saroyan is not mechanical, Saroyan
is the real thing; he tells you this over and over again in
the prefaces to his two plays. It is true. If you compare
him with his contemporaries, Odets and Steinbeck, the
purity of his work is blinding. Puerile and arrogant and

sentimental as he may be, he is never cheap. Both Odets and Steinbeck are offering the public a counterfeit literature: Odets is giving an imitation of a lacerated Bronx boy named Odets who once wrote a play; Steinbeck is giving an imitation of a serious novelist. Saroyan as a public figure does an impersonation of Saroyan, but as a writer he plays straight. Moreover, both Odets and Steinbeck suffer from a kind of auto-intoxication; they are continually plagiarizing themselves; and their frequent ascents into "fine writing" are punctuated with pauses for applause that are nearly audible. Now Saroyan, as I say, has created a public character for himself, and the chief attribute of this character is exhibitionism, but he has incorporated this character boldly into his work and let him play his role there. Vanity has become objectified and externalized; it has no need to ooze surreptitiously into the prose. Saroyan's writing remains fresh and crisp and never has the look of having been pawed over by the author. Furthermore, though Saroyan's work is all of a piece, and the same themes and symbols recur, you will rarely find a constellation of symbols repeating itself, you will rarely get the same effect warmed up for a second serving.

It may be that Saroyan's world of ice-cream cones and toys, of bicycles and bugles, and somersaults and shotguns, of hunger and of banquets that appear out of the air, of headlines that tell of distant disasters, of goodhearted grocers and lovable frauds, of drunk fairy princes and pinball games that pay, is naturally more at home in the theatre than in fiction. Or it may be that, his scope being necessarily as narrow as it is, he has exhausted the permutations of the short story and requires the challenge of a new medium. At any rate, he has written these two plays *; one caused a furore and the other is a hit.

* *My Heart's in the Highlands, The Time of Your Life.*

My Heart's in the Highlands, produced by the Group
Theatre on a geometric set, was the source of some dis-
tress to the New York critics, who had been getting ac-
quainted with "fantasy" and "the poetic drama" through
the agency of Maxwell Anderson. The meaning is in the
title, "My heart's in the Highlands, my heart is not here,
My heart's in the Highlands a-chasing the deer." It is a
story of poor people and their hunger for poetry and music
and theatre, which persists in the teeth of want, but can
only be partly satisfied because society will not pay for
these things. There are three principal characters: a poet
and his son, and a fugitive from the Old People's Home,
an ancient Shakespearean actor who plays the bugle. The
critics talked about "experimental theatre" and "surreal-
ism," but neither of these terms was quite satisfactory,
even to the critics themselves. Actually, the play is half a
pastoral and half a vaudeville. In *The Time of Your Life,*
which was produced this year by Eddie Dowling on a realistic set, the pastoral element has dropped out, and what is
left is almost pure vaudeville, a play that is closer to *Hell-
zapoppin* than to anything else in the theatre.

The action of this play takes place in a San Francisco
waterfront saloon in the year 1939. Again there is a group
of relatively simple people, a pure-hearted prostitute, a
boy out of a job, a pinball enthusiast, a nice cop, a nice
longshoreman, a Negro piano player, a hoofer, a mad old
trapper, the proprietor of the saloon, a nurse, and a stiff
young man who is desperately in love with her. All these
characters seem to be trailing clouds of glory; they are
beautiful and terrible just because they *are* people, Saroyan thinks. Each of them wants to do his own job, to do it
tenderly, reverently, and joyfully, and to live at peace
with his neighbors. Unfortunately, there are Frustrators
at work, monstrous abstractions like Morality, and Labor

and Capital, whose object is to flatten out these assertive individualists. The chief of these Frustrators is a Vice-Squad man named Blick, who stands for Morality, but Finance Capital is in the room in the shape of a gentleman slummer, and the voice of Labor can be heard outside in the waterfront strike. But if this universe has its devil in Blick, it has its God in Joe, the character played by Eddie Dowling, a charming, indolent alcoholic, whose mysterious wealth is the life-blood of the joint. Buying champagne, buying newspapers, ordering drinks for the house, giving handouts to the Salvation Army, to the boy out of a job, to the unfortunate prostitute, he keeps the people of the play going, but, being detached from the life of action, he is powerless to save them from Blick. This is left for one of their own numbers, the old trapper (God the Son), who shoots the interfering moralist as calmly as if he did it every day, and regretfully throws his beautiful pearl-handled revolver into San Francisco Bay. When Joe sees that everything is straightened out, and that the two main characters are ready to start life on their own, he goes home, and the understanding is that he will not be back tomorrow.

There is no point in commenting on this intellectual structure, for it is not an intellectual structure at all, but a kind of finger-exercise in philosophy. Whenever it makes itself explicit, its juvenility is embarrassing; when it is allowed to lie somewhere behind the lines, it gives the play a certain strangeness, another dimension that is sensed but not seen. The real living elements of the play, however, owe nothing to philosophy; they stem straight from the Keith Circuit. Saroyan is still drawing on the street-life of his adolescence; it is inevitable, therefore, that his plays should belong to the theatre of that street-life, that is, to vaudeville. *The Time of Your Life* is full of vaudeville; indeed, almost every incident and character in it can be translated back into one of the old time acts. Kit Carson, the trapper, is W. C. Fields; the pinball machine that plays "America" and waves a flag when the jackpot is hit is out of Joe Cook; the toys Joe buys are a visual reminder of the juggling turn, and his money, deriving from nowhere and ostentatiously displayed, makes you think of the magic act; the young man who keeps telephoning his girl is the comic monologist; Harry the hoofer is Jimmy Durante; the boy out of a job is the stooge; and Joe (or God), as played by Eddie Dowling, who is himself an ex-hoofer, has that slim, weary, sardonic, city-slicker look that was the very essence of the vaudeville artist. Even the serious part of the play, the soul-searing drama involving Kitty, the beautiful prostitute, and the boy who wants to marry her, and Blick, takes you back to those short problem melodramas starring a passée actress that were occasionally interspersed with the regular acts. And *The Time of Your Life,* like an evening of vaudeville, is good when it engages the fancy and bad when it engages the feelings. *My Heart's in the Highlands* was a slightly different case. The sentiment there was a little cloying but not false. It proceeded from a different and more untainted source, the folk tale or pastoral that was also a part of Saroyan's Armenian-American boyhood.

Saroyan is in love with America, and very insistent about it. Just as a girl in his plays will be an ordinary girl and at the same time "the most beautiful girl in the world," because Saroyan is young and feeling good when he looks at her, so America is an ordinary place and at the same time "the most wonderful country in the world." This excessive, rather bumptious patriotism has created a certain amount of alarm; it has been suspected that Saroyan has joined the propagandists of the second crusade for democracy. The alarm is, I think, unjustified. Actually, the second statement is no more realistic than the first; it is not the literal fact but the state of mind that the reader is asked to believe in. And there is a kind of pathos about both statements that arises from the discrepancy that must exist between the thing described and the description of it. How far, in the second case, the pathos is intentional it is impossible to tell, but the contrasts in Saroyan's work show that he is at least partly aware of it.

In each of these plays there is a character that, more than the "gentle people" he talks so much about, represents the America he loves. This national type, exemplified by the bugler in *My Heart's in the Highlands* and by the trapper in *The Time of Your Life,* is an elderly boaster who is both a fraud and not a fraud, an impostor and a kind of saint. In *My Heart's in the Highlands* the bugler, with all his pretensions, is just a fugitive from the Old People's Home; yet, from the point of view of the people in the play, he is everything he purports to be, and more; he is the light-bringer. The same thing is true of the trapper in the second play, but the point is better made. Beginning with "Did you ever fall in love with a midget weighing thirty-nine pounds?" Kit Carson moves along through the plot telling one tall tale after another. At the end, after he has shot Blick offstage, he comes into the saloon and begins a narrative that sounds exactly like all the others: "Shot a man once. In San Francisco. In 1939, I think it was. In October. Fellow named Blick or Glick or something like that." This statement is a bombshell. It gives veracity to all the improbable stories that have preceded it, and at the same time the improbable stories cast a doubt on the veracity of this statement, which the audience nevertheless knows to be true. A boast becomes a form of modesty, and the braggart is maiden-shy.

This kind of character undoubtedly belongs to the tradition of American life and especially to the tradition of the West. It is Paul Bunyan and it is also the barker. But the tradition is dead now; it died when the frontier closed on the West Coast at some point in Saroyan's childhood. The type, if it exists at all outside of W. C. Fields, is now superannuated, for such anomalous human beings could only thrive under nomadic conditions of life. Today the barker has become an invisible radio announcer, and the genial, fraudulent, patent-medicine man has turned into a business house, with a public relations counsel. The America Saroyan loves is the old America, and the plays he weaves around it are not so much daring innovations as legends.

THE SKIN OF OUR TEETH

Tʜᴏʀɴᴛᴏɴ ᴡɪʟᴅᴇʀ's latest play, *The Skin of Our Teeth*, is a spoof on history. For all its air of experimentalism, its debt to Joyce, as yet unacknowledged, its debt to Olson and Johnson, paid in full, it belongs to a tradition familiar and dear to the Anglo-Saxon heart. That is the tradition of *The Road to Rome, Caesar and Cleopatra, Hamlet* in modern dress, *Julius Caesar* in uniforms. Its mainspring is the anachronistic joke, a joke both provincial and self-assertive, a joke which insists that the Roman in his toga is simply a bourgeois citizen wearing a sheet, and that Neanderthal man with his bear-skin and his club is at heart an insurance salesman at a fancy-dress ball. The joke has a double fascination which it exerts on the middle-class public and the middle-class playwright alike. In the first place, it is conservative: it affirms the eternity of capitalism, which it identifies with "human nature," and it consoles us for the flatness of the present by extending that flatness over the past, so that whatever our sufferings, we shall at least not be racked by envy, that most dangerous of human passions. In the second place, it is sacrilegious, for it denies time and history, and this, to the modern ear, is the moral equivalent of hubris, of ancestor-desecration, of the sin against the Holy Ghost. Hence it is that such works as *The Skin of Our Teeth* almost invariably have an appearance of daring: the shock value of *The Private Life of Helen of Troy*, say, did not derive from its rather mild sexual impropriety. Moreover, art and culture generally find themselves within easy range of the blasphemer (and this is only logical, since culture is an historical phenomenon); you get Mark Twain or Mr. Wilder's third act where the philosophers appear as half-audible quotations from their works, quotations which can only be introduced after a great deal of apologetic discussion: "I don't suppose it means anything," says the stage-manager. "It's just a kind of poetic effect." Mr. Wilder, being a professor, wants to have it both ways: he wants to sponsor the philosophers, but at the same time he does not want the audience to think that he is an ass.

The plot and structure of *The Skin of Our Teeth* must by this time be in the public domain. Everybody knows that the play deals with three great crises in human history, the return of the Ice Age, the Flood, the War, any war at all or this war in particular. It is Mr. Wilder's fancy that all these events happened to a man named George Antrobus of 216 Cedar Street, Excelsior, New Jersey, father of two, President of the Ancient Order of Mammals, inventor, soldier and occasional philanderer. Man, then, enlightened ape, is seen as the eternal husband, whose destiny is an endless commuter's trip between the Home and the Office, the poles of the human sphere. The trip may not be broken on pain of flood, ice, fascism; a stopover with the Other Woman will result in a disaster of millenial proportions. "Oh, oh, oh! Six o'clock and the master not home yet," says the maid, opening the play. In other words, if George misses the five-fifteen, Chaos is come again. This is the moral of the piece. Man, says Mr. Wilder, from time to time gets puffed up with pride and prosperity, he grows envious, covetous, lecherous, forgets his conjugal duties, goes whoring after women; portents of disaster appear, but he is too blind to see them; in the end, with the help of the little woman, who has never taken any stock in either pleasure or wisdom, he escapes by the skin of his teeth. *Sicut erat in principio.* . . .

It is a curious view of life. It displays elements of Christian morality. Christ, however, was never so simple, but on the contrary allowed always for paradox (the woman taken in adultery, the story of Martha and Mary, "Consider the lilies of the field") and indeed regarded the family as an obstacle to salvation. No, it is not the Christian view, but a kind of bowdlerized version of it, such as might have been imparted to a class of taxpayer's children by a New England Sunday School teacher forty years ago. And here we find again Mr. Wilder's perennial nostalgia, a nostalgia not for the past but for an eternal childhood, for the bedrock of middle-class family life, for *"the old Sunday evenings at home with the tinkling piano our guide."* It is a nostalgia which found a pure and lyrical expression in *Our Town,* but which has made its way more furtively into *The Skin of Our Teeth* and lurks there as an impediment both to action and to thought, for at the end of each act the play hits the suburban family group, stumbles over it, and comes to a halt; the repetition is inevitable, but not dramatic: the only conflict is the conflict between the submerged idea and the form. The play in general suffers from a certain embarrassment and uneasiness, as if its author were ashamed of the seriousness with which he adheres to his theme. Surely Miss Bankhead's asides to the audience and the whole conceit that the end of the world is only a play that some actors are putting on serve no other purpose than to relieve the author's sense of awkwardness. "I don't understand a word of this play,"

Miss Bankhead complains again and again, but actually there is not a word in the play which Miss Bankhead cannot and does not perfectly comprehend. All this aspect of the play is, to put it frankly, fraudulent, an illusionist's trick; an elaborate system of mystification has been, as it were, installed in the theatre in order to persuade the audience that it is witnessing a complex and difficult play, while what is really being shown on the stage is of a childish and almost painful naiveté. To some extent, the illusion is successful: middlebrow members of the audience are, as usual, readily induced to disregard the evidence of their own ears and consider the play either monstrously profound or monstrously bewildering. Simpler people, however, who have never heard of Aristotle, see nothing difficult about it. They accept the performance as a sort of lark, which at best it is, a bright children's pantomime, full of boldly costumed figures out of Bible history. As the daily drama critics have said, over and over, with all the relish of Lucifer admitting a new registrant into hell, Mr. Wilder has become a *real* man of the theatre.

THE RUSSIAN SOUL IN WARTIME

IN REVIEWING the current version of *The Three Sisters,* The New York drama critics, almost to a man, congratulated Miss Cornell on her all-star production and deplored her choice of play. What integrity, what generosity, what talent, and all, alas, wasted on an inferior play by a dramatist whom we all revere but who, it must be confessed, seems dull and bookish in these stirring times. The general impression was that Miss Cornell in her devotion to art had committed an act of desperate, if winning, folly; like a great lady who loves the poor so much that she gives away her fortune to a beggar on the street. This inversion of values is a phenomenon that appears regularly at the revival of any classic, with the eternal exception of *Hamlet. Hamlet,* it is conceded, is a play for the stage: it is, in fact, *the* play for the stage; the other classics belong in the library, where the scholarly critic can study them at leisure—in the dramatic perspective of *The Eve of St. Mark.*

The fact is, of course, that *The Three Sisters* is not an inferior play of Chekhov, at least not strikingly so; it is earlier and cruder than *The Cherry Orchard,* but it is, on the other hand, more mature than *The Sea Gull,* and since Chekhov wrote only five full-length plays the choice was not a wide one. The fact is also that Miss Cornell, whose devotion to art is indeed painfully sincere, has given us a production that erupts heavily, like a slow volcano, over the topography of the play, so that the playgoer who would like to know what Chekhov was doing here must perform a considerable work of archaeology. There are intimations, it is true, of the original Chekhovian landscape, particularly in the performance of Tom Powers as the schoolteacher, Kuligin, and the text itself survives as a map. Leaving aside questions of talent—for Ruth Gordon as Natasha gives a striking, even terrifying performance that is nevertheless as injurious to the play's values as Miss Cornell's awkward and sentimental Masha—the main difficulty is that American actors cannot understand why Chekhov called many of his plays comedies. To the American theatre mind, a play that culminates in disastrous events is, by definition, a tragedy; the murder in the last act gives the director his clue. If you add to this the fact that the characters are unhappy, it is plain sailing! The funereal note is struck in the opening speech and the play is driven—at a respectable speed—to its last resting place in the fourth act. The critics then join the mourners in lamenting the fact that the play is dead.

Mme. Litvinoff (an Englishwoman) remarked to newspaper reporters that *The Three Sisters* is an absurd play about three grown-up women who spend four acts not going to Moscow when they have the price of the ticket. This description, though derogatory in intention, is perfectly exact. That is what the play is about, and the failure of the three sisters to get to Moscow (and indeed the whole nostalgic dream of Moscow) is not tragic, but pathetic, touching, absurd. The play is a study of the romantic character, and the city of Moscow is the earthly paradise, for which no railroad company can issue a ticket, no mat-

ter how prosperous the passenger may be. It is the illusion
of happiness, nobility, and freedom, pursued abstractly
in dreams, the mirage seen in the desert that dazzles the
eyes of the thirsty traveler till he loses his bearings and
no longer remembers what his real destination was. The
three sisters rise superior to the realities of a provincial
town and become its most abject victims. Their eyes fixed
on Moscow, they allow themselves to be plundered by a
vulgar sister-in-law, whose objectives are only too real and
hence readily attainable. This is the fate of all the romantic characters in the play. The brother, whose heart
is set on an enormous career in science (that is, on Fame)
accepts an insignificant post on the local school board
from his wife's lover, the ineffable Protopopov. Vershinin,
the idealistic colonel, who talks of the beautiful world
that will come into being in two or three hundred years,
is the slave of his two little girls and of a wife who is continually embarrassing him by attempting to commit suicide. And Tusenbach, the serious little Baltic baron, who
dreams of a life of hard work in his own brickyard, is killed
in a frivolous duel by the brutal and oafish Solyony, who
himself is acting out a dream in which he is a character in
Lermontov.

These unfortunate people are charming, but, in a certain sense, not to be taken seriously. Morally speaking,
they are all a little hollow, and their dreams of nobility
and hard work have in them an element of pretense.
There is an ugly scene in the third act where the sisters
fail to defend their old nurse against the bad temper of
their sister-in-law, and another painful scene in the last
act, where Irina, the youngest sister, who knows in her
heart that her fiancé is going off to be killed in a duel,
refuses to speak to him a final word of love. "What? What
am I to say to you?" she asks, innocently. These human

failures are the true crises of the play, and in the end it is only the eldest sister, Olga, who by accepting against her inclination the post of headmistress in the school, rises genuinely superior to circumstances, for by taking financial independence in exchange for her dream of Moscow, she is able to provide for the old nurse who has been driven out by Natasha. In Miss Cornell's production, however, none of this is to be found: the moral lapses of the sisters appear as aberrations or accidents; they are the innocent victims of a villainous woman, of fate, of provincial society, and the tragedy is, indeed, their failure to get to Moscow.

What is missed also is the comic element in the play. Chekhov's characters are both witty and amusing, and they have, in addition, a flickering awareness of the absurdity of their position, an inconsequent but nonetheless real irony which raises the whole problem from the level of action to the superior level of consciousness. It is Chekhov's peculiar use of a kind of modified soliloquy to treat the theme of self-consciousness that is his dramatic signature; Miss Cornell and most of her fellow actors handle these delicate passages as though they were either so many yards of plain expository material or interpolated operatic dirges.

It is curious to find the Chekhovian themes popping up in an improbable melodrama called *Counter-Attack,* which by a further irony is a play by a Russian named Vershinin that has been adapted by Janet and Philip Stevenson to American tastes. The revolution Colonel Vershinin anticipated has taken place, ahead of schedule, and the Red Army is defending its beautiful new world against the Germans on the Eastern Front. In reality, the new world might have afforded the Colonel his final disillusionment; in the play, the only flaw in the new world is the presence of Nazi troops on its territory: democracy and freedom prevail and the Russian soldier dreams of the "strong firm hand" of Comrade Stalin pressing him gently on his weary shoulder. Nevertheless, the obsessions that dominate *The Three Sisters* persist. Of the two Russian soldiers in the play, one is obsessed with the idea of correctness, military and ideological, and the other, who is a peasant and therefore more old-fashioned, is obsessed with the idea of heroism. One difference between this play and *The Three Sisters* is that both dreams come true. In trying circumstances, in a bombed dug-out with six Nazi prisoners, the soldiers are correct and heroic, and, after the war, I suppose, they will get a trip to Moscow at government expense. As Mme. Litvinov hints, if the three sisters had lived under Stalin, their problems would have been non-existent.

By looking hard enough, one can even find touches of Chekhov in *Dark Eyes,* a comedy by Elena Miramova and Eugénie Leontovitch. This is a play about three irresponsible Russian ladies and a rich Long Island factory owner who is giving his all, under severe handicaps, to the War Production Board. Here the Russian character is burlesqued for the carriage trade, in what I presume is a gesture of amity to our victorious allies. The play is both coarse and reactionary: references to governmental red tape and Mrs. Roosevelt bring down the house and the appearance of a colored butler with an enema bag provides a suitable curtain at the end. Yet traits of the true Russian character, which is here called the Russian Soul, occasionally make themselves felt. Solyony, in *The Three Sisters,* goes off to a duel with a quotation from Lermontov on his lips. Nick, a dubious White Russian member of café society, in habits not unlike Solyony, is inspired by another quotation from Lermontov to enlist in the Canadian army. It is apparently easier for Russians to do things if they are under the impression that they are someone else. And Chekhov may be distinguished from Miss Miramova and Miss Leontovitch by his belief that action induced by such intoxicants is not likely to be of the highest social worth.

BROADWAY'S SPRING OFFENSIVE

Of two spring plays on war themes, it is, oddly enough, the more conventional one, the stodgy little play with a single, inexpensive set and a small, inexpensive cast, that makes the more effective claims on its audience's attention. Irwin Shaw's *Sons and Soldiers,* at the Morosco Theatre, has Max Reinhardt, Norman Bel Geddes, Geraldine Fitzgerald, Stella Adler, and a revolving stage, it has the tradition of Chekhov via Clifford Odets, it has the modern urban sentimentality of the *New Yorker* magazine, it has a number of "terrific" scenes (a mother nursing a prop baby onstage, chanting, "Drink, drink, when you grow up, you will go to the best restaurants and make your own French dressing," a middle-aged husband, drunk, laying bare his heart to his wife's young lover, and the wife, under a symbolic street lamp, turning off the young idealist with a streetwalker's sneers), it has passages of the most strenuous rhetoric ("I have swum in the Atlantic Ocean, I have read the poetry of John Keats, and loved a woman to the point of madness"), it has all this, and it is both too much and not enough—the audience sits squirming in its seats, bored and embarrassed and uneasy, as though it had been impressed by some unhappy chance into the role of eavesdropper on a highly painful and in-

timate spectacle. That is the trouble with the new sensa-
tionalist school of writers, which is headed at the moment
by Mr. Shaw: the impulse that produces the work appears
to be purely exhibitionistic, the subject of the play or
the short story is not a character or a situation or an idea
but the author's own cleverness, his modernism, his culture, his irony, his political humanity, and the audience
is obliged to complement his performance by itself assuming the part of the *voyeur*. Thus the spectator is condemned to remain the spectator, he is turned into a pair
of large round eyes; participation is forbidden him, the
feeling and the will are paralyzed, and it is all like a bad
dream or like the stories of atrocities in the Gestapo pris-
ons where the victims are compelled to witness the tor-
tures of their comrades and can neither act nor betray
human sympathy. But of course this is a democracy, and
the playgoer, if he is not a dramatic critic, is at liberty to
go home.

Naturally, to a playwright with Mr. Shaw's objectives,
all the old considerations, the principles of dramatic construction, of character drawing, are irrelevant. *Sons and
Soldiers* has not a single character who is plausible even
as a stage figure; as for plot, the element of conflict is
present, theoretically, in the mind of the heroine, but it
never reaches the level of action. The point at issue on the
stage is whether a young woman in the year 1913 should
go on and have a baby, at some risk to her life, if she can
look ahead and see what the world has in store for him in
1943. The answer, of course, is Yes, and the audience is
aware of this from the beginning since it sees the young
man's life unrolling and knows, therefore, that the choice
has been made. The only possible interest, then, lies in
the Why of the decision. Earlier in the season, Thornton
Wilder tried to give a philosophical answer to the Why

of the human race's decision and found it in the male principle of intellection where Joyce had found it in the feminine creative principle. Mr. Shaw's affirmation, however, is not philosophical but Hollywood-practical. The child must be born because, in 1943, he will become engaged to the girl next door and wear the uniform of the United Nations. At an earlier point in the play, when the boy has been carrying on with a married woman, the answer has been decidedly No. The tragic acceptance of life is not for Mr. Shaw; he is humanity's fair-weather friend.

Needless to say, the war is not taken seriously by this author. The uniform is the costume of virtue, and that is all. In *Tomorrow The World,* by James Gow and Arnauld d'Usseau, at the Ethel Barrymore Theatre, the problems of fascism and democracy are, at any rate, opened for discussion in an atmosphere reminiscent of a radio Round Table. This is the play about the Nazi child, a paratrooper of the spirit, who steps from a plane into the home of a middle-western American college professor, bringing terror and evil and darkness with him. Before he is cured by the straightforwardness of a child and the discreet sympathy of a progressive school teacher, a picture has been slashed to pieces, a child has been hit on the head with a bronze ornament, an engagement has been broken, a spy discovered, and the professor has nearly committed a murder. This play is so wholeheartedly within the conventions of the American theatre that it exudes a certain stuffy yet innocent charm. We know this professor so well, we have seen him on the stage so many times that he has become our legendary culture-hero, and his house, with its flowered chintzes, its wall of books, its comfortable sofa, its comical maid, has become our American Valhalla, whether we like it or not. And we feel it as a kind of national outrage that this sacred home, this shrine of the *Nation* and the *New Republic,* should be violated by a goosestepping child. The play, then, gives a limited satisfaction; its aim is to entertain and instruct, and it does so with moderate success. The symbolism is obvious but well maintained. The fifth column which throws off its disguises at the appearance of Emil exists in the heart of the professor and his old-maid sister as well as in the person of a Bundist janitor named Muller, who is trying to get the key to the professor's laboratory, where experiments of military importance are being carried on. What the audience carries home is the conviction that fascism is a disease which can be cured by patience, toler-ance, intelligence, and by casting out the mote in one's own eye. This view is at least humane, and the spectator, here fully participating, feels his own humanity swell with a kind of pleasant ache in his bosom. Unfortunately, the catharsis, though real enough, is incomplete. The prob-lem has been solved in a vacuum, in a pure ether of melodrama and progressive education, or, rather, *a* prob-lem has been solved, but it is not precisely the problem we thought we were wrestling with. The child is not nor-mal; he has had a traumatic experience, and his case is therefore not typical. In the same way, the question of anti-Semitism, which appears to have been mastered by the characters, turns out upon examination never to have been properly raised. The professor's Jewish fiancée, who is socially accepted by everyone on the stage, including, in the end, the Nazi child, is a young lady named Miss Rich-ards; she is played by Shirley Booth, a blond actress whose last role was My Sister Eileen.

WARTIME OMNIBUS

IN THE NEW YORK THEATRE, this is a big sad year. Every night is New Year's Eve on Times Square. It is hard to walk along Broadway, hard to get tickets, hard to get dinner. To find oneself installed in a seat before a curtain is in itself a triumph; what the curtain discloses, when raised, is not so important; the means have supplanted the end. Much of our pleasure this year comes from the sense of our own achievement; in the foyer, during the intermission, we are as likely to compare our strategies as ticket-buyers as to compare our experiences of the play. Our experiences have in fact been thin; the theatre has rationed itself, drawing heavily on its own staples, on Shakespeare and Bizet, German expressionism, barbershop harmony, the Whiffenpoof song, the character of Dorothy Parker, which belongs as firmly to the theatre as a caricature in Sardi's. There are on the stage this year only two things which do not remind you of something else—Mary Martin and the character played by Margaret Sullavan in *The Voice of the Turtle*. Everything else is derivative, frankly so in *Othello*, where it is a question of a revival, a restoration of a classic; mockingly so in *Carmen Jones,* where an opera of passion becomes a "hot" show and a dark theme, given to dark actors, becomes by paradox light; perversely, sentimentally, uneasily so in *One Touch of Venus,* where the tradition of the ballad, the tradition of barbershop harmony, the tradition of German expressionism, are both parodied and asserted; corruptly so in *Winged Victory,* where the play is a bad imitation of a bad movie, and where the playwright can, at his big moment, find no more suitable musical outlet for his democratic emotions than the song of the Yale Whiffenpoofs.

This is not a war phenomenon. Since the collapse of the proletarian theatre as an art-form eight years ago, the theatre has been plagiarizing itself. Revivals have come thick and fast; there have been the straight revivals of Shakespeare, Shaw, Chekhov and Ibsen; and the revivals-with-a-difference, *Julius Caesar* in uniforms, *Romeo and Juliet* as a ballet, the Negro *Macbeth*—it is significant that our white culture has had to draw so heavily on the Negro (witness the *Macbeth,* Jack Carter as Mephistopheles in Orson Welles's *Dr. Faustus,* and now Paul Robeson and the cast of *Carmen Jones*) for the revivification of its classics; as in the days of the Empire in Rome, it is the son of the freedman who believes most in the national past, and the élite must depend on the feelings and energies of its ex-slaves to experience its own artistic inheritance. The revival itself is not new. What did seem to come in with the war is another kind of borrowing, more abject, and more desperate than the appropriation, which is perfectly legitimate, of a treasure from the collective storehouse. Actors, after all, must work, and producers must produce; no doubt it is better all around for their talents to be employed on the good and old, rather than on the bad and new. The habit, however, has spread; the playwrights have taken it up; they do not imitate the masters;

they lift quotations, particularly from the poets, to do what ought to be their own work.

Last year Mr. Thornton Wilder used quotations from Spinoza, Plato, Aristotle and the Bible (spoken, incidentally, again by Negro actors) to finish a play for which he himself had no outcome; the device was perhaps forgivable since the subject of the play was the history of culture, and since the words were beautifully spoken and dramatically introduced. And in *The Eve of St. Mark,* Mr. Maxwell Anderson, having already taken his title from Keats, presented one of his characters with the whole of Eliot's *Sweeney Among the Nightingales,* which was recited *twice* and served once to bring down a curtain which might otherwise have stayed up forever; the lines were badly read and their appropriateness to the situation on the stage was never indicated (it is true that young men sometimes recite poems but, in the particular case, why Eliot, why *Sweeney?*—one was left with the hypothesis that Eliot was the most *poetic* poet and *Sweeney* the most *poetic* poem that Mr. Anderson could think of). This year quotation from the poets has become a mania on the stage: Milton and Shakespeare and the Bible make their appearance in *The Voice of the Turtle,* and in *Winged Victory* a poem from an unknown source carries a crucial scene, symbolizing, rather inadequately for the audience, the values for which the Air Forces are fighting; while in *Over Twenty-one,* by Ruth Gordon, it is the corpus of Dorothy Parker's work, as it exists, not in quotation, but in the memory of the audience, that provides the *donnée* of the play, and what the spectators laugh at is not so much the rather heavy quips of Miss Gordon as the light and legendary quips they themselves have heard ascribed to the wit of Miss Parker.

All this is merely symptomatic. In theory there is nothing against the use of quotation in drama—it might well serve as it formerly did in the essay as decoration or embellishment. It cannot, however, support the dramatic structure, provide curtains, assert values, define character —a quotation from Milton or Shakespeare does not in itself guarantee the *bona fides* of the juvenile; the man with a verse on his lips is quite as likely as not to be a scoundrel. Quotation has been used by Eliot and Pound to do some of the poetic work; but in these cases, particularly in Eliot's, the use of the quotation is itself part of the subject of the poem, and there is deliberate pathos and irony in the fact that the artist has had to resort to quotation: *these fragments have I shored against my ruin.* Moreover, as in collage, the arrangement of the excerpted material constitutes an aesthetic problem and consciousness is everything; quotation becomes a kind of wry understatement, as when an actor who has already shown his powers proves them by throwing a line away—an actor incapable of speaking the line in the first place gains nothing by tossing it aside.

In the authors who are bandying verses on the current stage there appears to be no consciousness of a predicament; it is the audience, rather, which discovers the dramatist's impasse. Only in *One Touch of Venus* does the element of consciousness protrude; here three sophisticated artists, Ogden Nash, S. J. Perelman and Kurt Weill, acknowledge the fact that you cannot write a modern love song or a modern ballad or a modern ballet, you cannot, that is, write it straight; what you can do is to take over an old form and parody it, and at the same time make love to it surreptitiously, keeping always a poker face. These old forms, the ballad, the barbershop sweet music, the rigid mechano-set movements of the expressionist ballet, are all treated so; and in one case, "The Ballad of Dr. Crippen," which makes the first act finale, something which is at once grotesque, absurd, and morally terrifying is created. The authors have here produced both a parody of *Hamlet* (there is the idea of a play within a play, a murder drama enacted on a marionette-scale stage to catch the guilty conscience of the hero) and a parody of the Victorian moral ballad; there are also, in the staging, reminiscences of waxworks, the *Eden Musée* and the Chamber of Horrors at Coney Island. The refrain goes something like this:

> "This is Dr. Crippen, Harley Harvey Crippen
> Lying in a felon's grave;
> He gave his life and that of a wife
> For the love of Ethel Le Neve."

Several impressions are combined: the idea that man is a marionette pulled by the strings of passion, the idea that man is a wax figure, i.e., that there is no life in him, the idea that love and murder are antiquated pastimes, like your Aunt Ida's tatting, the idea that love and murder are frightening and that the fate of the outlaw (the felon's grave) is the ultimate horror—the ideas are superimposed one on the other, but as in a cubist painting all are visible simultaneously; they interpenetrate each other, and the total effect is one of envy, of Dr. Crippen, of Dr. Crippen's judge, which was the whole of society, and envy of an imaginary ballad-writer who might at one time have written the song in all seriousness. This number is beautifully produced, and sung with marvelous shading by John Boles, who belongs in style and spirit to the gas-light tradition but here by mockery transcends it. "The Trouble With Women," sung by a male quartet in a barbershop, strikes off another effect of the same kind, but lighter, less complex. It is also worth noticing that in this musical there is a harmony of subject matter and style that our regular stage writers cannot give us, that is, the idea of the play, at least at the beginning, is that Venus, if she were to come alive today, could not rouse the blood or even the attention of the normal young man who is her true love; only the dissolute art connoisseur has a cold, lubricious eye for her—she was better off as a statue. This theme is rather lost sight of as the show progresses, but its relevance to the authors' collective problem is apparent. Unfortunately, Perelman's humor is, on the whole, too nervous for the stage; the embarrassment of the authors drops the show into a kind of mumbled witticism, and the radiant Mary Martin has to come too often to the rescue, like the hostess at a teen-age party. Nevertheless, at its best, in its moments of self-laceration and parody, *One Touch of Venus* is the most interesting production of the season.

Ruth Gordon's play, *Over Twenty-one,* deals with a character like Dorothy Parker who is married to a character like Ralph Ingersoll and endures for his sake the trials of army life in Miami Beach to help him get his commission. It is dull, rough stuff done in what appears to be the atelier of George Kaufman; there is not the slightest respect paid to character, on which comedy after all is founded: you create a church-social kind of old lady and then, when you need a laugh, have her say "Damn" or "Hell"—anything goes. The most hilarious moments of the evening are when Miss Gordon is locked outdoors in her panties, and when the trays stick in the icebox while the colonel is paying a call. Mr. Kaufman himself directed and contributed his usual touches: two large irascible men stand facing each other, stage center, and yell insults

back and forth; this is supposed to be funny, and it is true
that the audience laughed. Miss Gordon is an accomplished but very mannered actress who, in classic roles
(The Doll's House, The Country Wife), gets wonderful
contrapuntal effects by the impact of her style on the
author's style; with only her own material to work with,
she seems monotonous, though the sureness of her technique is pleasurable.

Winged Victory is the show about the Air Force, written by Moss Hart, and played by actual members of the
service. The boys who have not been too long in or too
much affected by Hollywood are convincing in their very
lack of skill, and there are two or three good performances
which do not arise from technical inadequacy. The play,
however, is shocking in its false sweetness, its false democracy (sure there's room for everybody in the Air Force
and one man is as good as another, but the Jewish boy
from Brooklyn is only good for a laugh while the real
hero, the impeccable young pilot, is the son of a West
Point man). Some one has said of this play that it is the
Rover Boys' version of the war; this is accurate, and one
cannot help imagining with embarrassment, all through
the performance, what the people of England, let alone
Poland or Greece, would make of the problems which
agitate Mr. Hart and his characters.

As for *Othello*, Margaret Webster, using Paul Robeson,
has directed it, with a new emphasis on the black-and-
white theme. Mr. Robeson, unfortunately, is not an actor.
His voice is beautiful, and in the early scenes, where
Othello need only be magnificent, he is not over-taxed
by the character. When Othello, however, cracks open,
Mr. Robeson can no longer follow him, but remains at

a distance from the role; even in murder he is courteous and dignified, the well-trained concert performer. The direction is bad, clumsy especially in the handling of groups. It is Jose Ferrer's Iago that is the star-piece of this production. He manages in his soliloquies, to demonstrate the trance-like, solitary, almost visionary character of Iago's dream of evil, which, like God's dream of the world, he makes incarnate on earth. The division of Iago's nature between the man as good fellow and the man as destroyer is well established by Mr. Ferrer; this distinction is usually lost by actors who play Iago as Mephistopheles.

The Voice of the Turtle, while not a serious or particularly well-written play, makes an original contribution to the stage. John Van Druten has discovered for the theatre a new American type, a type with whom we are all familiar in life but have not seen behind the footlights. This is the character played by Margaret Sullavan; she is the well-brought-up American girl who, at twenty-one, has had two affairs, yet remains at heart a virgin, an innocent, a perennial spinster who will always be more in love with her apartment, her flowers, her possessions, her treasury of quotations from poetry, than with any man she sleeps with, whose bed the morning after a sexual adventure will always be made up, with the spread indented under the pillows, while coffee for two drips in the Silex and toast pops out of the electric toaster. This is the eternal college girl, who will be windswept and hatless at forty, and whose old age no one so far can predict. Mr. Van Druten has been both honest and observant in recording the details of this girl's behavior; he does not shrink from showing the audience the realistic underpinnings of her romantic affair with the soldier who happens to arrive at her apartment; he sees that it is all a matter of propinquity, of *faute de mieux,* an evening on one's hands, a girl who has stood one up and a married man who has got tired of one's intensity. Mr. Van Druten goes so far but no further; he presents the type and weaves a light, rather cute, comedy around her; he does not venture on into analysis or satire, with the result that the play has no third act and remains a play for women, a play at which women can smile tenderly and a little fatuously, relaxing happily in self-love as the heroine relaxes in her bath. Men are out of place at this play, just as a real soldier would find himself violently out of place in that apartment.

WE MUST HAVE FAITH

If it were possible to make any coherent remark about the theatre this season, you might say that this was a year of apparitions. Actually, in 1944, the stage presents such a spectacle of confusion, disintegration and despair that no generalization can cover the case. This is not a year of musicals or of nostalgia or of war plays or of plays dramatized from *New Yorker* sketches or of dirty plays or of sophisticated plays about marriage, though single specimens of each of these genres can be found listed on the dramatic page. Among theatrical managers there appears to be no agreement as to what will go; they do not even pay each other the sincere compliment of imitation. Money pours in, but each success has a fortuitous character. *Harvey,* with its rabbit six feet tall, is the talk of the country, but this will not insure the next producer against the failure of a play about a short giraffe.

The real heroes today are the play doctors, principally George Kaufman and George Abbott; younger writer-directors have copied their methods, with the result that in the Times Square district there are more doctors than patients available.

Out of this chaos, during the current season three plays have emerged that deal with the same theme. This does

not, however, constitute a theatrical trend, though it may
be symptomatic of a social tendency to which the three
authors have been particularly sensitive. Superficially,
Harvey, The Streets Are Guarded, and *A Bell for Adano*
bear no resemblance to each other. The first, by Mary
Chase, is about a drunk who has an invisible rabbit friend
named Harvey whom he finds more human than the other
characters on the stage. Of the three, this is the only one
which has any genuine theatrical tradition behind it; it
reminds one intermittently of *Our Town, On Borrowed
Time, Blithe Spirit, The Devil Passes,* and a whole vague
group of plays which took the supernatural lightly and,
in the interests of whimsy, defied the laws of time and
space. (Since the conventions of the theatre are, precisely,
concerned with time, space, and visibility, plays which violate these laws are naturally of perennial interest to playwrights who enjoy the métier and take its restrictions as a
challenge, and it is interesting that Miss Chase, who is a
relative outsider, a lady from Colorado, is virtually the
only author on Broadway this year to find inspiration in
terms of the medium itself.) The second play, by Lawrence Stallings, takes place somewhere in the Pacific during the present war and deals with an old seaman, a pharmacist's mate with a religious turn of mind, who, stranded
on an island with a few companions, and suffering from
fever, imagines that a stray Marine who appears in a boat
is the Lord Jesus Christ come to the rescue. This play
has biographical ties with *What Price Glory,* which Mr.
Stallings wrote with Maxwell Anderson, and like Mr. Anderson's *The Eve of St. Mark,* it demonstrates that the
authors exploited the First World War, but that the
Second World War exploited the authors. When *The Eve
of St. Mark* was produced two years ago, some of its
harsher critics concluded that the realism and humor of

What Price Glory must have been injected by Mr. Stallings—the production of *The Streets Are Guarded* imperils this position. The third play, as everybody knows, is a dramatization of John Hersey's novel about the Amgot administrator who brings democracy in the shape of a bell to a demoralized Sicilian town. It has been transported with the greatest care to the stage of the Cort Theatre; yet it remains more at home in the pages of *Life* magazine, where several pages were recently devoted to it. The conventions of the theatre are not those of the Luce magazines, and it is rather startling to hear characters on the stage talking to each other in that patient parental style (explaining everything so very, very carefully, look, dear, here is a picture of it), which may be appropriate to the relation between the editors of *Life* and their presumably semi-illiterate readers, but which does not suit the theatregoer's idea of relations between ordinary human beings. The third dimension, moreover, makes us apply the test of truth to what is in actuality a fable, and Fredric March's Major Joppolo is infinitely more convincing in glossy black and white as a photograph.

But what is interesting about these three plays is not their artistic merit, for they have none (though *Harvey*, which appears to have been heavily play-doctored, gives evidence of mutilated fancy), but the fact that they all tell exactly the same story. In each case, there is a man (the pharmacist's mate, Elwood P. Dowd, Major Joppolo) who believes in a supernatural object (the Marine, Harvey, the Bell). Other more pedestrian characters question either the efficacy of the object or its actual existence. There follows a drama of faith and resistance. In every instance, the man of faith is regarded by most or all of the other characters as crazy. "You're raving," the sailors tell the pharmacist's mate. "You crazy boss," the Italians tell Major Joppolo, and Elwood P. Dowd is actually incarcerated in a lunatic asylum. But in the end the man of faith wins out. Resistance is abandoned, belief embraced, indeed, by the more susceptible characters positively wallowed in; at this point, happiness is achieved.

Now this is an old enough pattern of drama or fiction; it is, after all, the story of the New Testament. What is remarkable in these three plays is that the virtue resides, not in the object, but in the believer. It makes no difference, according to these authors, whether the belief is objectively a delusion. In *Harvey*, the rabbit is, at long last, accepted by the other characters as real; but the audience, of course, knows better. In *The Streets Are Guarded*, the Marine is admittedly not Jesus, but the son of a marine colonel in Washington—the pharmacist's mate was wrong. With *A Bell for Adano*, the case is a little more complicated, for the Bell is not conceived by the author as having supernatural powers but only treated as if it had. But here too the Bell cannot live up to what is expected of it. The Bell is not democracy; indeed, it is precisely the kind of symbolic substitute for communal well-being that Mussolini was so expert at supplying the people of such towns as Adano. If *A Bell for Adano* celebrates anything real at all, it is the jubilant return of fascism with its bells, medals, certificates, portraits of great men, to a people which had been briefly deprived of it by the chaotic conditions of war; and the figure of Major Joppolo is an Americanized version of the *duce*, a great little man, as opposed to the Italian townspeople who are very small little men, dressed in very small absurd little clothes. The Bell does not bring democracy, but belief in it will give the feeling of democracy, which is all that is necessary.

It is the same with the other two plays. Objective conditions are recognizedly hopeless, they say. Nevertheless, we must have faith, for if we have faith, we will feel better and not notice the objective conditions so much. Elwood P. Dowd, with his rabbit, had ceased in any true sense to live in his sister's middle-class household. Therefore, it did not inconvenience him at all to be put into the lunatic asylum—if you have a wonderful white rabbit to talk to, what difference does it make where you are? Less outspokenly, the other plays with their apparitions, their bells and images of Christ, are invitations to madness, to systematized delusions of a harmless kind. But three swallows do not make a summer, and it is doubtful whether the theatre will turn itself to the business of supplying the public with fantasies and secular myths. The truth is (and the weakness of these plays demonstrates it) that the drama is incorrigibly concrete; it cannot, like the movies, deal in shadows, or in reverie, like the novel. It demands that its conflicts be settled; it cannot, by its very nature, dissolve them away, as the camera can. It is the only one of the arts whose medium is the living flesh, and this sets a certain limit on belief—one is always more conscious of what is excessive in a stage performance than one is of the same kind of thing in a movie or a novel. In fact, the very plainness, conclusiveness and realism of the stage have unfitted it to deal with this period of irresolution, evasion and ambiguity.

EUGENE O'NEILL—DRY ICE

THE CRUCIAL FIGURE of O'Neill's new play is a mad hardware salesman. Consonantly, the play itself is like some stern piece of hardware in one of those dusty old-fashioned stores into which no Pyrex dish or herb shelf or French provincial earthenware had yet penetrated, which dealt in iron-colored enamel, galvanized tin, lengths of pipe and wrenches, staples, saws, and nails, and knew nothing more sophisticated than the double boiler. Ugly, durable, mysteriously utilitarian, this work gives the assurance that it has been manufactured by a reliable company; it is guaranteed to last two-and-a-half hours longer than any other play, with the exception of the uncut *Hamlet*.

The Iceman Cometh is indeed made of ice or iron; it is full of will and fanatic determination; it appears to have hardened at some extreme temperature of the mind. In the theatre today, it is attractive positively because of its defects. To audiences accustomed to the oily virtuosity of George Kaufman, George Abbott, Lillian Hellman, Odets, Saroyan, the return of a playwright who—to be frank—cannot write is a solemn and sentimental occasion. O'Neill belongs to that group of American authors, which includes Farrell and Dreiser, whose choice of vocation was a kind of triumphant catastrophe; none of these men possessed the slightest ear for the word, the sentence, the speech, the paragraph; all of them, however, have, so to speak, enforced the career they decreed for themselves by a relentless policing of their beat. What they produce is hard to praise or to condemn; how is one to judge the great, logical symphony of a tone-deaf musician? Pulpy in detail, their work has nevertheless a fine solidity of structure; they drive an idea or a theme step by step to its brutal conclusion with the same terrible force they have brought to bear on their profession. They are among the few contemporary American writers who know how to exhaust a subject; that is, alas, their trouble. Their logical, graceless works can find no reason for stopping, but go on and on, like elephants pacing in a zoo. In their last acts and chapters, they arrive not at despair but at a strange, blank nihilism. Their heroes are all searchers; like so many non-verbal, inarticulate people, they are looking for a final Word that will explain everything. These writers are, naturally, masters of suspense.

O'Neill has neither the phenomenal memory which serves Farrell as a substitute for observation, nor the documentary habits which, for Dreiser, performed the same service. In *The Iceman Cometh,* the scene is a cheap bar somewhere in downtown New York in the year 1912; the characters are the derelict habitués of the back room—a realist's paradise, one would think. But it needs only a short walk along Third Avenue today (or the armchair method of inquiry) to solidify the suspicion that, unless drinking *moeurs* have changed in the last thirty-five years, O'Neill is an incompetent reporter. In the day and a half that elapses on the stage of the Martin Beck, none of the characters is visibly drunk, nobody has a hangover, and, with a single brief exception, nobody has the shakes; there are none of those rancorous, semi-schizoid silences, no obscurity of thought, no dark innuendoes, no flashes of hatred, there is, in short, none of the terror of drink, which, after all, in the stage that Harry Hope's customers have presumably reached, is a form of insanity. What is missing is precisely the thing that is most immediately striking and most horrifying in any human drunkard, the sense of the destruction of personality. Each of O'Neill's people is in perfect possession of the little bit of character the author has given him. The Boer is boerish, the Englishman english, the philosopher philosophizes, and the sentimental grouch who runs the establishment grouches and sentimentalizes in orderly alternation. So obedient indeed are these supposed incorrigibles to the play's thematic dictation, so well behaved in speech and in silence, that one might imagine, if one shut one's eyes, that one was attending the Christmas exercises in some respectable school ("I am Wind, I blow and blow," says little Aeolus with his bag).

And the didactic tone is, in fact, the play's natural mode. The "realistic" scene that stretches, rather Moscow Art style and friezelike, across the stage is no more than mood or *décor*. The play quickly calls itself to order, the drunkards awake and embark on an elementary study of the nature of reality and illusion. Each drunkard, it seems, has his "pipe-dream": he imagines that tomorrow he will get a job, take a walk, marry, see the anarchist millennium, go home to England or South Africa. A hardware salesman, beloved of all, who is expected to arrive for one of his periodical benders, finally does appear on the dot of the dramatist's excellent schedule; he is changed, sober, exhilarated, he has a mission to perform; he will cure Harry Hope and his customers of the illusions that are making them unhappy. In the course of the play, he obliges each of the characters to test himself. All fail to carry out the actions projected in the pipe-dream, but self-knowledge, the recognition of failure, does not bring them the freedom the salesman promised. On the contrary, it kills whatever life was left in them; disgruntled, despairing, demoralized, they cannot even get drunk, though they are full of red-eye whiskey. Fortunately, it turns out that the salesman had attained his own state of freedom and euphoria by killing his wife; the police come for him, and Harry Hope and his clients, perceiving that he is mad, can dismiss the truths he has taught them and feel their liquor again (though this statement must be taken on faith, since here, as in the rest of the play, alcoholism does not have its customary sour breath, and the characters, like the actors who are impersonating them, seem to have been swallowing ponies of tea). As the happy derelicts carouse, one character who is without illusions, the boy who has betrayed his anarchist mother to the police, goes out and commits suicide, and another character, the philosopher, who is also capable of facing truth, indicates that he will soon join him in a plunge from the fire-escape. Life, then, consists of illusion, and if death is reality, reality is also death.

The odd thing about *The Iceman Cometh* is that this rather bony synopsis does it perfect justice; in fact, it improves it by substituting, whenever possible, the word *illusion* for the word *pipe-dream,* which recurs with a crankish and verbally impoverished tastelessness about two hundred times during the play. What shreds of naturalism cling to this work are attached to and encumber the dialogue; the language has the wooden verisimilitude, the flat, dead, echoless sound of stale slang that makes Farrell's novels and the later works of Sinclair Lewis so stilted. O'Neill here has not even the justification of sociological pedantry, which these other writers might bring forward. His intention is symbolic and philosophical, but unfortunately you cannot write a Platonic dialogue in the style of *Casey At the Bat*. O'Neill might have studied the nature of illusion through the separate relations to illusion of a group of characters (*The Three Sisters*), but his people are given but a single trait each, and they act and react, in the loss and recapture of illusion, not individually but in a body. Bare and plain, this play has the structure of an argument; its linguistic deficiencies make it maudlin. How is your wife getting along with the iceman, the characters roar, over and over again, and though death is the iceman, the joke is not appreciably refined by this symbolic treatment; rather, it is death that is coarsened.

Yet it must be said for O'Neill that he is probably the only man in the world who is still laughing at the iceman joke or pondering its implications. He is certainly the only writer who would have the courage or the lack of judgment to build a well-made play around it. This sense of one man's isolation is what, above all, gives *The Iceman Cometh* its salient look. Though it is full of reminders of Saroyan (the barroom, the loose-witted philosophical talk, the appearance of the Redeemer at the middle table), of O'Casey (again the drunkards, and the tense, frightened young man who has betrayed the Cause), of Ibsen, Thornton Wilder, and even of Maxwell Anderson (the ripples of the Mooney and Sacco-Vanzetti cases which lap at the edges of a distant slum, and again the home-made philosophy) *The Iceman Cometh* seems nevertheless estranged from all influences and impressions. Its solitariness inside its rigid structure suggests the prison or the asylum or the sound of a man laughing in a square, empty room.

(The following article appeared in the book section of the *New York Times* for Sunday, August 31, 1952.)

In the mid-nineteen forties *A Moon for the Misbegotten* was tried out on the road by the Theatre Guild but never brought to New York. "Casting difficulties" were spoken of, which is generally a theatrical euphemism for loss of interest in a property. Yet the play, as it appears in book form, seems very much like the New England farm plays of the O'Neill apogee, and in particular like *Desire Under the Elms,* which was revived last winter in New York. The spectacle of a mature play by a renowned dramatist vainly haunting the managers' offices while revivals of his early successes close and open has a certain sardonic pathos, a note of *Enoch Arden.*

A Moon for the Misbegotten is *Desire Under the Elms* grown old and hoarse and randy. There is the familiar puritan triad of greed, land and sexual repression. There are a demonic old man, a stony unrewarding farm, a vital Demeter of a woman. The finale is lit by an apocalyptic dawn, and the whole play is reddened by whisky, like a bloodshot eye. There is an opening which is really a prologue, with the cunning son (two in *Desire Under the Elms*) deserting the farm with a sum of money stolen from the miser father. This opening imparts to both plays a curious, desolate aspect, as if normal self-interest, in the person of the departing sons, had stealthily forsaken the vicinity; those who are left are survivors in a waste.

A Moon for the Misbegotten, however, is not laid in the period-past of the gold rush but in the golden bootleg twenties, on a Connecticut tenant farm, an old box of a house raised up on blocks of timber. The characters are not New Englanders of the original stock but Irish supplanters. The heroine is a gigantic young woman, one hundred and eighty pounds broad and tall, who carries a club to defend herself; as the daughter of a bootlegger and shifty, shiftless farmer, she is known throughout the neighborhood for her herculean sexual prowess. A sort of Olympian knockdown comedy is enacted between the trickster father and the virago daughter, but this comedy is at bottom sad, for the daughter is in actuality a virgin with a strong maternal heart and the father a grimy cupid with benevolent matrimonial plans for her.

These plans center on a middle-aged alcoholic of educated pretensions, the son of a well-known Thespian who owned farm property. Here the theme of puritanism suddenly appears, like an elemental blight. Behind the pagan façade of Irish boasting, drinking and ribaldry is revealed a wheyey sentimentality and retching hatred of sex. With the nuptial couch all readied in the tar-papered lean-to, James Tyrone Jr., man of the world and Broadway rakehell, makes his true confession: he is a man who, like Stephen Dedalus, has wronged his dying mother, and wronged her again, a thousand times over, when, escorting her body home on the train, he entertained a prostitute in his drawing-room while Mama was in the baggage car ahead. In his moment of opportunity, he sobs himself chastely to sleep, a guilt-sickened altar-boy.

This moment, in which the bootlegger's daughter discovers that this middle-aged man is really "dead," emotionally speaking—an exhausted mummified child—is a moment of considerable poignancy. The defeat of all human plans and contrivances is suddenly shaped in the picture of the titaness sitting staring at a stage moon with a shriveled male infant drunkenly asleep at her side. The image of the survivors takes on a certain grotesque epic form; the woman, stage center, like a gentle beached whale, appears for an instant as the last survivor of the world.

What disturbs one here, however, as in so many of O'Neill's plays, is the question of how far the author himself is a victim of the same sentimentality and self-pity that is exhibited clinically in the characters; how far, specifically, O'Neill himself is taken in by the "tragic" figure of James Tyrone Jr., who is merely a pitiable wreck. My impression is that O'Neill himself does not know, that he puts the character forward like a question, which he hopes may be answered favorably. The crudity of the technique makes it hard to descry intention. Nevertheless, despite this, despite the tone of barbershop harmony that enters into all O'Neill's work, this play exacts homage for its mythic powers, for the element of transcendence jutting up woodenly in it like a great home-made Trojan horse.

FIVE CURIOS

THE G.I.'s have gone home and Broadway is at peace. The Rolls Royces of former days like large perambulators gently deposit their muffled elderly couples before the lighted marquees; the noise of the big musicals is drowned in the spoken word, and, taking advantage of this general atmosphere of armistice, culture emerges from its wartime shelter—Oscar Wilde and Eva Le Gallienne find the enemy departed.

For the first time in many years, the New York theatregoer this season can step into almost any theatre lobby with that sense of virtuous expectation, of responsibility and enlightenment, that the drama peculiarly awakes and that makes the theatre for New York what the café is for Paris, a pleasure and also a pride, a habit and a ritual, a diversion and a duty. To the extent that America has any communal life at all, it is centered in the New York theatre; here is the last refuge of sociability and humanism —the ordinary middling man, who has given up nearly all universal pretensions, still considers himself a competent judge of acting and a competent critic of plays. The movies annihilate him in their darkness and do not ask his opinion; the symphony is over his head, and if he participates at all in it, it is with the largest and limpest of his emotions. Only the theatre can he approach with his faculties alert and unabashed; he sees it as a kind of courtroom and himself as a qualified juror whose verdict is, from moment to moment, solicited.

This little arena of judgment was commandeered by the war. Despoiled of its provincialism, which was a necessity to its mood and its identity, the theatre became a great barracks and entertained the boys from Arkansas and Minnesota with imitation movies *(Winged Victory, Lady in the Dark, The Eve of St. Mark)*, pasted-up magazine stories *(Junior Miss, My Sister Eileen, Life With Father)*, and high-salaried burlesque shows. The sound of talk, which since the eighteenth century has been the normal tone of the drama, the tone, that is, of rational intercourse, was seldom heard, and though there were revivals of classics, these classics were, for the most part *(Hamlet, Othello, Macbeth, The Tempest)*, staples of the high school curriculum which were free from the minority taint. Chekhov, possibly because of the interest in Russia, was visible in three productions; Shaw in two, and the second of these, *Pygmalion,* was probably believed by many to be a stage adaptation of a movie.

Demobilized, the theatre has returned to its antique habits with fresh energy. The old boxlike stage is back, confining its group of people to the limits of a single room; the interest in the mechanics of production (the revolving stage, the stage on different levels, the use of a movie screen, the use of a loudspeaker) has been replaced by an interest in the details of costume and décor or else by an interest in acting: Lady Windermere's fan becomes an *objet de virtu* as powerful as Desdemona's handkerchief; on the other hand, Maxwell Anderson does a play about Joan of Arc which declines to avail itself of the medieval license for pageantry, but uses a bare rehearsal stage and makes a corselet or a helmet do for a full suit of armor. Except in the neighborhood of Moss Hart and Lillian Hellman, there is everywhere in the theatre this season a sense of restored dignity, of limitations accepted and formal conventions embraced. The return of O'Neill and George Kelly and the predominance of revivals sets the tone; it is an old man's season, garrulous, unsentimental, reasonable, pessimistic, and, in the manner of Lear and the late Yeats, contradictory, willful, and adventurous.

The list of revivals this fall is as eccentric as an old man's reading. *John Gabriel Borkman, Henry VIII, Lady Windermere's Fan, The Duchess of Malfi, The Playboy of the Western World, Cyrano de Bergerac*—what a bizarre assortment, yet they all, with the exception of *The Playboy,* which is a recognized favorite, have something in common. They are all curios. Minor works of an established author, like *Borkman* or *Henry VIII,* or *Lady Windermere's Fan* (*The Importance of Being Earnest* is the classic), major work of an author who is out of fashion (*Cyrano de Bergerac*), major work of an author who is unknown to the public at large (*The Duchess of Malfi*), they represent collectively a certain hardihood on the part of their producers. Unfortunately, like a number of other neglected works, most of them are not very good.

Of *Henry VIII,* the American Repertory Theatre made it impossible to form a literary opinion, for between the text and the audience Miss Le Gallienne and Miss Margaret Webster, the co-sponsors of this project, laid down a barrage of dust: dirty costumes which seemed to have been bought complete from a theatrical warehouse flapped across the stage, windily reciting lines; the Field of the

Cloth of Gold was badly tarnished. This production had a pathos of its own, and Miss Le Gallienne, playing Katharine of Aragon, seemed to feel herself a tragedy queen whom the public as well as her husband had long misunderstood.

John Gabriel Borkman, revived by the same group, had the advantage of fresher costumes, and the weariness of the acting did not so sharply distinguish itself from the matter of the play. The play is a debilitated *Peer Gynt,* another study of the self-isolated superior man who loses his humanity in an abstract passion for excellence. Borkman embezzles money, confusing this crime with his destiny; he returns from prison to his bourgeois home a pariah and a god. The action of the play is over before the curtain rises, yet it thrashes about the stage, questioning, demanding, recalling, as impotently as old Borkman in his chamber, and finally, in a last spurt of the will, it moves from realism into symbolism and drags itself with its hero out onto a crag to die. This work might have seemed a little more substantial had Miss Webster and Miss Le Gallienne, playing Borkman's wife and his sister-in-law, dropped the airs of Cassandra, the antiphonal responses, the glare of prophecy, and asked themselves, for a single instant, what a Norwegian housewife was like.

Lady Windermere's Fan, in contrast, is as pretty and professional as a box of French chocolates. The Cecil Beaton sets have the succulent vulgarity of a Wilde epigram; the ladies' costumes seem to have been dipped in those vegetable dyes used for frostings and are as dainty and miraculous as if they were squeezed out of a pastry-tube. The play, too, is like some expensive confection, hard and shiny on the outside and soft and runny at the center. Wilde, as an author, did not have the courage of his convictions. The cruelty and cynicism of the dialogue is quickly atoned for by the virtuous sentimentalism of the plot, and what begins as a monstrous study of the initiation of a strictly brought-up young wife into the profligate realities of London society becomes not a comedy but a rather shoddy melodrama in which there is no vice but only scandal, and the mysterious bad woman turns out to be the heroine's unfortunate mother. Before the plot, however, has been rectified to suit the conventional morality that the dialogue affects to disdain, there is one truthful and shocking scene, played by Penelope Ward and Henry Daniell, in which the young wife, learning of her husband's infidelity, hardens her own heart. And though it later appears that the husband was not *really* unfaithful, the memory of Miss Ward's acting leaves the audience unconvinced: the transition between innocence and knowledge she has made as terrible as death.

The Duchess of Malfi has been modernized by W. H. Auden. The effect of the poet's alterations has been to date the play more securely than history had yet done. He has made it into a period-piece, accentuating its peculiarities by adding horrors and pathos of his own: dead bodies fall out of armoires where, in the original, wax effigies were shown through a curtain; a child is made the witness of his father's death, where an adult companion was used by Webster; the incest theme is openly stated, and at a particularly harrowing moment, where in Webster it is altogether hidden; the *Lyke Wake Dirge,* a death chant of the early Tudor period, is introduced to heap the terror of medieval superstition upon the barbarism of the Renaissance; and, finally, the selection of Canada Lee, a Negro in white-face, to play Bosola, goes in the same

direction as these other improvements. It directs this tragedy of blood and passion toward the ghoulish, the unnatural, the perverse. Auden's *Duchess* is more Gothic
than Jacobean; from this springs a gain in pace and intensity and a loss of somber seriousness. What is missing
from the Auden-Elisabeth Bergner version is a certain
hardness and realism, a sense of character that is more
modern than Shakespeare's, if less poetic. The Webster
Duchess of Malfi is an advance over Ophelia, on the one
hand, and Lady Macbeth, on the other; she is, in fact, the
transition, the connection, between these two women;
she is the whole world of ordinary women, of which they
are but the poles. Unfortunately, Miss Bergner's acting,
while admirable for the tragic scenes is too heavy for the
everyday ones; furthermore, the cutting done by Auden,
while it enhances the Duchess's plight as the play's victim,
misunderstands her character by making her its dead
center. Similarly, the character of Bosola is brutalized by
Canada Lee's acting; this man, in Webster, is a fiend only
in the sense that every shrewd, purchasable man is a
fiend; unlike Iago, he has a heart; he has scruples; he can
be shocked—he is not a nature-devil.

If these four plays in the aggregate constitute an aberration from some norm of choice, they each individually
in their subject matter contemplate an aberration from
some norm of conduct. There is the incest theme in *The
Duchess of Malfi;* in *Lady Windermere's Fan,* the relations between mother and daughter do violence to family
feeling, and there is a suggestion throughout, which gives
the play a certain spice, that the husband is going from
the daughter's bed to the mother's as regularly as he
would go to his club. In *John Gabriel Borkman* twin sisters are fighting for the possession of a father and a son;

the domestic history of *Henry VIII* is well known, and even in *Cyrano de Bergerac,* which I have not seen, there is the pronounced aberration of the nose, which cuts the hero off from the norm of love and marriage.

It is as if in the closed room of the theatre a morbid situation had suddenly been discovered; the drama, returning to the individual instance, finds him poisoned in the library. This predicament is not new to the novel, but the drama, which is concerned with action and hence with health, which gives the ability to act, has been obliged to look along its periphery, in the works of its minor writers, its aging writers, its great writers temporarily impotent, to find the contemporary mood. That this mood is also a fashion does not deprive it of significance; there are patients who boast of their symptoms who are nevertheless ill; the theatre, of all the arts, has, with its parochial, sheltered, and rather high-minded and unfashionable audience, been the last to succumb to the mode of the morbid and perverse. The fact that it now does so is perhaps an index of the world's extremity, another example of which is to be found in the play of Sartre, *Huis Clos,* produced in New York under the title *No Exit.* Here a modernist philosopher, to present his view of the modernist predicament (the damned soul in the locked room), resorts to the most ancient theatrical methods. A collaborationist who is really a coward, a society woman who is really a murderess, and a lesbian who is really a sadist die and go to hell, which they find is simply a hotel room where their own characters hold them prisoner as in life. Of this play, however apt its subject, it need only be said that M. Sartre's sense of sin is rudimentary. The crimes his characters confess to are so crude as to appear innocent and artless—a clergyman in the course of a five-minute solitary walk commits sins graver, more multifarious, more subtle, than are dreamed of in M. Sartre's philosophy. Only in the acting of Ruth Ford can a glimpse of evil be caught. She endows the society girl with a rattling silliness and vanity that is surely more repugnant to God than the infanticide M. Sartre ascribes to her. Those older writers, who were not existentialists, had, even in their failing moments, a less journalistic sense of the horror of existence.

March–April 1947

GEORGE KELLY

GEORGE KELLY is the unique case of a writer who is a box office success, an esoteric excitement, and a name utterly unregarded by the serious intellectual public, which imagines, in all probability, that he is George Kaufman. About twenty-five years ago he wrote three plays, *The Show-Off, The Torch-Bearers,* and *Craig's Wife,* which have been filed away in the memories of such veteran dramatic critics as Joseph Wood Krutch as superior but normal examples of American realism. Today he is being discovered by *Theatre Arts Monthly,* while independently and indeed irrelevantly, Ina Claire is playing in his *The Fatal Weakness* and Judith Evelyn has opened in a revival of *Craig's Wife,* to audiences whose aesthetic faculties have settled gluttonously in the stomach and whose sole anxiety is the gain or loss of *a good evening's entertainment.*

This after-dinner sluggishness on the part of his public must explain the fact that he has been allowed to pass unremarked, for he is the queerest writer on view in America. His plays, though they are set in drawing rooms, are not polite comedies; though they make a fetish of observation, they are not realistic; though they are performed by actors, their complete cast of characters is not

97

listed on the program, their real heroes and heroines being glasses of water, pocketbooks, telephones, and after-
dinner coffee cups. It is difficult to describe a George
Kelly play to anyone who has not seen several, simply because it is not like anything else while on the surface it
resembles every play one has ever been to.

The curtain goes up on what is recognizable as a drawing room; a recognizable Irish maid comes in and begins
to set things straight on the tables. The telephone rings;
the maid answers it. Soon the lady of the house appears,
a plausible matron in a girdle; before long, her husband
is on the stage, a hearty, successful American businessman.
He pecks her on the cheek; they start to discuss some family matter or local event: someone is expected on a train,
the drama league is giving a play, the man across the
street has married a new wife. A plot begins to form; the
wife is jealous of the bride across the street; she is to play
the leading role in the amateur theatricals; she opens an
anonymous letter which tells her that her husband is being unfaithful to her with an osteopath out near the
Merrick Memorial; she reads in the paper that a man her
husband plays poker with on Willow Avenue has just been
found dead with his wife. The play continues. The widow
from across the way brings over a bunch of roses; the
daughter, whose child goes to progressive school, drops in
to report a quarrel with her husband; a woman friend
calls and cannot make up her mind whether or not to
dine at the golf club; the telephone keeps ringing; the
maid fetches a glass of water. Meanwhile, the plot moves
forward: the husband asks his wife for a divorce, or breaks
an expensive ornament, or has a heart attack from seeing
his wife on the stage. An event has happened, and the
playgoer, when the curtain drops on his first George Kelly
play, may notice nothing unusual, except that there has

been rather a lot of stage business, and that something about the story seems not quite resolved.

It takes a second or a third George Kelly play for the spectator to perceive, with the horror he remembers from dreams, that the stage business is everything. "Tell them to say something, Nelly," shrieks the directress, Mrs. Pampinelli, in *The Torch-Bearers,* during a humiliating pause in her production, when the amateur actors sit frozen on the stage waiting for the prop fountain pen that nobody has remembered to put on the desk. "Anything at all! Something about the weather!" Mr. Kelly, as a playwright, has taken Mrs. Pampinelli's advice. The George Kelly play is, in essence, a long ad-lib. Its subject is inanity. Stage-time here, like lifetime, is an interminable gap which must be bridged by desperate conversational maneuvers, remarks about the weather, the time of day, vital statistics, golf scores, menus, clothes, train schedules, people's addresses ("I don't know where all this rain is coming from. . . . You can't tell, it might not be raining in Albany. . . . Aren't those roses lovely? . . . I heard her telling Miss Austen she's got over two hundred rose bushes in her garden. . . . 2214, that must be out near the lake . . . I think there's nothing in the world so exhausting as train-riding . . . Have you got the time?"). This gabble is the chorus which speaks the meaning of the play; and like a chorus it has its pantomimic expression in a compulsive dance of pocketbooks, pencils, fancy work, glasses of water, hats, timetables, and newspapers. The pocketbook is the leader of this chorus. This "accessory," with its self-possessed air of indefinable value, its bulging, flappy, serviceable exterior, and its obscene interior jumble of scraps and bits, is the prime repository of concern here. The loss of one of these vital objects is the subject of one of Mr. Kelly's early vaudeville plays; and though it never again assumes such open thematic prominence, the heroine's pocketbook is always resting on a lower shelf of the audience's mind. All action halts on the stage while the heroine fumbles in it, opens it or closes it, loses it, finds it; the heroine's maid does not feel that it is safe to leave the stage without telling her mistress that she has put her pocketbook in the drawer. The maids in Mr. Kelly's plays have a kind of weight and portentousness that does not derive from the plot, to which they make no contribution. Their masters and mistresses dally with them in obsessive conversation; offstage maids answering offstage telephones are greeted ceremoniously by name ("Hello, Selina, this is Mrs. Espenshade"). They are laden with gravity because they are the servants of the objects which are the plays' gods; they tend the telephones, the tables, the cigarette boxes, the suitcases; they know the time of day and carry in the inevitable glass of water, reverently, like a communion cup; they have devoted their lives to the weather report and the evening news. Mr. Kelly's heroines have come and gone; Ina Claire has succeeded Tallulah Bankhead and Chrystal Herne; but the Irish maid, Miss Mary Gildea, who is acting in *The Fatal Weakness,* was answering the door in *The Torch-Bearers* in 1922, in *Craig's Wife* in 1925, in *Here Comes the Bridegroom* in 1917, in *The Deep Mrs. Sykes* in 1945. Presumably, Mr. Kelly, like his own matrons, "would not know what to do without her."

Early in Mr. Kelly's career, this pedantry of ceremonial and vacuous busyness was related to the official subject of his plays. In *The Show-Off,* the hero is a ritualistic greeter who lives on small talk, idle boasts, and gratuitous lies; in *Craig's Wife,* the heroine is a house-proud woman

who lives through her furniture and will not let her husband smoke in the parlor. Both of these people are mad;
they are monsters in the Jonsonian manner; a human
trait has been carried in them to the point of inhumanity.
But they have at any rate a consistency of character that
respects the conventions of the human personality; their
personalities are overdeveloped but intact. Mrs. Craig is
in love with her house, but she is not a house; Aubrey
Piper is a compulsive stream of words, but he is also a
man who listens to them. In *The Deep Mrs. Sykes* and
The Fatal Weakness, however, character has become utterly disassociated, and it is hard to say whether this is
an advance or a regression. In these plays, type with its
simplicities disappears. One lady may be designated as
jealous or proud of her intuition, and the other as romantic, but these traits are weak, stunted, undeveloped, like
rudimentary organs of character that have not been able
to complete their growth, or like vestigial remains of some
extinct race of beings that went by the name of humanity.
The personalities of these late heroines are fluctuating
and discontinuous. With complexity comes a loss of stabil-
ity. Emotion with these characters is a kind of bird-
mimicry of emotion; and, like amateur actors, they cannot hold a pattern. Mrs. Sykes wobbles between jealousy,
masochism, and mediumistic vanity, while Mrs. Espenshade, who is supposed to be a romantic nature, cannot
remember for five minutes to feel regret for the infidelity
of her husband. The people acquire strange names, as
though they were queer botanical specimens, outside ordinary classification. Motive, so prominent in Mrs. Craig,
has vanished, naturally enough, in this incoherence of
personality; motion replaces it, a kind of nervous twitching of the will which survives the death of the character:

Mrs. Sykes hatches a series of plots that have no conceivable object; Mrs. Espenshade energetically gathers evidence for a divorce that she has no wish to obtain. Curiosity is the only incentive that remains to these women, their friends, and their servants, curiosity of the kind called idle, that is, curiosity without motive or concern, a senseless twitching of the intellect. It fastens as readily on the affairs of strangers as on the affairs of friends, on an address, a birthplace, a telephone number, or an item in the morning paper. It shows itself most singularly in a pointless interest in the clock; there is not a play of George Kelly's in which the characters do not ask the time of each other, as though this knowledge were a pressing necessity. The passion for exact and irrelevant information is not a mere function of leisure here. The husbands, as well as the servants, participate in this acquisitive literalness. "I've been out in Milwaukee visiting my family," says Mrs. Sykes. "Milwaukee, Wisconsin, you mean?" asks a gentleman visitor. "Yes," answers Mrs. Sykes, "I have a mother and two brothers out there."

This reply is, somehow, reassuring, and the question, prehensile, groping, had an anxious pathos. It was an attempt to possess a void. In these last plays, the American family is seen as a nomadic integer, lost in time and space, inquiring, placing, dating, its only impulse a locative one, its brain a rudimentary map on which, several times a day, through hearsay or direct information, new points are marked, new connecting lines traced between them. The plots in these late plays falter, a technical failure which, however, has its own appropriateness, for the plots take on the aspect of deceptively well-marked roads that trail off ineffectually in the wilderness of chaos.

This sense of the American family as floating placeless in its solid living-room is intensified by the fact that the Kelly play is set in no recognizable city and yet always in a different city and a city so particularized that it cannot be every city, so that the spectator's mind as he watches travels hurriedly from Scarsdale to Cleveland, from Philadelphia to Rochester, from Chicago to Hartford, searching for the residence of Mr. Oswald Sykes. In the same way, the class locus of Mr. Kelly's families is by no means definite. Except in the case of *The Show-Off*, where the family is lower middle class, the stage directions always specify a "comfortable room suggestive of good circumstances," "gorgeous gold-colored rugs . . . rich brocaded satins," "a handsome little armchair, upholstered in buff," etcetera; yet the habit-ridden family which is discovered in this setting would seem more at home in less opulent circumstances—Mrs. Craig, for example, is really inconceivable as a great lady with a staff of three house servants, while she is quite easy to imagine as a woman who does her own work. There is a continual tension between the spectator's sociological memory and Mr. Kelly's taste in decoration which also keeps the Kelly family constantly on the move.

And here the question enters of how far conscious selection and intelligence have directed Mr. Kelly's work. The printed versions of his plays are prefaced by little gnomic sayings, quotations from himself, which imply that he is under the impression that he is writing problem plays. In *Behold the Bridegroom*, he did write a problem play about the modern girl who, having loved many men, is incapable of the love of one; in *Reflected Glory*, he treats the actress as a problem and concludes that the life of the entertainer is incompatible with the life of love. But even here the glass of water, the pocketbook, the maid, and the wristwatch intrude on these commonplaces, just as, in the family plays, other commonplaces out of sentimental drama plop into the glass of water. It is possible that Mr. Kelly's best effects are nervous tics which, in the course of years, have encroached more and more upon the territory of his plays, pushing the plot to one side, in the same way that the nervous tics of his characters have left them no room for feeling: Mrs. Espenshade, trying on a white hat with a veil for her ex-husband's wedding, is diverted from her "natural" emotions. It seems probable indeed that the conscious and voluntary drive of Mr. Kelly's talent is, like his "social" plots, an avenue of platitude that misdirects his material. Yet, as in the case of the *naif* painters, his very faults, the crudity of his conceptions, the innocence of his allegories, become part of the subject, and, while distorting it, add to its grace. The distinction between form and content vanishes; Mr. Kelly's phrasing, now stiff, now soft and mawkish, sinks like a wax into the wooden images he is creating. He remains an oddity, a manifestation of nature, from which he cannot be disengaged, as a free artist can, for judgment.

Born Yesterday, by Garson Kanin, the smash-hit comedy that pimps for progressivism, brings sadistic farce and a *PM* editorial into closer association than one would have thought possible. The little people's spokesman here is a *New Republic* writer with glasses and a set of Tom Paine who undertakes, for pay, the education of a gangster's mistress. The unsuspecting enemy of the people is swindled out of his girl and his private papers, not to speak of his money, and the curtain falls on a victory for democracy. Coming out boldly against people who push other people around, the play is ready with its own night stick, borrowed from George Kaufman, whenever truth or integrity of characterization tries to read its bill of rights. The infantile blonde and the big, rich, mindless thug do, at one moment, makes a true picture of brute violence and pathos, very much like the scene in *Frankenstein* where the sentimental monster by the pond unwittingly kills the child that attracts it. Violence is not this play's enemy, but its *alter ego,* and this moment symbolizes Mr. Kanin's own aggressive and tender approach to political innocence quite as aptly as a page of *PM* type.

View magazine, under the name of the *Theatre Ubu,* has begun a series of avant-garde evenings in the theatre. Ramon Sender's *The Key* was presented recently in a comic style so robust and vigorously American as to disconcert some avant-garde sections in the audience which had counted, apparently, on a less amused and more "amusing" evening. The acting, particularly Miss Mary Welch's, had a wonderful gaiety and bounce, an energetic directness that is never felt today in the professional theatre. This suggests that real acting, like real poetry and fiction, has become the property of amateurs, that is, of people who are not doing it for a living. The actors here were professionals, but they did *The Key* under unprofessional conditions, with improvised scenery and costumes, insufficient rehearsals, and to an audience for which the play was not a performance but a party, in short, an unprofessional audience. *The Key* is a ferocious comedy about avarice and sex. With its stock types and loose structure, it too had something artless, negligent, and spontaneous about it, as though it were a scenario for a modern *commedia dell'arte.*

THE UNIMPORTANCE
OF BEING OSCAR

ONE OF OSCAR WILDE's acquaintances wrote of him that he could never be quite a gentleman because he dressed too well and his manners were too polished. The same criticism can be made of his art. There is something *outré* in all of Wilde's work that makes one sympathize to a degree with the Marquess of Queensberry; this fellow is really insufferable. Oscar's real sin (and the one for which society punished him, homosexuality being merely the blotter charge) was making himself too much at home. This is as readily seen in his comedies as in his epigrammatic indorsement of socialism or his call on a Colorado coal mine. He was overly familiar with his subjects. Shaw said of him that he did not know enough about art to justify his parade of aestheticism. Certainly, he was not intimate enough with poverty to style himself an enemy of riches. In this light, the Marquess of Queensberry's libel, that he went about "posing" as a sodomist, speaks, in the plain man's language, the true word of damnation. In his comedies, it is his audience whose acquaintance he presumes on. Where the usual work of art invites the spectator into its world, already furnished and habitable, Wilde's plays do just the opposite: the author invites himself and his fast opinions into the world of the spectator. He ensconces himself with intolerable freedom and always outstays his sufferance—the trouble with Wilde's wit is that it does not recognize when the party is over. The effect of this effrontery is provoking in both senses; the outrageous has its own monotony, and insolence can only strike once.

In *The Importance of Being Earnest* (Royale Theatre), the tedium is concentrated in the second act, where two young ladies are rude to each other over tea and cake, and two young gentlemen follow them being selfish about the muffins. The joke of gluttony and the joke of rudeness (which are really the same one, for heartlessness is the basic pleasantry) have been exhausted in the first act: nothing can be said by the muffin that has not already been said by the cucumber sandwich. The thin little joke that remains, the importance of the name Ernest for matrimony, is in its visible aspects insufficiently entertaining. That the joke about the name Ernest is doubtless a private one makes it less endurable to the audience, which is pointedly left out of the fun. To the bisexual man, it was perhaps deliciously comic that a man should have one name, the tamest in English, for his wife and female relations, and another for his male friends, for trips and "lost" week ends; but Wilde was a prude—he went to law to clear his character—and the antisocial jibe dwindles on the stage to a refined and incomprehensible titter.

Yet, in spite of the exhausting triviality of the second act, *The Importance of Being Earnest* is Wilde's most original play. It has the character of a ferocious idyl. Here, for the first time, the subject of Wilde's comedy coincides with its climate; there is no more pretense of emotion. The unwed mother, his stock "serious" heroine, here becomes a stock joke—"Shall there be a different standard for women than for men?" cries Mr. Jack Worthing, flinging himself on the governess, Miss Prism, who had checked him accidentally in a valise at a railroad station twenty-five years before. In *The Importance of Being Earnest* the title is a *blague,* and virtue disappears from the Wilde stage, as though jerked off by one of those hooks that were used in the old days of vaudeville to remove an unsuccessful performer. Depravity is the hero and the only character, the people on the stage embodying various shades of it. It is deepest dyed in the pastoral region of respectability and innocence. The London *roué* is artless simplicity itself beside the dreadnought society dowager, and she, in her turn, is out-brazened by her debutante daughter, and she by the country miss, and she by her spectacled governess, till finally the village rector with his clerical clothes, his vow of celibacy, and his sermon on the manna, adjustable to all occasions, slithers noiselessly into the rose garden, specious as the Serpent Himself.

The formula of this humor is the same as that of the detective story: the culprit is the man with the most guileless appearance. Normal expectations are methodically inverted, and the structure of the play is the simple structure of the paradox. Like the detective story, like the paradox, this play is a shocker. It is pure sport of the mind, and hence very nearly "English." The clergyman is the fox; the governess the vixen; and the young bloods are out for the kill. Humanitarian considerations are out of place here; they belong to the middle class. Insensibility is the comic "vice" of the characters; it is also their charm and badge of prestige. Selfishness and servility are the moral alternatives presented; the sinister impression made by the governess and the rector comes partly from their rectitude and partly from their menial demeanor. Algernon Moncrieff and Cecily Cardew are, taken by themselves, unendurable; the meeching Dr. Chasuble, however, justifies their way of life by affording a comparison—it is better to be cruel than craven.

Written on the brink of his fall, *The Importance of Being Earnest* is Wilde's true *De Profundis*; the other was false sentiment. This is hell, and if a great deal of it is tiresome, eternity is, as M. Sartre says, a bore. The tone of the Wilde dialogue, inappropriate to the problem drama, perfectly reflects conditions in this infernal Arcadia; peevish, fretful, valetudinarian, it is the tone of an elderly recluse who lives imprisoned by his comforts; it combines the finicky and the greedy, like a piggish old lady.

Fortunately, however, for everyone, there is a goddess in the play. The great lumbering dowager, Lady Augusta Bracknell, traveling to the country in a luggage-train, is the only character thick and rudimentary enough to be genuinely well-born. Possibly because of her birth, she has a certain Olympian freedom. When she is on the stage —during the first and the third acts—the play opens up. The epigram, which might be defined as the *desire* to say something witty, falters before her majesty. Her own rumbling speech is unpredictable; anything may come out of her. Where the other characters are hard as nails, Lady Augusta is rock. She is so insensitive that the spoken word reaches her slowly, from an immeasurable distance, as if she were deaf. Into this splendid creation, Wilde surely put all the feelings of admiration and despair aroused in him by Respectability. This citadel of the arbitrary was for him the Castle; he remarked, in his later years, that he would have been glad to marry Queen Victoria. Lady Augusta is the one character he could ever really imagine, partly, no doubt, because she could not imagine *him*. Her effrontery surpasses his by being perfectly unconscious; she cannot impose on the audience for she does not know they are there. She is named, oddly enough, after Bracknell, the country address of the Marchioness of Queensberry, where Wilde, as it turned out, was less at home than he fancied. The irony of the pastoral setting was apparently not lost on the Marquess of Queensberry, who arrived at the first night with a bunch of turnips and carrots.

Jean Cocteau, it is said, has modeled his life on *The Portrait of Dorian Gray*. If this is so, one cannot help but feel that *The Eagle Has Two Heads* (Plymouth Theatre) was written by the Albright portrait. Grandiloquent and lurid in the old-fashioned royalist mode, this story of a poet and a queen suggests that the attic of Cocteau's mind was never as smart as the downstairs: a schoolgirl was there all along reading romances and trying on costumes. "Dressing up" has been, all along, M. Cocteau's subject; the romantic temperament in *Thomas the Impostor, Les Enfants Terribles,* and *Le Grand Écart,* revealed itself as an heroic fraud, a shabby and magnificent lie. The beauty of these works trembled in the equipoise between truth and falsity; comedy was the predicament of his suffering figures, an irony enforced by the age. In *The Eagle Has Two Heads,* the tension has broken, posturing is no longer serious; it is solemn. The eagle is *not* double-faced.

June 1947

THREE PLAYS WITH MUSIC

Beggars Holiday, book by John Latouche, music by Duke Ellington, inspiration by John Gay, enjoyed neither critical renown nor box office popularity. For me to condemn it now would be simply a tautology. It might be said, however, that the error of this production was fundamental: it lay in an over-enthusiastic identification of Mr. Latouche's subject matter (twentieth century Harlem low-life) with John Gay's subject matter (eighteenth century London low-life). In one important respect, the highwayman differed from the modern mugger—he was a hero, and not only to his accomplices. The vitality and stylishness of Gay's opera comes from the vitality and stylishness of Macheath, a scoundrel of magnificent proportions who is noble because he is free. All of the original Macheath's crimes are attributes of his freedom: he murders and steals subversively, as if the penal code were an invasion of his liberties; he is inconstant in love in the manner of a manifesto—fidelity is a bungalow-heaven to this luciferian spirit. The final scene, where he is about to be hanged, has the aspect of a gay crucifixion; the law seizes Macheath but cannot possess him, for the man has chosen to die. Mr. Latouche has moved this story to Harlem piece by piece and assembled it there as rich an-

tiquarians carry an old house off on a truck to locate it in
a more fashionable environment. But the opera's essential element, freedom, is violently absent from Harlem;
the salient fact about the Harlem man is that he is born
the prisoner of his color. His music is the dolorous accompaniment of his fixed and limited state: prison songs,
work songs, blues, not to mention spirituals, all groan and
yearn for a Heaven Macheath already inhabits. From Mr.
Latouche's insensitiveness to this point, his assumption
of an equality of opportunity between the rogue and the
Lenox Avenue mobster, came the confused tastelessness
of the production, which was "daring" enough to exploit,
for a song or a dance number, the brutal features of Harlem life, and "advanced" enough to drop a tear for the
killer as the product of social conditioning, but never bold
enough to spend the theme it borrowed and show crime as
a happy occupation.

With *Brigadoon,* the case is different. The critics liked
it; "nice people" will continue to go to it for six months
or a year. Criticism could not deter them from it because
its vice, an absolute vacuousness, is to them a virtue. A
fantasy about two American soldiers chancing on a seven-
teenth century Scotch village that comes to life for a
day once every hundred years, it offers all the comforts of
familiarity, uniting the Highland fling, the Scotch joke,
and the twice-told ghost story in an eternity of the trite.
How it has happened that Scotland, the national home of
prudence and foresight, should have become, for middle-
class imaginations, the seat of the exotic, is a curious
question. Dr. Johnson, a middle-class man himself, found
it barbarous and uninteresting; but other views have prevailed and from the time of Scott and Burns, it has been
the *locus classicus* of the mild dirty story, the mild clean

story, the mild supernatural story, and the mild clean romance. In my childhood, there was James M. Barrie and Harry Lauder, to whom we used to listen on the gramophone. The deterioration of the reality principle from that day to this may be measured by the fact that Harry Lauder was, at least, a real Scotchman, while today in *Brigadoon* a troupe of Broadway actors *imitate* Scotchmen. In this sense *Brigadoon* is a new product like enriched flour, from which the nutrients are removed by milling and then synthetically restored.

Street Scene is another matter. It was worth putting Elmer Rice's former stage success into operatic form if only to make the play visible once again, embedded in music as in an oyster shell. The story has not aged, except where the author has tried to rejuvenate it: references to the housing shortage and jitterbug youth seem already dated before the immemorial brownstone, the neighbors at the windows like historic fixtures, and the *crime passionel* in the bedroom with the flower-pots outside it. In certain places, it is true, one feels a hint of the passage of time, which only intensifies, however, the mood of city desolation which the play so strongly creates. The seducer from the real-estate office, for example, with his promises of a stage career, belongs now to the age of innocence: this is the age of consent and the working girl, generically speaking, no longer dreams of the footlights, just as the boy on the farm no longer believes he can be president. Similarly, the part of the old socialist, haranguing gently from the first-floor window, has lost its prophetic conviction—as if in deference to world events, Mr. Rice has cut it to a murmur. The brownstone, it appears, has outlived its disaffected inhabitant; the revolution, like the job in the chorus, was too extreme a demand.

Time has, as it were, been absorbed by this play and given it a classical appearance which it did not possess in 1928. Nearly twenty years have passed, and these people are still there, sitting ritually in the evening on the stoop: suffering wears shirt sleeves and house dress like a uniform of endurance. The play is more dispassionate than it seemed—there is a sense of justice toward all the characters and of the crime as pursuing the criminal. From the very beginning, as in the classical drama, it is plain to the audience—and the man himself seems to know it obscurely, by a gloomy instinct—that the exacerbated stagehand will kill his pretty, faded, unfaithful wife. This event is awaited with pity and terror, pity for the criminal and terror for the crime. The plot, like the old plots of Hamlet, Oedipus, and Orestes, is not a conflict of persons but a contest between a man and a fearful action which everything wills him to commit but which he himself repels as inadequate to his complexity of being. The climax is a release. The murder being committed, the murderer is freed of it and can become human again through regret. This liberation, this convalescence, makes a very beautiful tableau at the end of *Street Scene,* where the father, singing, explains his crime to his daughter while the police and the neighbors stand back, respecting the moment of rest. Unfortunately, the words he is forced to use at this moment are a lyric called "I Loved Her Too," which sounds like a singing telegram.

And that, it must be admitted, is the trouble throughout. The production has no style to speak its subject, or rather its style is precisely the one that a character in *Street Scene* would use if something moved him to write an opera. This is particularly true of the lyrics, but true to some extent of the libretto and of the acting of the minor roles. There is a general slackness of technique

that reflects all too well contemporary urban civilization—
Sophocles is sitting in the window dressed in his under-
wear. Take the matter of accents, for example, which,
rendered pure and true, should have furnished the opera
with a kind of spoken music: the slovenly casting of the
production has an Irishman playing a Jew, an American
playing a Swede, and, worst of all, two Americans playing
Italians, a choice which can hardly have been dictated by
scarcity, considering the number of unemployed Italian
divas and tenors in metropolitan New York. It is only on
the visual plane that the play is worthy of itself. In the
massing and the isolation of figures, in the somber lighting, above all in the stage set of Jo Mielziner, a style *is*
achieved that commemorates the matter, a style grave and
composed, faithful to nature, full of justice and proportion, which uses the tawdry human body as a kind of
bitter yet lyric ornamentation. It is a new mode of seeing
—Tenement Renaissance.

WHAT A PIECE OF WORK IS MAN!

Proceeding backward down the arcade of English comedy, John Gielgud and his company arrive, in Congreve's *Love for Love* (Royale Theatre), at a bay of felicity. From this point, it is possible to look in one direction toward Jonson and the Elizabethans and in another toward Sheridan and Wilde. William and Mary were on the throne when Congreve wrote this comedy; commercial expansion had begun but the receding rural England was not forgotten, and the marriage of a Stuart princess of romantic heredity to a businesslike Dutch burgher expressed on the dynastic plane this equivocal moment in English history which is arrested in *Love for Love,* a play which has no graspable subject but is like an equation in balance. The whole world of nature is still present in these London lodgings. Ending in a dance, and interspersed with songs, the play has strong masque suggestions, with the sea being danced by Brother Ben, redfaced and marine as Poseidon, the stars by old Foresight, the astrologer, and the earth by the country girl, Prue, a stumpy little sex fetish rabid with desire of generation. Here, as with Dogberry and Verges, Shallow and Silence, and the innumerable troupe of clowns and rustics, rural idiocy is on the one hand the butt of the playwright and on the other a source of vitality. This ignorance is bliss, a gift of the Muses, country girls from Pieria themselves, to the urbanized author. In much the same way, the stock types from the earlier comedy are present here, like simples handed down from one play-doctor to another. The Alchemist survives in Foresight, Orlando in Valentine, and all those primitive vices and humors in Mr. Tattle, Mrs. Frail, and Sir Sampson Legend, whose very name proclaims what he is—an indomitable old myth.

Looking the other way, in what must be admitted is a diminishing perspective, toward Sheridan, Wilde, Coward, one sees at the end of the vista a drawing-room in which Tattle and Scandal will still be drinking Valentine's sherry and being wicked and fastidious and selfish and fatigued. Plato and Epictetus will no longer be found on the table (Valentine Discover'd Reading would be Valentine discovered dead), and Jeremy, the manservant, will now be called by his surname, Fetch, but Angelica's fortune will still be the object, and comfort a necessity to gentlemen without employment. Those who find Wilde original would do well to return to Congreve—it is *Love for Love,* truly, which ushers in the age of insolence. Hardness of heart (Valentine turning off his old mistress when she comes to see him with one of his children), greed (Valentine's designs on his father's property), voluptuousness (Valentine and Mrs. Frail) are here presented for the first time as ornaments of the male character. From the days of Plautus and Terence, comic plots have frequently turned on money and inheritance, but this is the first major comedy in which a mercenary attitude is struck charmingly by all the principals, as though fortune-hunting were as pretty and pathetic as love. There remains, however, in Valentine's nature something of the Renaissance gentleman, a touch of chivalry and desperate bravado, particularly in

the scenes where he simulates madness, that wafts the
Mayfair tea-table back onto the battlements of Elsinore
and reminds us that Hamlet, too, was the glass of fashion
and Mercutio a fop. And insofar as Valentine is a man of
parts, his position is that of a latter-day Hamlet. He is the
humanist hero surrounded by a swarm of monsters, the
nature-monsters of the past, personifications of appetite,
and the unnatural monsters of the future, dolls with
sand inside them. Scandal, half-doll, half-human, is his
Horatio.

But this view of the play is too somber. Valentine's
pathos is merely a shadow that life casts for a moment on
this art. The truth is that the play is slapstick, and the
Hamlet echo is part of the joke, like a Mona Lisa on a
moustache. The peculiar quality of *Love for Love* is that
it is not comedy in the classic sense, comedy critical of
manners and morals, aiming to delight and instruct according to the precepts of Horace, but parody, and parody
not of man's work but of God's. Where Shakespeare and
Molière, say, hope for correction or improvement, Congreve sees his people as mannerisms of Creation. This
lèse-majesté is what gives the play its atmosphere of dan-
ger, its wonderful headiness and elation. Something of the
spirit was inherited by Wilde, but Wilde's parody is too
catty; it caricatures experience and then parodies *that*.
Congreve makes truth absurd; he is not afraid of the serious. The situation in *Love for Love* is not a construction;
it is horrid probability itself. The disinherited heir, the
tradesmen with bills at the door, the cold mistress, the
false friends, the insensate father, these are no Algys and
Gwendolyns and Cicelys—Congreve here, like Beerbohm
in his famous Henry James parody, has hit off the style
of the Master in His richest and most tragic period. And,
as with Beerbohm or any fine parodist, the joke comes

with the unexpected withholding of sympathy—a rug is
jerked from under the performer in his moment of splen-
dor. This withholding of sympathy (which in Congreve
is identical with the absence of censure) ought, one would
think, to make the play unpleasant. But in fact it is not
so. The author has participated sufficiently in the subject
to rise above it in triumphant laughter: mind has eluded
matter, and the play's mirth is a kind of high spirits, as
after a narrow escape.

This sense of freedom is a great gift to actors. Congreve,
unlike Wilde, has left them something to act. *The Importance of Being Earnest* was, in both senses, too *finished*
a play for the stage. There is nothing for the actors to
do but read the lines correctly, and Mr. Gielgud, trying
to make room for performance, could only add a lean-to
of parody to what was already a parody structure, as
though the Wilde play had been a naïve effusion like *The
Drunkard*. The results were a little wintry, and Mr.
Gielgud himself, lacking sportiveness, showed particularly
to bad advantage. With the Congreve, everything is different. The play is not closed. The dialogue must be well
and stylishly spoken, but beyond that there is a whole
field of stage business in which the actors can inventively
romp. The contrast, in fact, between the precision of
speech and the horse-play of action is the point; physical
existence itself is the jest, and the curl of Valentine's wig,
the turn of Scandal's neat calf begin that parody of Man
that ends in the act of copulation. Anything the actors
can be or do, therefore, accrues to the play's interest. Mr.
Gielgud's gravity, his sensitive, melancholy profile, here
become exquisitely comic—he looks like a tiglon with a
heart. And Pamela Brown's acting style, the words drop-
ping measuredly from her lips as from the most refined
and expensive eye-dropper, her beauty, the bland, egg-

shaped face sliding gracefully down into the long goose neck with no decision of chin interrupting, become an image of the declension of form into the sensual inane. The notion of the human being as a work of art is played on wittily throughout the performance by pantomimic allusions to painting. The poses and gestures appear to come from the conversation-pieces of Zoffany, and the scene when Valentine is found in a Disordered Bed is a plate out of Rowlandson. These continual references to painting not only set the play, visually speaking, in a social world the eye can remember, preserving it thus from abstraction; they also force the spectator into the mood of the connoisseur, a mood, that is, of detachment, to which parody appears not an indignity but the truest compliment to an Author. This production is, in all its details, a buoyant act of perception unique in today's theatre.

January 1948

FOUR "WELL-MADE" PLAYS

Bᴜꜱɪɴᴇꜱꜱ ɪꜱ ʙᴀᴅ this fall in the theatre. Behind time, as usual, the entertainment industry is just now feeling the slump which began last year for the book trade and the department stores. There are fewer openings; empty rows of seats compromise plays that are classified as successful; a school has been organized for the benefit of unemployed "name" actors to provide them, like patients hooking rugs in a mental institution, with some therapeutic occupation.* Plays which have weathered the season display, for the most part, a certain workmanlike solidity. The well-built stage set of *The Heiress*, the safe, well-constructed plots of *Command Decision, The Druid Circle,* and *The Inspector Calls,* all reassure the playgoer against the prevailing storms; they are built to last, for an evening. As the value of houses and land, of what is called "real" property, becomes inestimable during a dangerous inflation, so the "real" property of the theatre, sound plotting, plausible characterization, a balanced outlook, appears to be quoted during this crisis at an almost exaggerated premium—there is something slightly ridiculous about those open, well-padded boxes of experience into which, at the rise of a curtain, we can gain

* Now the Actors' Studio.

admission for a few hours in the evening. These plays are
not contemptible: upon a modest segment of human life,
a family, a school, an air-force unit, a temperate beam of
justice plays impartially—a small truth is told. But the
heavy workmanship of these structures is out of all proportion to their function; it is as though one were to make
an umbrella out of solid marble. These plays are honest
but not serious. The playgoer can participate in them
with a mild sense of satisfaction, but he hesitates to recom-
mend them to others; the experience has been too re-
laxed, as it were, and domestic for public comment.

The Heiress is an adaptation of Henry James's *Washington Square*. It has a stage-set of such massive authenticity that it is almost a contribution to the housing
problem, a wind blowing in freshly from the square,
whipping the white curtains, fine intimacies of lighting,
and one of those evening scenes, simple, melancholy, and
uncorseted, at which Mr. Jed Harris, the director, excels,
a scene in which the masks of the day, the postures of
action and decision, are laid aside for the night and two
middle-aged people, brother and sister, facing each other
wearily in a dishabille of gesture, yawning, intermittently
conversing, their voices slowly decelerating, acknowledge
the failure of all things, the daily death of belief. The
interjection of fatigue, with its nullification of "problems," has a peculiar poignancy in the theatre, where
action is the *sine qua non*: Brutus in his tent, Emilia
combing Desdemona's hair and offering to go fetch her
nightgown, Sonya and the doctor, too tired to feel, sitting
glassy-eyed over the samovar toward the end of *Uncle
Vanya*—such intermissions of conflict are the musical rests
of the drama. There is the murmur of all those lingering
good nights in Dr. Sloper's conversation with Mrs.

Almond; what is unfortunate about *The Heiress* is that
its sound is less real than its silences.

It would be idle to complain that the authors of *The
Heiress,* Ruth and Augustus Goetz, had missed the point
of James's story, if only they had missed it completely.
This, however, they failed to do. The vague, large, awkward figure of Catherine Sloper is still dimly there at the
center, embarrassing the playwrights as she embarrassed
her father and her aunt Lavinia, who, like Mr. and Mrs.
Goetz, wanted to "make" something of her. Her father
wished her to be a sensible woman; her aunt wished her
to be a romantic heroine; Mr. and Mrs. Goetz wish her
to be a thumping Freudian case-history, a repressed libidi-
nal impulse which, thwarted, destroys itself. But it is poor
Catherine's fatality that she cannot "be" anything; a great
block of recalcitrant material, she confounds all efforts to
mold her. She has the stubbornness of inert matter, lacking both the power to move and the power to resist movement actively; she can be carried along, dropped, and re-
trieved, but nothing can really happen to her—she is too
unwieldy. Dr. Sloper's failure to perceive this is the tragic
error that keeps the story in motion; he has observed that
he himself cannot alter her, but, neglecting to reason from
experience, presumes that the fortune-hunter who courts
her can actually affect her destiny. His parental firmness,
based on this mistake, has an arbitrary and almost impious
character; the reader opposes him, for the reader divines,
through his instinct, that the doctor's fears, however ap-
plicable they might be in any ordinary case, are in this
instance groundless—nothing can happen to Catherine.
And the doctor's death, in the novel, has the irony of a
pure irrelevance; he dreaded what would happen when he
left her, but everything goes on as before.

Catherine, clearly, is a square, that least dynamic of all

shapes, the shape that gives the book both its pattern and its title. Yet this unbudging entity can feel—this is the miracle of the novel, which has a charm truly pantheistic: the hills are skipping with Catherine, and a rock can quiver at a slight. In James, there is a delicate tenderness toward Catherine that is a courtesy extended to all inanimate objects and inarticulate creatures. The coercion attempted on Catherine by each of those interested parties, father, and suitor, and aunt, appears, in the light of this tenderness, as a cosmic want of refinement, a crass insensitiveness on man's part to life of a lower order. All plans made for Catherine must of necessity deny her nature, and the well-meaning efforts of Aunt Penniman are quite as cruel in this respect as the selfish schemes of the suitor and the father's clever maneuver. But this cruelty, too, like everything impinging on Catherine, fails to dent its object. A cry of pain, a silence, and then Nature resumes its habits. Human beings, the past, sympathy itself are defeated in the serene middle age of the heroine, which knows no grudges or regrets, but smiles placidly back on its memories like a blue and empty day.

In the problem of awareness it sets itself, the recognition of consciousness in a creature mute and inglorious, this story is, in essence, a poetic feat of personification. To "humanize" the tale in the vulgar sense, which is the task Mr. and Mrs. Goetz have undertaken, to make Catherine, that is, sympathetic by making her socially presentable, teaching her how to walk and speak, like a DuBarry Success Salon neophyte, how to do her hair and respond to the advances of a lover, is to undo, with infinite labor, the work of the original author. If the playwrights are not wholly lacking in invention, a fresh start would have been more advisable, for though a passable melodrama results when the adapters have got their hand in—cruel father, abused daughter, deceitful lover, Victorian setting, crashing psychological finale which calls for a subtitle, The Spinster's Revenge—yet enough of the novel is still protruding, particularly in the first act, to throw the sequel into very flat relief. The audience which has beheld Basil Rathbone, a tired, trenchant practitioner, handing his bag to the maid and turning to face, once again, the friendly image of opaque good nature presented to him by Wendy Hiller, can only be disappointed that it sees no more of these people as the play proceeds; it wonders what can have happened to them and feels the boredom and restlessness that follow an unwanted interruption. Later in the evening, when passion is understood to have awakened her, Miss Hiller floats gracefully about the stage in arabesques of womanly feeling, and still later she burns with anger and her eyes flash terrible meanings (she has gotten to resemble her father), but all this appears a little tawdry and professional after those first few insights into the clumsy joys and lumbering sorrows of an amateur. Mr. and Mrs. Goetz, I understand, are being congratulated for their integrity in resisting a happy ending, but the temptations the devil labels for us as evil are not usually the most dangerous.

An Inspector Calls is a middle-class sermon on responsibility which uses a detective-story plot formula, like bingo in the church basement, to reach the un-spiritual man. A poor girl kills herself, and a comfortable industrialist's household is disturbed at its revels by a detective, who has been sent to affix the blame. Suspicion falls on each of five people in turn, and each is found guilty; the detective turns out to be a supernatural agent, and the curtain goes down. The symmetries of this plot are as Sunday-school strict as its message: one by one, as in a chain-reaction, the actors are called upon to look smug, to start with guilt, to feign unconcern, to bluster, to go to pieces, to admit all, and to bluster again. It is Cock Robin done as a round. The sins and omissions and cruelties are all offstage, in the past; and with the art of acting in its present state of innocence, pantomime is hardly adequate to make a guilty memory bear witness to guilt. Guilt, therefore, is revealed not by the action, not by the actors' faces, but by the police-inspector, who comes to force it out. The worm of conscience, here, is a worm indeed, and the play, for all its firm structure, has a strangely soft and spineless character. Fear of implication becomes a guide to conduct. Be careful what you say, the characters keep warning each other. Be careful what you do, Mr. J. B. Priestley, the author, admonishes them; watch your step with Labor or God will give you a parking ticket.

Many people who saw *Command Decision* imagined that here too they were witnessing a kind of moral *causerie*—on the expendability of human life in war. What they actually saw, however, was a dramatization of the *story* of expendability, which is quite a different matter. A tough air-force general is sending out bomber-missions, beyond range of fighter-protection, to destroy three jet plane factories that lie in eastern Germany. This operation, vital to Allied air superiority but entailing terrific losses on three successive days, is opposed, from self-interested motives, by a journalist, a staff bigwig, and a Southern congressman, all of whom are more concerned with public opinion and personal advancement than with the prosecution of the war. The public will not stand for these losses, the general is told by his critics, and in deference to these spokesmen of the public, the general is finally deprived of his command. The operation, however, is carried through, for the staff officer who replaces the general is converted overnight to his project; once he is in the general's place, he sees with the general's eyes. This play, of course, can be construed as justifying all on-the-spot military decisions; certainly, it denies the public the right of exercising judgment in an emergency or protesting the sacrifice of life. Yet the effect of the play as a whole is not to justify all on-the-spot decisions, but only a particular one, one, in fact, which is purely fictional and which is explained by the playwright to the public in the fullest detail. There can be no doubt whatever, if war itself is accepted as moral, that the stage general created by Mr. William Wister Haines took the correct course in the stage circumstances Mr. Haines contrived for him. This, however, leaves General Patton exactly where he was.

Of the hopelessness of drawing moral inferences from any specific military action, *Command Decision* provides a striking illustration. Mr. Haines perhaps wishes to whitewash some actual general, but this could only be accomplished by an actual board of inquiry. Killing men can never be good, and all that can be pleaded in its favor is that there were extenuating circumstances. There can be no analogues here, for the act, if it is to be palliated at all, must be seen in its concrete setting; theft as a principle is not condoned if a hungry man is pardoned for stealing a loaf of bread. Moral speculation, in fact, has no place in the military scene: one cannot say how many lives should be expendable for the sake of an x objective unless one knows precisely what the objective is worth, what alternative methods there are of taking it, and how much time there is. But this implies an omniscience that can be only *ex post facto*. Once one accepts the principle that any life is expendable, the principle, that is, of war, then no life has an established value, and everything is tested by results. Humanitarian considerations may be a factor in a military decision; they cannot, obviously, govern it, for war is inhumane. Tenderness for the lives entrusted to him is a good quality in a commander, but only in moderation, as a deterrent to military folly. So treacherous indeed are all moral footings where the problems of war are concerned that the atomic bomb can actually be represented as a life-saver by those who wish to defend it; it shortened the war, they insist, and since no one knows precisely how long the war would have lasted without it, the argument is, on this level, irrefutable.

Plays against war can evoke moral feeling, and plays about the common soldier may also do so, but a play like *Command Decision,* which concerns itself with the higher military processes, the big strategic decisions, has moved up into a sterile room from which ethical anxiety is brusquely excluded. The word *operation* is the clue. These generals of Mr. Haines's are really surgeons, disputing operational techniques over the etherized form of an invisible patient; no one questions their *right* to make the incision, but they argue with each other as to its medical *necessity.* The two congressmen hustle in like interfering relations of the patient, and the specialists show annoyance; these laymen ought not to be allowed to wander unchallenged through the premises. Professional jealousies intrude also but these are the *scandals* of a service whose ideal is an absolute colorlessness, an instrumental efficiency. Like *Yellow Jack,* like *Men in White,* this play conveys, not feeling, not thought, but information, in the manner of a feature article. With its neat and clear plot line, its ups and downs of suspense, it holds the spectator's interest without involving his emotions, and bears the same relation to war that the temperature chart of a patient bears to his human identity and his ethical worth.

In the academic life, as in the army, personal affairs are a scandal, almost by definition—that is why there is so much gossip in college communities. That a teacher should have a wife or a mother, to say nothing of a vice or a weakness, is *unthinkable* to those who look up to him; his very bodily existence, his shaving, sleeping, going to the toilet, jeopardizes his classroom standing from moment to moment; he himself, the intimate man, is the perpetual object of his students' obscene curiosity, for it both shocks and excites them to imagine him as human. The indecencies of the academic position, the shame of being a man when one would prefer to be a pure omniscience, the cowardly attempts at good fellowship, the hatred and disparagement of students which is the professor's revenge for the daily belittlement of his image that private life imposes on him, all this is the subject of *The Druid Circle,* a play that would have been better if craftsmanship had not fashioned it so expertly, if it had avoided high climaxes and dramatic confrontations and remained insistently on the plane of the ordinary, where the teacher's tragi-comedy really takes place. The atrocity committed by the professor, who makes a student read aloud a very intimate loveletter, is robbed of its proper shabbiness by the hysterical emphasis Mr. Van Druten, the author, puts on it; what is horrible about the academic life is not that a teacher should do such a thing in a crisis of passion and jealousy, but that he would do it as a matter of course, without any sense of emergency, as a routine disciplinary measure. That a teacher should be a tyrant is not so terrible as that he should be a petty tyrant, yet the whole tendency of his profession is to narrow his actual opportunities while investing him with sovereign powers. Jealousy, consequently, is the pedagogue's occupational habit, jealousy of his colleagues, of his pupils, of the world, of the very authors he elucidates; to present this ever-present irritant as a kind of fit arising from sexual causes, as a folly, a momentary aberration, is to divest it of that daily meanness which is its distinguishing mark. In the professor's *descent* to persecution of the ugly little pair who are his victims lies the play's real pathos and squalor, but a false nimbus of pathos is drawn about this smug couple by the author's inveterate stagecraft, which transforms a timeless study of character into a rather belated defense of youth and its sexual rights. Here, as in *The Voice of the Turtle,* Mr. Van Druten encases a certain amount of realistic observation within a sentimental convention without appearing to notice the leak of meaning that results.

A STREETCAR CALLED SUCCESS

You are an ordinary guy and your wife's sister comes to stay with you. Whenever you want to go to the toilet, there she is in the bathroom, primping or having a bath or giving herself a shampoo and taking her time about it. You go and hammer on the door ("For Christ's sake, aren't you through yet?"), and your wife shushes you frowningly: Blanche is very sensitive and you must be careful of her feelings. You get sore at your wife; your kidneys are sensitive too. My God, you yell, loud enough so that Blanche can hear you, can't a man pee in his own house, when is she getting out of here? You are pretty sick too of feeling her criticize your table-manners, and does she have to turn on the radio when you have a poker game going, who does she think she is? Finally you and your wife have a fight (you knew all along that She was turning the little woman against you), you decide to put your foot down, Blanche will have to go. Your wife reluctantly gives in—anything for peace, don't think it's been a treat for *her* ("But let me handle it, Stanley; after all, she's my own *sister!*"). One way or another (God knows what your wife told her) Blanche gets the idea. You buy her a ticket home. But then right at the end, when you're carrying her bags downstairs for her, you feel sort of funny; maybe you were too hard; but that's the way the world is, and, Boy, isn't it great to be alone?

This variation on the mother-in-law theme is the one solid piece of theatrical furniture that *A Streetcar Named Desire* can show; the rest is antimacassars. Acrimony and umbrage, tears, door-slamming, broken dishes, jeers, cold silences, whispers, raised eyebrows, the determination to take no notice, the whole classic paraphernalia of insult and injury is Tennessee Williams' hope-chest. That the domestic dirty linen it contains is generally associated with the comic strip and the radio sketch should not invalidate it for him as subject matter; it has nobler antecedents. The cook, one may recall, is leaving on the opening page of *Anna Karenina,* and Hamlet at the court of Denmark is really playing the part of the wife's unwelcome relation. Dickens, Dostoevsky, Farrell rattle the skeleton of family life; there is no limit, apparently, to what people will do to each other in the family; nothing is too grotesque or shameful; all laws are suspended, including the law of probability. Mr. Williams, at his best, is an *outrageous* writer in this category; at his worst, he is outrageous in another.

Had he been content in *A Streetcar Named Desire* with the exasperating trivia of the in-law story, he might have produced a wonderful little comic epic, The Struggle for the Bathroom, an epic ribald and poignant, a *comédie larmoyante* which would not have been deficient either in those larger implications to which his talent presumes, for the bathroom might have figured as the last fortress of the individual, the poor man's club, the working girl's temple of beauty; and the bathtub and the toilet, symbol of illusion and symbol of fact, the prone and the upright, the female and the male, might have faced each other eternally in blank, porcelain contradiction as the area for self-expression contracted to the limits of this window-less cell. Mr. Williams, however, like the Southern women he writes about, appears to have been mortified by the literary poverty of such material, by the pettiness of the arena which is in fact its grandeur. Like Blanche Du Bois in *A Streetcar Named Desire* and the mother in *The Glass Menagerie,* he is addicted to the embroidering lie, and though his taste in fancywork differs from these ladies', inclining more to the modernistic, the stark contrast, the jagged scene, the jungle motifs ("Then they come together with low, animal moans"), the tourist Mexican (*"Flores para los muertos, corones para los muertos"*), to clarinet music, suicide, homosexuality, rape, and insanity, his work creates in the end that very effect of painful falsity which is imparted to the Kowalski household by Blanche's pink lampshades and couch-covers.

To illustrate with a single instance, take the character of Blanche. In her Mr. Williams has caught a flickering glimpse of the faded essence of the sister-in-law; thin, vapid, neurasthenic, romancing, genteel, pathetic, a collector of cheap finery and of the words of old popular songs, fearful and fluttery and awkward, fond of admiration and over-eager to obtain it, a refined pushover and perennial and frigid spinster, this is the woman who inevitably comes to stay and who evokes pity because of her very emptiness, because nothing can ever happen to her since her life is a shoddy magazine story she tells herself in a daydream. But the thin, sleazy stuff of this character must be embellished by Mr. Williams with all sorts of arty decorations. It is not enough that she should be a drunkard (this in itself is plausible); she must also be a notorious libertine who has been run out of a small town like a prostitute, a thing absolutely inconceivable for a woman to whom conventionality is the end of existence;

she must have an "interesting" biography, a homosexual
husband who has shot himself shortly after their marriage,
a story so patently untrue that the audience thinks the
character must have invented it; and finally she must be
a symbol of art and beauty, this poor flimsy creature to
whom truth is mortal, who hates the feel of experience
with a pathologic aversion—she must not only be a symbol
but she must be given a poetic moment of self-definition;
she who has never spoken an honest word in her life is
allowed, indeed encouraged, to present her life to the
audience as a vocational decision, an artist's election of
the beautiful, an act of supreme courage, the choice of the
thorny way.

In the same manner, Stanley Kowalski, the husband,
who has been all too enthusiastically characterized as the
man who wants to pee, the realist of the bladder and the
genitals, the monosyllabic cynic, is made to apostrophize
sexual intercourse in a kind of Odetsian or tin-pan alley
poetry. Dr. Kinsey would be interested in a semi-skilled
male who spoke of the four-letter act as "getting those
colored lights going."

If art, as Mr. Williams appears to believe, is a lie, then
anything goes, but Mr. Williams' lies, like Blanche's, are
so old and shopworn that the very truth upon which he
rests them becomes garish and ugly, just as the Kowalskis'
apartment becomes the more squalid for Blanche's attempts at decoration. His work reeks of literary ambition
as the apartment reeks of cheap perfume; it is impossible
to witness one of Mr. Williams' plays without being aware
of the pervading smell of careerism. Over and above their
subject-matter, the plays seem to emanate an ever-growing
confidence in their author's success. It is this perhaps
which is responsible for Mr. Williams' box-office draw:
there is a curious elation in this work which its subject-

matter could not engender. Whatever happens to the characters, Mr. Williams will come out rich and famous, and the play is merely an episode in Mr. Williams' career. And this career in itself has the tinny quality of a musical romance, from movie usher to Broadway lights, like *Alexander's Ragtime Band* or *The Jolson Story*. Pacing up and down a Murray Hill apartment, he tells of his early struggles to a sympathetic reporter. He remembers his "first break." He writes his life-story for a Sunday supplement. He takes his work seriously; he does not want success to spoil him; he recognizes the dangers; he would be glad to have advice. His definition of his literary approach is a triumph of boyish simplicity: "I have always had a deep feeling for the mystery in life." This "Hello Mom" note in Mr. Williams' personality is the real, indigenous thing. He is the Aldrich Family and Andy Hardy and possibly Gene Tunney and bride's biscuits and the mother-in-law joke. The cant of the intelligentsia (the jargon, that is, of failure) comes from his lips like an ill-learned recitation: he became, at one point, so he says, "that most common American phenomenon, the rootless, wandering writer"—is this a wholly fitting description of a talent which is as rooted in the American pay-dirt as a stout and tenacious carrot?

LITTLE THEATRE

THIS REVIEW is dedicated to three repertory groups, the company headed by Richard Whorf and José Ferrer who put on *Volpone, Angel Street,* and a bill of four Chekhov comedies at the New York City Center, the Dublin Gate Theatre, which brought a festival of Irish comedies to the Mansfield, and New Stages, Inc., which is performing Sartre's *The Respectful Prostitute* and Lennox Robinson's *Church Street* at the New Stages Theatre on Bleecker Street. Since the Dublin Gate Theatre and the City Center group are no longer on the boards, my notice is chiefly a labor of love, a bread-and-butter letter addressed to the absent. The reader must forgive me for speaking in his presence of pleasures from which he is now forever cut off, but it would be thankless to allow these players to pass unsung into oblivion; in any case, if he hurries, he may still find the box office open at the little theatre on Bleecker Street.

In an ideal state of affairs, the performances of these companies might have been looked on in a critical spirit and even with a certain severity. Richard Whorf and José Ferrer made *Volpone* into a kind of raucous collegiate romp, more reminiscent of a Marx Brothers film than of that terrible Noah's Ark of carnivora that Jonson, mastercarpenter, beached on the English stage. The Dublin Gate players, at any rate in the minor parts, had a slapdash style of acting that suggested an Irish housemaid flailing about with a dust-cloth—they gave their roles a lick and a promise and trusted to the audience's good nature to take the will for the deed. And the younger male actors with New Stages, Inc. are a wretched lot, feeble and uncertain in technique, miserably deficient in ease and charm; they seem to be the victims of a vocational delusion.

Yet the very shortcomings of these companies were allied to their most amiable qualities. Toward these groups an audience has been able to feel, for the first time in many seasons, an unguarded emotion, a sense of camaraderie and friendly give-and-take which may in part have been excited by a "popular" price policy at the box office or by Irish-American in-feeling, but to which the blithe spirit of the players themselves made the principal solicitation. These players asked your indulgence where the American Repertory Theatre DEMANDED YOUR SUPPORT, and where the commercial theatre (*Medea, The Heiress, A Streetcar Named Desire, Antony and Cleopatra*) manipulated your emotions for two hours in a thorough yet perfunctory manner, as though your object in attending the theatre was not to give anything at all, even understanding or tolerance, but to receive a certain bargained-for satisfaction, like a customer in a whorehouse. A modesty of ambition, a limitation of purpose, an acknowledgment of weaknesses characterized all the repertory performances; perfection was not aimed at, but only a generous sufficiency; there was no truculence, neither the boorish truculence of financial success nor the weak truculence of artistic failure. The theatre was not treated either as "entertainment" in the Broadway sense or as a moral imperative in the manner of Miss LeGallienne or

Piscator. The tone taken by these productions was one of pleasant seriousness or of serious pleasantry; the final impression left was one of the humane and the droll.

John Bull's Other Island, The Respectful Prostitute, The Old Lady Says "No!", the four Chekhov comedies, none of these plays are masterpieces, and *Volpone*, as I have indicated, was played as if it had never been one. They are intelligent and witty fancies, located in some region of the mind between the sentimental and the sardonic, even the Sartre play (surely the French *Born Yesterday*), whose political stridencies have been moderated by the direction of Mary Hunter and by the equable performance of Meg Mundy as the prostitute with the vacuum cleaner, till the play seems not quite so much a crude indictment of the American South as a dream that a French savant might have had on the subject of the Scottsboro case, a dream full of distortions and confusions, half-digested facts and conventional notions, moments of terror and interludes of ribaldry, a wonderful hodgepodge, in fact, in the brain of a clever man, to which this company has lent credibility by treating it as a parody which nevertheless speaks truth.

The Old Lady Says "No!" is frankly a nightmare (based on Stephen Dedalus's witticism) which mixes up an eighteenth-century costume piece with a modern expressionist drama. The curtain goes up on romantic Robert Emmet with a price on his head, in the green jacket and top boots, declaiming in blank verse from a garden to his lady-love in the window above. He is surprised by Major Sirr and his redcoats; swords are drawn; he falls to the ground; and at this point the story suddenly collapses. A doctor is summoned to the stage. In history brave Robert

Emmet would have gone on to make his famous speech
to his judges, to be hanged, drawn, and quartered, but
Irish history in this Denis Johnston version is a play in
which a ham actor is performing. The man in the plumed
hat and lace sleeves, suffering from concussion, wanders
through the streets of modern Dublin, among the drab
and uniformed citizens of the De Valera state. He is looking for Sarah Curran, his sweetheart, for Rathfarnham
and the lost garden, which is now a trolley-stop, for the
lines that he cannot remember, and the freedom for which
he died. Everywhere his questions are met with totali-
tarianized responses, with mass recitatives, the stiff salute
of law and order, and an old crone's obscene cackle. But
the jeering crone is Sarah Curran, and a statue of Grattan
in the Square which begins to harangue him with the
arguments of the great Parliamentarian is his old nemesis,
Major Sirr. The beauty of the play is that this is not a
one-way irony. Emmet's predicament is half-comic, and if
the plumed and booted figure calls into question modern,
regimented Dublin, dispirited Dublin itself questions the
validity of this tattered hero, this green, lace-bordered
Valentine which it has kept so long in its parlor. Romantic Ireland's dead and gone, but is not Emmet himself the
father of the brutal lie which confounds him now in the
streets? The debate between Emmet and Grattan, between
the insurrectionist and the parliamentarian, between
violence and peaceable action, arrives at no conclusion,
but the difficulty of posing the problem in terms of any
absolutes is symbolized by the fact that it is a debate between an actor and a statue—as everyone who has tried to
grapple with the question knows, it tends to vaporize into
the rhetoric of the gesture or solidify into the marble of
abstract thought.

The staging of this production (reminiscent in part of

the WPA theatre) was very direct, very simple, very funny, very moving; it slipped easily from the heroic to the mock-heroic, from the conversational to the grand, giving each genre its due, without burlesque or inflation; the fall from the sublime to the ridiculous is not such a very great one for the Irish, possibly because they have experienced it so often. This production was the high point of the Dublin Gate's short stay: the play was the most interesting in itself (the Shaw was a little parochial, an Englishman-Irishman joke) and made fewer demands than the others on the subordinate members of the cast. Micheal Mac Liammóir, the star of all three productions, is a real Jack-of-all-trades as an actor: he can play a gentleman, a servant, and a legend with the same nonchalant facility. He might be a fine actor, if he were willing to work at it; he contents himself instead with being a plausible one and with exercising every night an easy and affluent charm; a man accustomed to please, he has a rather serviceable and accommodating air, like a familiar guest in a household who will pass the sandwiches or oblige on the piano. A good-sized, sparkling fish in a small and sociable pond, he brings to the theatre a little poetry, a little polish, and a great deal of gregariousness. Here in America he was certainly a fish out of water; the critics were antagonized and bewildered by those pleasant and insular manners, just as they were repelled by the Chekhov one-act plays; the modesty of the undertaking alerted their suspicions.

A PRINCE OF SHREDS
AND PATCHES

"You *liked* the Laurence Olivier *Hamlet?*"
breathed a young woman the other day in a shocked under-
tone, when I mentioned the fact at a party. She herself
had not seen the film, the news that it did not employ "the
full resources of the cinema" having reached her in time.
"And I hear Fortinbras has been cut," she continued, with
an inquiring glance into my features, "not to mention
Rosencrantz and Guildenstern. And that the Queen is too
young, and the Oedipal theme over-emphasized." From
these objections one could not wholly dissent. The film is
indeed a photographed play, though why a photograph of
a play by Shakespeare should be such an inferior article, it
is hard to know—would a movie that had "liberated"
itself from the text be really preferable? The other objections are more forceful. The Queen, who looks a buxom
thirty-five, *is* too well preserved: if the gravedigger's memory does not betray him, Hamlet himself is thirty, middle
age to an Elizabethan, a fact, however, which Shakespeare
himself seems unmindful of, moved as he is by the poignancy of Hamlet's youth, his blighted studies, and un-
seasonable death. In the openly erotic scenes between
mother and son, the film is all too cinematic—what can the

Court be thinking, the audience asks itself; why does no one appear to notice these scandalous goings-on? The omission of Rosencrantz and Guildenstern no one greatly complains of, but Fortinbras is a different thing. He is as necessary to the play as Hotspur to the first Henry Fourth. Insofar as *Hamlet* is a study of different kinds of young men, he, Hamlet, and Horatio make a triad of *virtus,* as Osric, Rosencrantz, and Guildenstern make a triad of puerility. The play's frame, moreover, is *the soldier's music and the rites of war;* beginning with an armed watch, it ends on a peal of ordnance. Horatio is unfitted to sound the martial note. Military funerals are not in his line; he is the perennial student, like Raskolnikov's friend, Razumikhin, the honest pedant, a little Germanized, the uncouth and good-hearted intellectual. And it is characteristic of the Shakespearean irony and tenderness that peace should descend on the play to the sound of drum and bugle: the simplicities of war, the rules of the field are order and blessed tranquillity when set against the drama of blood and perfidy that has played itself out in the castle. To Fortinbras, the outsider, the man who happens to be passing, the heap of corpses in the hall is a prodigious and unnatural sight. Clean up this mess, he commands, and, touched by something in the dead young prince's aspect, remarks that he might have made a fine soldier, too bad he never had the chance. Without this tonic fresh presence, the dead march at the finale is merely a pageant of woe.

There are other times when the Olivier *Hamlet* is perhaps over-sumptuous with the décor of feeling, too interpretive, heavy on the pathos and light on the ethos, as in the bedroom scene, the To be or not to be speech, the drowning of Ophelia, and, above all, in those taffeta glances slid by the camera over the marriage couch. Yet the temptation to the picturesque, the scenic, is in the text itself. There is no tragedy of Shakespeare in which so much play is made with hand-props: Enter Hamlet reading, Hamlet writing in his tables, Hamlet with the mirror, Hamlet with the recorder, Hamlet with the skull. Hamlet's appearances in the play are a succession of pictorial attitudes, as though the glass of fashion were reflecting what was being worn heraldically that year by the model Renaissance man. Reading the uncut *Hamlet,* one cannot fail to be struck by the efficiency with which the hero is put through his paces. Not the least baffling aspect of Hamlet's character is that it often appears to be a mere congeries of "parts": the soliloquies themselves, so disturbing to the line of the action, seem half displays of virtuosity, just as if they had been inserted to show off to best advantage the powers of the principal actor. And the great anomaly, Hamlet's madness, is the actor's supreme opportunity.

What might be called the Mannerist style in which the hero is presented, moreover, is not the only example of a kind of showmanship and professionalism in this otherwise Orestean tragedy. The play is a veritable county fair of attractions. There are the two recitations, Hamlet's and the First Player's, the Dumb Show, the Play, a Danish March, flourish upon flourish of kettledrums, sound of cannon, Fortinbras' army on the Plain of Denmark, Ophelia's flower-strewn mad scenes, the Ghost—a profusion of stage-effects, a mime-show of marvels. In a sense *nothing* happens in *Hamlet* because everything happens on the same level of interest and thus, so to speak, simultaneously. What is seen is a series of pictures, vivid, brief, isolated. Hamlet, his mother, Claudius are so many shivered fragments. "A king of shreds and patches," Hamlet says of Claudius in a line that has been omitted from the Olivier version. He might also have been speaking of himself or of the play which he gives his name to. Hypocrisy, broken faith, play-acting, imposture are the characterological norm of reeling Elsinore. The fissure between *is* and *seems* cracks the world open. *Hamlet* is enigmatic because it is completely histrionic—everybody is playing a part.

This peculiar jerkiness, both in Hamlet's character and in the play as a whole, may be explained by the assumption, put forward by one scholar, that the play is a hasty composite of several earlier lost *Hamlets* pieced together so haphazardly that the discordances were never noticed. The text may have been improvised to serve the needs of an acting company or it may express some interior derangement on the part of the author or, very likely, both. In any case, this unsteadiness, which is the most striking feature of *Hamlet*, is the thing which most acted versions begin by trying to eliminate, either by "interpretation" or by a kind of glaze imparted to the diction that makes it (a) inaudible and (b) all of a piece. Sir Laurence Olivier's is the only *Hamlet* which seizes this inconsecutiveness and makes of it an image of suffering, of the failure to feel steadily, to be able to compose a continuous pattern, which is the most harrowing experience of man. Hamlet, a puzzle to himself, is seen by Olivier as a boy, whose immaturity is both his grace and his frailty. The uncertainty as to what is real, the disgust, the impulsiveness, the arbitrary shifts of mood, the recklessness, the high spirits, all incomprehensible in those middle-aged, speechifying Hamlets to whom our stage is habituated, here become suddenly irradiated. The play appears to be not so much a drama but a kind of initiation ceremony, barbaric like all such rituals, in which the novice is killed.

Already, in his first scene, Hamlet is grieving for the death of his father, but woodenly, uncomprehendingly, bitterly, as a child grieves who refuses to countenance that such things can happen in the world. The Ghost's appearance is to him almost an adventure. He rushes down from his interview full of jokes and wildness; his boredom is gone—at last he has something to do. But the Ghost's commission is not really Quixotic. The enterprise loses its zest with Hamlet's recognition that it is an actual man he must kill, his uncle, whom he knows very well, a sleazy piece of the old, tedious reality. Bored, sullen, and angry, he diverts himself by tormenting Ophelia, whom he suspects of being One of Them. He baits her father, pretends to be mad, and then promptly sloughs his ennui when the players come, gives them a lecture on acting in the patronizing tone that comes easily to precocious, gifted young dilettantes, loses interest shortly, and sends them off for the night. Thoughts of suicide engage him; he wishes himself dead. Meanwhile, a marvelous plan has occurred to him; he will trap his uncle with the play. He draws Horatio into the game, but before the play is over, he has ceased to care about the result. Repelled by the sight of his uncle praying, he lets pass his opportunity and instead makes a row with his mother, kills Polonius and two minutes later has forgotten about *him* in the interests of a new idea—to get his mother to promise not to go to his uncle's bed. At this point, the forces of reality—middle-age, and cunning—themselves take charge of the action, and Hamlet, who has provoked them, is done for.

Whether or not this is the authentic creature of Shakespeare's imagination, it is impossible to say. Behind the gesture and the impulse is there a Hamlet at all? That is the question which in Olivier's unique performance is kept open and aching, like a wound.

February 1954

THE LITTLE GATE

Love's Labour's Lost, an early play of Shakespeare opening Wednesday at the City Center, is seldom seen on the stage. When the talented Brattle Theatre produced it last year in Cambridge, Mass., with an Edwardian décor and costumes, the public sat up and rubbed its eyes: many people had never heard of it or supposed it was a "youthful exercise." A confused impression prevailed that the Brattle Theatre's directors had made an epochal discovery. Who would have thought the old bard had so much blood in him?

Why *Love's Labour's Lost* is so rarely done is a mystery, since it is both extremely actable and full of exquisite poetry; but perhaps, on the whole, it is a good thing that some of Shakespeare's plays should come to the audience fresh, with the dew still on them. Custom, it must be admitted, has done something to stale *As You Like It* and *A Midsummer Night's Dream* and *Macbeth* and *Hamlet* for us, so that we can hardly see these plays for the dust of old productions they have gathered, like costumes in a theatrical warehouse.

But *Love's Labour's Lost* has a special, spring-like quality that sets it off from the other so-called neglected plays:

146

*Two Gentlemen of Verona, All's Well That Ends Well,
The Comedy of Errors,* to mention only the comedies.
Whether or not it was Shakespeare's first play or second or
fourth (there is a dispute about the dating), it has something about it that makes one want to imagine it as the
first, something pristine and dazzling new, like the first day
of Creation. The King of Navarre and three attendant
gentlemen have decided to make Navarre the wonder of
the world by turning the court into a little hermitage or
academe, in which they will dedicate three years to study
and contemplation, vowing to see no women during this
exalted period.

Instantly, like the gods' punishment for folly, there appears the French king's daughter, with her suite of three
ladies; love supervenes; the vow is broken; a troop of rustics intrudes itself, multiplying confusion; letters are
mixed up; the ladies, disguised, extract declarations from
the wrong gentlemen, who find themselves again forsworn
(that is, false to a pledge); a play is put on; a braggart is
discomfited; in the end all comes right but a penance is
laid on the gentlemen. And a rough country girl is got
with child.

Here is the Shakespeare world, new-born, with its themes
and persons perambulating in wondering delight and as-
tonishment; even the serpent, jarred from his prehistoric
nap, is stretching his coils in a tree. Cruelty and time enter this Eden, foreshadowing the tragedies; at the end, un-
expectedly, with all its troubles resolved, the play turns
forlorn. The winter's wind whistles through, and Armado,
the magnifical, breaks off curtly, "The words of Mercury
are harsh after the songs of Apollo."

The spectator who comes to the play fresh is startled by
a series of almost uncanny recognitions, as if he had
stepped into a Shakespeare mirror-maze. Navarre's aca-

deme will be the forest of Arden, but it will also be the Vienna of *Measure for Measure,* where Angelo, the unjust judge, will try to impose an inhuman chastity on a human population; and it will be the court of old Lear in Britain, where an impossible filial love will be exacted.

Berowne and Rosaline, as lovers in *Love's Labour's Lost,* will appear again as Orlando and Rosalind and Benedict and Beatrice; of these three pairs, Berowne and Rosaline are, in many ways, the most charming, witty and redoubtable. Berowne, in his own person, is an early Mercutio and a Hotspur; Rosaline is not only Rosalind of *As You Like It,* but the dark Rosaline, Romeo's first love, and the dark lady of the sonnets.

Shakespeare's sonnets, indeed, are just offstage in *Love's Labour's Lost.* The young men write sonnets and read them aloud in the wood; the whole conception of the academe (harking back to Lorenzo's platonic Academy in Florence) belongs to the platonizing mode of the sonnets; moreover, in the very language of the play, with its insistence on perjury and forswearing, there is a light, yet persistent, echo of the note of personal betrayal that obtrudes in the sonnets like an angry allusion. Perhaps it is the reminder of the sonnets that makes *Love's Labour's Lost,* despite its frame of satire, seem so curiously personal.

But it cannot be only that. Remonstrating with the king on his bookish pursuit of wisdom, Berowne tells him, in effect, that the proper study of mankind is man; to retire into solitude to seek knowledge is to "climb o'er the house to unlock the little gate." This piece of proverbial wisdom provides an image of the play that seems to come straight out of Lewis Carroll. *Love's Labour's Lost* is the little gate that, once unlocked, opens into Shakespeare's wonderland. Light and tinkling as the play is—a concert of lutes and virginals or "a consort of voices," as someone called it—

quick in repartee as a set of tennis ("Well bandied both! a set of wit well played"), full of games and manage, it holds nevertheless the clue to Shakespeare's gravity.

"Now, to our perjury to add more terror, We are again forsworn in will and error." This jingling couplet of Berowne's swells to a demonic aria in the tragedies. In *Love's Labour's Lost,* the young king's will is only the arbitrary whim of youth seeking to violate nature in pursuit of its own ends, and it is corrected, in the end, by the women, like a childish fault. But it is a foretaste of future horrors, of Lear on the heath, Lady Macbeth and the monstrous Angelo and Timon of Athens.

In *Love's Labour's Lost,* will or wilfulness is tied to perjury and forswearing in a way that seems merely whimsical until one realizes that swearing an oath really expresses the will in its most extreme form; it is an assertion that one can rule the future. "Swear," says the ghost to Hamlet, and Hamlet swears to commit a crime that his soul shrugs away from—at bottom, he is too critical a spirit to believe in such absolute acts as murder.

When anybody in Shakespeare swears an oath or tries to extort its equivalent from somebody else, you can be sure there is trouble ahead, trouble materializing almost instantly, out of the air, like the Princess of France and her court, who arrive as though on a magic carpet. Throughout the plays, as in *The Merchant of Venice,* the will is always trying to gouge a pound of flesh from life, and life retorts with blood. There is no blood in *Love's Labour's Lost,* for here everything is play and lightheartedness, and Cupid is shooting, not at a real heart, but at a valentine that obediently drips sonnets.

For Shakespeare, the counter-forces to this male will are women. In *Lear, Timon, Hamlet, Macbeth,* where the abstract will is strongest and darkest, the power of women is enfeebled—the unsexed Lady Macbeth is not a woman but a man in woman's clothing. But in *Love's Labour's Lost,* the vow's antagonists, from the very start, are women, Nature's cohorts, in full tournament array, armed with the brightest weapons of wit and beauty and pity that Shakespeare ever gave them in ensemble.

SHAW OFF BROADWAY

THE PHOENIX THEATRE production of *The Doctor's Dilemma* had a cast of veterans: Geraldine Fitzgerald, Shepperd Strudwick, Frederic Worlock, Roddy McDowall, Philip Bourneuf. Mr. Worlock, the eldest of the group, was celebrating his fiftieth anniversary in the theatre; Mr. McDowall, probably the youngest, has been acting since he was eight years old. On the average, this cast had twenty years' stage experience. They had been seen in Shaw and Shakespeare and Ibsen and Sophocles, in the movies and on television. They still represent, in a curious, petrified way, the younger element—the serious element—in the commercial theatre. Their very names on a playbill are an announcement of honorable intentions on the part of the producer. But the chief thing that struck me, watching them in *The Doctor's Dilemma,* was a sort of wonder: whatever made most of these people want to go on the stage? And what keeps them there, undiscouraged, year after year? One is tempted to think of a conspiracy, like the medical conspiracy described by Shaw in the play—a plot against the public, schemed up by quack actors, quack directors, quack critics. The old words of dispraise—ham, hack—will not do for these performers. "Amateur" is wrong, for they are paid for what they do, and they lack, moreover, the one quality that makes amateur performances attractive: a certain *zeal* for acting, even if misguided. Whatever else may be said about him, the amateur actor is always acting, with might and main. But these professionals are not only without talent, for the most part, but without the slightest desire to impersonate anyone or anything. They could not, one feels, get up a charade or play Santa Claus. If they wish to impersonate anything, it is to impersonate actors. Hence this production, which had no relation to miming, was at the same time intensely stagey. It made me think of the movie of *Julius Caesar,* where all the busts of Caesar used in the décor repeated in a mirrored infinity Louis Calhern's double chins.

This is a play about doctors. There are six of them in the cast, each, as pinned down by Shaw, a collector's specimen of his type: fools, by and large, or charlatans, each with his panacea or trademark, except for the old doctor, who has lost his belief in medicine. They illustrate the pathology of medicine, like so many blisters and carbuncles, for Shaw treats doctoring as a disease. Yet the actors playing these "doctors" felt, apparently, that they had done their duty when they put on a false mustache or whitened their hair with cornstarch and spoke in a gruff voice. There was not an attempt, even a feeble one, to suggest the actual practice of medicine or the habits and mannerisms of live doctors—the way they rub their hands, for instance, their bustle in entering a room, the style they have of listening, with the head slightly cocked. To study a real doctor or doctors would be repugnant to actors of this sort. They want to have nothing to do with real life. Once I talked with a "younger" actor who had just been cast in *Detective Story.* He was worried about his characterization. "Well," I said, "I suppose you can go around to the police station and spend a little time with the detectives there." He was horrified by the proposal. That, he cried, would be imitation. True acting, he explained, came from within yourself. He did not want to know how live detectives looked and dressed and walked. It might introduce an impure element.

Assuming he was right, assuming that acting can be achieved by the armchair method, by sheer introspection, even here the veterans of *The Doctor's Dilemma* failed to put to themselves the questions that any amateur would ask: how would I react, for instance, if someone gave me some drawings to look at and they turned out to be rather good? The way Shepperd Strudwick does it, playing the great Sir Colenso Ridgeon, is to take young Dubedat's drawings to a window and give a violent start, as if a horse had kicked him, but meaning merely, "This fellow has talent." When the other doctors, his colleagues, examine the artist's work in a later scene, they go through the same routine: picture held at arm's length, galvanic start, picture passed on, to next colleague, repeat. Sir Colenso has been established as an art-connoisseur, but what sort of doctors are these others supposed to be, to know art so well that they are electrified by a single glance at a drawing? No one asked this question; it was left for the audience to speculate about.

Throughout the play, in fact, the burden of questioning was on the audience. What sort of man did Shepperd Strudwick imagine Sir Colenso to be? It was impossible even to guess. He played by fits and starts, seeking desperately for his laughs, alternately boyish and elderly, vacillating and decisive; he had evidently never taken a temperature, felt a pulse, or stood at a bedside. Yet he was supposed to be a great doctor. Or was he? The audience never knew. Among the lesser doctors, the only one who was recognizable as a man was Frederic Worlock, as Sir Ralph Bloomfield Bonington. He played the ignorant old impostor as a thespian, which at least was close to Shaw's idea. Bright-cheeked Roddy McDowall, playing the artist, Dubedat, was right in his early scenes. He gave very well the feline, animal alertness that Dubedat's impudence needs to make his demands bearable. But he lost hold of the part in the death scene, where Dubedat delivers his artistic credo: "I believe in Michelangelo, Velasquez, and Rembrandt. . . ." As this scene was played and directed, it was a sentimental apotheosis of the artist-figure. Mr. McDowall, spotlit, was rapt as he pronounced his exordium, as if he were about to be floated off on invisible wires to a stage heaven. But the point of this scene, as I understood it, should have been different. The religion of art was not sympathetic to Shaw. And Dubedat is amusing himself, even on his deathbed. When he recites his artist's creed, he is mocking the moralists grouped around him; it is partly exaltation and partly naughtiness and teasing. Dubedat is not the hero; there is no hero.

The real daring of this play, in fact, is that no one is heroic and nothing is sentimentalized, not even death. Dubedat dies, so to speak, baldly and matter-of-factly, surrounded by his medical chorus. It is not an emotional moment. It carries a shock because of the lack of emotion. "Was that death?" inquires the artist's widow, almost curiously. Death is a sort of anti-climax, a disappointment. One is tempted to echo the widow. "It that all?" "All this fuss about *that?*" Dubedat's funeral oration is promptly spoken by the quack who killed him: old Sir Ralph Bloomfield Bonington, who mouths a pastiche of Shakespeare and keeps reiterating, "He died *well.*" There is a good deal of irony in this, but no tragedy. And the death scene becomes pure comedy when the young widow appears, dressed in a white evening gown and flashing with jewelry, this being her interpretation of her husband's injunction not to mourn for him.

Jennifer, the artist's widow, is a fool. She is the perennial wife of the Great Man—ardent, admiring, uncomprehending. She believes she understands her husband and sets her love for him, like a *défi*, against the whole world of philistines. But she does not understand her husband any more than the philistines do; she is taken in by him, so that she makes him into a noble, sentimental lie. This greed for punishment, this obdurate gullibility, this craving to admire, can satisfy itself only in one way: the wife must become the widow. Jennifer does not directly cause Dubedat's death, but she, as they say, asks for it, by her tenacity in pursuing the great Sir Colenso Ridgeon, whose medical powers she believes in with the same hero-worship she gives her artist-husband. She thrusts herself in Sir Colenso's way, to get him to save Dubedat's life, at the expense of other lives, mere ordinary ones, which appear to Jennifer much less valuable. But she thus furnishes Ridgeon with a motive for killing her husband; Ridgeon has fallen in love with her, though she is too blind to see it. Sir Colenso does not do the deed himself; he behaves with professional correctness and turns the patient over to Sir Ralph Bloomfield Bonington, who kills in all the innocent fervor of his medical quackery. But once Dubedat is dead, Jennifer really enters into her element. If there is an apotheosis in the play, it is that of Jennifer, in the final scene, in a red gown and furs and feathers, in the art gallery, where Dubedat's pictures are being shown and the memorial volume about him, "The Story of A King of Men. By his Wife," is stacked, ready for sale. She finally owns Dubedat, who was unfaithful to her in his lifetime; his pictures at last are making money;

and she has a new husband. Her devotion to Dubedat has paid off; her hero has not disappointed her. The real fool, it appears, is the clever Sir Colenso, who is left empty-handed for his pains. He has killed Dubedat for nothing.

Very little of this was hinted in the performance. Neither Geraldine Fitzgerald nor the director appeared to realize that a type—the artist's wife—is being presented with a certain comic sharpness. In Miss Fitzgerald's performance, Jennifer's metamorphosis as the widow is bewildering. But for Shaw, though he is charmed by his heroine, the widow exists larvally in the figure of the ardent wife. Sir Colenso perceives this; that is why he can kill her husband without remorse. He is doing her a good turn by removing Dubedat with all his shabby frailties from the scene and leaving only "a beautiful memory."

Shaw calls this play a tragedy, which I take to be a jest. It is a very dry comedy, a little sour and chilling. The first act is a classical satire on the medical profession, which is seen to be composed of charlatans, naïve quacks, or unbelievers. The conclusion appears to be nihilistic: nothing is known in medicine; fads succeed each other in eternal cycles; patients are cured by accident or by being given the wrong medicine through the doctor's carelessness. Sir Colenso, with his new discovery for "buttering" the disease germs sounds as big a booby as his colleagues. Only the old doctor, Sir Patrick, who has retired from practice, dares to speak the truth, which is that they are all bunglers and murderers.

The second act presents the doctor's dilemma. Sir Colenso's cure for tuberculosis is still in its early stages, so that he can take only a limited number of patients. He has room for one more. Given two lives, Dubedat's and that of a colleague, Blenkinsop, a poor general practi-

tioner, which should he save? Which is worth more to
humanity, that of the gifted artist, who is also a bad man,
dishonest, sponging, fickle, or that of the plain man, who
is good, hard-working and selfless? If there is a choice of
a world of good pictures and bad people or a world of
bad pictures and good people, which would you elect?

Shaw evades the question, as he so often does his own
queries. He changes the subject. In fact, it would seem
that he had changed it once already, for the premise of
the second act is not the same as that of the first. If all
doctors are bunglers, then a discussion between a doctor
and his colleagues as to which life is to be saved becomes
ludicrous, for they are incapable of saving any. Indeed,
on the first act's premise, the life they chose to save would
be the one they would lose and vice versa. But Shaw
shrinks from his own logic. He *believes* in Sir Colenso's
opsonin discovery. The preface leaves no doubt of this. It
is an additional irony, which Shaw himself only half-
foresaw at the time he was writing the preface (several
years after the play), that opsonin was merely another
medical fad, now remembered, if at all, because Shaw
pinned his faith in it when he wrote *The Doctor's
Dilemma*. Other fads succeeded it, and there is still no
cure for tuberculosis—according to the latest bulletins, the
antibiotics are only effecting a temporary improvement.
The old doctor, Sir Patrick, was right, when he said he had
known seven men with cures for tuberculosis and yet people still kept dying of it.

But in any case, the ethical dilemma presented by the
second act is brushed aside in the third. Sir Colenso decides, but not on the basis of which life is worth more to
humanity. He chooses to save Blenkinsop because he has
fallen in love with Dubedat's wife. Other things being
equal, Blenkinsop, the citizen, balancing Dubedat, the

artist, self-interest swings the scale. Dubedat is condemned
to death, at the hands of Bloomfield Bonington. A new
movement of the plot begins, in which Sir Colenso will
get his come-uppance. This starts in the fourth act, where
the artist, by "dying well," embarrasses the doctor who
must witness it. Sir Colenso's fall is complete in the final
scene in the art gallery, where he learns that Jennifer has
remarried. Moreover, his character has deteriorated. Being
a murderer has made Sir Colenso something of a sardonic
humorist. He now stands outside the "eminent physician"
and smiles bitterly on him, as a licensed murderer. He is
a better doctor and a worse man than his colleagues, because he can kill or cure deliberately, while they do it
through inadvertence. The doctor's dilemma appears in a
revised form, as the patient's dilemma: which would you
rather have kill you, the doctor who does it on purpose
or the one who does not know any better? Behind the wit
of the play, in the Chinese box of the plot, there is a
somewhat enigmatic conception of the destiny of the
superior man. Dubedat and Ridgeon, the two supermen
of the cast, combine between them most of the crimes
and vices of humanity. The others, except for Sir Patrick,
are only fools.

Shaw's plays are said to be actor-proof, but this is not
true. This performance demonstrated only that laughs
will come from an audience, no matter what the actors do.
The plays are mined with laughs, and the actors cannot
help detonating them as they stumble through the text.
But the audience, half the time at Shaw revivals, does not
know why it is laughing; underneath its amusement, it is
puzzled and wary. The quicksilver of Shaw's temperament
makes his plays elusive and even dissatisfying, unless the
director and the actors take a firm line with them, as they
did last year with *Misalliance*. It was not altogether Mr.

Strudwick's fault that the part of Sir Colenso appeared to
be a cipher. How is the actor to reconcile the ingenuous
enthusiast of the first act with the diabolical Paracelsus of
the later ones? He will have to find a way to impose his
own authority on the character, to make it behave. Shaw's
characters are often refractory; they step out of themselves
to make speeches, to make a dramatic reversal, or merely
to make a joke. And Shaw himself keeps popping out of
them, like a Jack-in-the-box. In this play, he is in Sir
Patrick Cullen, in Schutzmacher, the Jewish doctor, in
Ridgeon, and in Dubedat. This does not matter in the
smaller roles, but in the case of Dubedat, it presents the
actor with a poser. Is Dubedat a great artist, as the doctors
and his wife are convinced? Or is he a "great artist" in the
same sense that they are "eminent physicians"? That is,
is he a bit of a hoax, not only in his personal dealings, but
in his role of the genius?

Shaw's greatest limitation was that he regarded himself
as a completely rational man—indeed, often, as the only
rational man in a world of fools and lunatics. His opti-
mism, such as it was, was a scientific and rational opti-
mism: he looked forward to a day not when people would
be better (he was too rational to expect that) but when
they would be more sensible, that is, when there would
be more people like himself. He had a diversity of opinions but only one simple idea: equal distribution of
money. He recognized the existence of other problems,
but these problems amused his mind without really en-
gaging it. He stated them wittily as dilemmas or para-
doxes. A dilemma or a paradox is eternal. When Shaw
looked at the cosmos under the aspect of eternity, he was
a pessimist. He saw warring antinomies, doomed to ever-
lasting strife, men against women, youth against age, in-

telligence against stupidity, the few against the many, the artist against the citizen. And the difficulty between them was a failure of communication, that is, of rationality: you could never get a woman to look at things from a man's point of view. But if rationality fails and must fail forever (except in the matter of money), the alternative is despair or a kind of nihilistic relativism, in which everyone is right, from his own point of view, and these points of view are isolated, each revolving on its axis in interplanetary space.

Shaw was personally a generous man, chivalrous, quick with sympathy and the kind of understanding known as feminine. He was always able to put himself in another person's place. In his letters, he appears to know his friends—Chesterton, Mrs. Pat Campbell, Florence Farr, the Irish actress—better than they know themselves. He gives them advice continually, sensitive, wise advice, the advice they would give themselves if they had Shaw's intelligence and clearsightedness. Yet this very clairvoyance becomes a source of despair to him. He sees and they do not. He tells them and they will not listen. It is the same with the public. The tragedy of a rational man is that the world is deaf.

The result of this isolation was that Shaw became a crank. His passion to simplify got the better of him, and he peddled panaceas: equal distribution of money as the sole immediate social remedy, vegetarianism, anti-vivisectionism, anti-vaccinationism, phonetic spelling. He himself came to prescribe like the chorus of physicians in *The Doctor's Dilemma*. "Stimulate the phagocytes," says Sir Ralph Bloomfield Bonington. "The nuciform sac," says Cutler Walpole. "Greengages," cries poor Blenkinsop. "Don't eat meat or take stimulants and you will live to my age," twinkles Bernard Shaw.

He played the barker of his remedies very early in life,
as soon, he says, as his critics convinced him that he would
not get a hearing unless he practiced the art of self-
advertising. In this respect, he was a deliberate charlatan
like Dr. Schutzmacher, with his country practice, who put
up a sign: "Cure Guaranteed." The charlatanism was
only a decoy, but was Shaw himself snared by it? It is hard
to be sure. He called himself a socialist all his life, but
his political infatuations with the dictatorships in the '20s
and '30s make one wonder whether he had privately lost
faith in the single, simple, easily digestible idea to which
he had reduced socialist theory. And did he really think
that he was an improvement, in many ways, on Shakespeare, thanks to a law of progress in art? In the end, did
he believe in anything? Including Bernard Shaw? As an
old man, he grew selfish, and his private sympathies dried
up; he did not like to be bothered. When he died, he left
his house at Ayot St. Lawrence for a museum, but it has
had to be closed down since so few paying visitors came
to see it.

There is something about Shaw that compels one's
admiration and at the same time elicits pity. He was a
world figure, the most gifted and original playwright of
his day, the best English playwright since Congreve. His
plays "entertain." They also provoke thought. But he
ought to have been better. He missed greatness while playing the great man. The sudden deflation of his fame, after
his death, like the air going out of a tire, was both unjust
and inevitable. He was one of those gods of his period,
like the "Copeys" and "Kitties" of the seminar room,
whose function was to disturb and subvert the youth of
the middle classes. But the "educational" side of Shaw is
dated, like health clothing. The sensible, spare, school-
masterish, whiskered figure in knickerbockers no longer

has the power to terrorize with a conundrum or a paradox. His own mystifications misled him. He took his intelligence and common sense for genius, even while he
knew better; indeed, he depreciated genius when he discovered he had what passed for it. "Is this all?" he appears
to say to himself in bewilderment, like Jennifer at the
death of Dubedat. "Is this all there is to it?"

July 1955 London

THE FAMILY TEA PARTY

THE EASE OF GETTING TICKETS, the small size of the theatres, which makes it almost impossible to have a bad seat, the modest price scale, the tea in the interval, the audibility of the actors, all this makes a delightful impression on the American visitor, in comparison with the Broadway stampede. To go to the theatre today is too complex an undertaking for the ordinary New Yorker, whose complaints fill the correspondence columns of the Sunday drama sections in the newspapers: he has been unable, he writes, to buy a ticket four months in advance or he has had to pay scalpers' prices (up to nine pounds a head) or he has been seated behind a pillar or he has been unable to hear a syllable because of the actors' diction or because of the audience's steady coughing or because of acoustical peculiarities due to the overhang of the balconies—correspondents write in, rebutting each other's theories and capping each other's experiences. These correspondents, like all letter-writers, are a minority; the majority has given up quietly and goes to the movies, at second-run houses. Plays and musicals on Broadway are seen by out-of-towners or by New Yorkers, on expense accounts, entertaining out-of-towners; any other members of the audience are movie scouts, agents, and actors who have got tickets through a friend in the cast.

Cut off from its metropolitan public, the Broadway theatre is linked to the Mid and Far West by a sort of air lift; stratoliners from Kansas City ferry in patrons for *Guys and Dolls* and *The Teahouse of the August Moon.* And the former New York theatregoer, a displaced person, may rediscover the lost pleasures of the stage in London's West End. It is a little like rediscovering childhood, a comfy, cosy, snug-as-a-bug story hour, with milky tea and cakes in the middle. The curtain rises on a seaside boarding house, a living room in Surrey, a temporary flat in Mayfair, and everybody settles down to a prolonged recognition scene: "Don't you *know* the type!" cries a woman in the row behind, of an officious female on the stage. The stage mirrors the audience, and the audience mirrors the stage. A general nodding and nudging, in the stalls and dress circle, accompanies the action; the ideal actor, for this theatre, is the one who makes himself instantly recognizable as someone the spectator has met, off the stage.

It is not the worst test, by any means, for acting. English actors, with their professional aplomb and solidity, are a welcome sight to Americans, who have seldom seen anything resembling a flesh-and-blood person on the stage: a fair example of "American style" productions is the Orson Welles *Moby Dick,* where there is only a tormented Caravaggist scene, of dangling ropes and shadows and sweat and staring eyes: toiling amateurism brought to a pitch of frenzy. A rare exception to the run of American performances was Ruth Gordon in *The Matchmaker* at the Haymarket, which was pure virtuosity, like a dazzling vaudeville turn. There are no people anywhere like Miss Gordon's red-wigged Mrs. Levi; and yet she is a whole breathless collection, a heap, a scramble, of people who keep speaking through her uncannily like ventriloquists' dummies, or climbing out of her like circus clowns out of the tiny wheezing old car that drives into the arena and disgorges eight or ten persons, concluding with a midget.

Danny Kaye, at the Palladium, is a possessed creature too, inhabited by foreign voices, accents, echoes, tags. There is somebody or something inside him that tickles him until the tears come and he breaks down altogether into a slumped jelly. His style is more monotonous than Miss Gordon's; he is an image of perpetual collapse, a phonograph running down, a radio-set fading out, while she is a prodigy of control and eternally resurgent energy, as suits the part of the matchmaker, who is never at a loss for a new combination.

Danny Kaye's Palladium show is distinctly an export product. It depends on an intimacy of rapport with the audience, that sense of family that is peculiar to the English stage. *The Matchmaker,* under the title, *The Merchant of Yonkers,* was a failure in New York some years ago. It requires a small house and a certain tolerant patience on the part of the spectators, for Mrs. Levi is a deadly bore, the sort of bore you put up with in the family. The play, an adaptation of an adaptation, is quaint and droll, like a sampler on which a proverbial moral is stitched.

This moralistic embroidery is proffered with a twinkle, by a playwright who celebrates perpetual innocence in all his works. In the Surrey living rooms and Bournemouth parlors of this season's English plays, a more modern outlook is advocated. Lessons in Modern Living are what you get in the West End this season, advice on How to Face the Problems of Our Changing World. To go to the theatre is like sitting in on a session of group-psychiatry.

You learn what to do when you meet a sexual deviant, how to approach an unmanageable child, how to marry off your uncooperative daughter. Whatever the play's plot, the problem underneath is the same; it is a question of cooperation. Somebody is not pulling his oar; somebody is rocking the boat, whether it is the wife in *Uncertain Joy*, the dragon-mother in *Separate Tables*, the over-protective, over-solicitous mother in *The Reluctant Debutante*. And the solution is always the same; what is needed is love and acceptance. Then we can all pull together. This theme crops up in Trojan dress in *Tiger at the Gates*, where it is the intellectuals, in the insensate figure of the poet, who are uncooperative, insisting demoniacally on war while the Big Four, Helen, Ulysses, Paris, Hector, have agreed on peace. One might even say that Ahab in *Moby Dick* is another such obstructive individual, who lives selfishly and grandiosely for his private obsession, the Whale, just as in *The Matchmaker*, the merchant of Yonkers lives meanly for his obsession, money.

But Wilder is dealing with a traditional figure, the Miser, and Melville was dealing with a Force or Will. The difference between the current English outlook and the American can be better seen by comparing two mediocre plays, *The Bad Seed* and *Uncertain Joy*, both of which contain a juvenile delinquent. In the American play, the delinquent is seen as hopelessly evil, a murderer by heredity; in the English play, the child is merely "unfortunate," and the grown-ups who protest his behavior are the ones who are anti-social. Similarly in *The Reluctant Debutante*, similarly in *Separate Tables*—grown-ups, society, the insistence on norms and standards, are shown as evil or ludicrous, and a finger seems to point at the audience: this means You. It is like the searching eye of

Danny Kaye that scans the audience to find out who is not singing, who is spoiling the show.

English audiences seem to respond to this treatment; they feel shaken up and aerated, like plumped sofa cushions after a brisk housecleaning. One senses good resolves in every breast as the house rises to "God Save the Queen." And why not? The message behind these plays is one of optimistic fatalism. You cannot change the world, the playwrights counsel; it has changed, without your permission. The best you can do is accept it with a good grace. You may feel a little puzzled about the direction things are taking, but it is simpler not to ask questions. Just keep in step.

THE WILL AND
TESTAMENT OF IBSEN

GINA. Wasn't that a queer thing to say—that he'd like to
    be a dog?

HEDWIG. I tell you what, Mother. I think he meant some-
    thing else by that.

GINA. What else could he mean?

HEDWIG. Well, I don't know; but it was as though he
    meant something else all the time—and not what
    he said.

This short catechism—from the second act of *The Wild
Duck*—is at first sight only a sort of road sign to the
audience to look out for curves ahead. Hjalmar Ekdal's
wife and daughter are discussing his friend, Gregers, the
meddling fanatic who has inserted himself into the family
speaking a dark language and pressing what he calls the
claim of the ideal. In the scene just before he has expressed the wish to be a dog—an "extraordinarily clever
dog. The kind that goes to the bottom after wild duck
when they dive down and bite fast hold of the weeds and
the tangle down in the mud." Translated out of this
idiom into plain speech, this means that Gregers sees himself as the rescuer of the household which his father (the
hunter) has wounded and sent down into the depths.

These depths, ironically, are located in an attic, where Hjalmar, who plays the flute and has a windy, "artistic" personality, also plays at being a professional photographer and inventor while his wife does the hard work. In the neighboring garret room, behind a curtain, Hjalmar's disgraced, drunken old father, wearing a brown wig and his lieutenant's uniform, plays at being a hunter with an old double-barreled pistol, some barnyard fowls, pigeons, rabbits, and a real wild duck. Father and son "go hunting" in this make-believe forest, which is rather like photographers' scenery. Hedwig, the percipient little girl, who is not Hjalmar's real daughter but the illegitimate child of Gregers' father, is going blind. This blindness is a metaphor for the state of darkened self-deception in which the little family lives. Gregers believes that he has the duty to *open Hjalmar's eyes* to the true facts of his marriage. At the house of Gregers' father, who is also losing his sight, they are drinking Tokay wine and playing Blind Man's Buff.

In short, as Hedwig indicates to her uninstructed mother, the dramatist means something else all the time and not what he says. Everything, Hedwig precociously understands, is symbolic. The real wild duck is the child, Hedwig, who picks up Gregers' "loaded" suggestion and shoots herself. The tragic climax of *The Wild Duck* is brought about, thus, by an act of over-interpretation. Gregers, for once, was speaking literally when he said to the little girl: "But suppose, now, that you of your own free will, sacrificed the wild duck for *his* sake?" But Hedwig, confused and terrified the next morning by her supposed father's harshness (for Hjalmar's eyes have at last been opened), thinks that she has finally grasped Gregers' under-meaning and, presuming that she is the "sacrifice" alluded to, goes into the garret room and puts the pistol to her breast.

This ending, like so many of Ibsen's dramatic finales ("The mill race! The mill race!"), seems a little heavy and strained, like the last crashing chords of movie music. Yet it is utterly just. The child's suggestibility has a semantic grounding. She has been led by the Higher Critics around her to look for the real reality under the surface of language—that is, to schematize her life as she lives it. Gregers, with his "claim of the ideal," Hjalmar, with his talk of "a task in life," are both inveterate schematizers, one a truth-speaker, the other an aesthetician. As his wife says of Hjalmar, "Surely you realize, Mr. Werle, that my husband isn't one of those ordinary photographers." Everything has conspired to make Hedwig distrust the *ordinary* way of looking at things. In a peculiarly sinister scene in the third act, Gregers has been talking to Hedwig about the garret room where the wild duck lives. She tells him that sometimes the whole room and all the things in it seem to her like "the ocean's depths," and then she adds: "But that's so silly."

GREGERS. No, you mustn't say that.
HEDWIG. It is; because it's only an attic.
GREGERS. (*looking hard at her*). Are you so sure of that?
HEDWIG (*astonished*). That it's an attic?
GREGERS. Yes. Do you know that for certain?
(*Hedwig is silent, looking at him with an open mouth.*)

Gregers preaches mysteries. Hjalmar's daily conversation is a flow of oratory. He always speaks of his brown-wigged bald father as "the white-haired old man." And his pretended "purpose in life" is a sort of parody of Gregers' "purpose to live for." Hjalmar too conceives of himself as a savior, the rescuer of his father. "Yes, I will rescue that ship-wrecked man. For he was ship-wrecked when the storm broke loose on him. . . . That pistol there, my friend —the one we use to shoot rabbits with—it has played its part in the tragedy of the House of Ekdal." Again, a flight of metaphors, more disjointed and *ad libitum* in Hjalmar's case, a fact which points to the difference between the two rhetoricians. Hjalmar improvises idly on the instrument of language, but Gregers is in earnest, with his single unifying metaphor, of the duck and the bird dog and the hunter, which he pursues to the fearful end.

The men are poet-idealists; Hedwig is a budding poetess. Gina, the uneducated wife, belongs to the prosy multitude that was patronized earlier in the century by Wordsworth: "A primrose by the river's brim, A yellow primrose was to him. And it was nothing more." "That there blessed wild duck," she exclaims. "The fuss there is over it!" When Gregers, true to his metaphor, speaks of the "swamp vapor" that is morally poisoning the Ekdal household, Gina retorts: "Lord knows there's no smell of swamps here, Mr. Werle; I air the place out every blessed day."

The Wild Duck was written in the middle of Ibsen's career, after *Pillars of Society, A Doll's House, Ghosts, An Enemy of the People* and before the sequence of plays beginning with *Rosmersholm*. Ibsen regarded it as a departure from his earlier work, and it is often taken to be a satiric repudiation of "the Ibsenites" or even of Ibsen himself as a crusading social dramatist. In the figure of Gregers Werle, an ugly man in a countrified gray suit who appears on his mission of truth to rip the veil of illusion from a satisfied household, it is certainly possible to see a cruel self-portrait of the dramatic author who sought to "let in the air" on the stuffy Norwegian community, to expose its hypocrisy and commercial chicanery, its enslavement to a notion of duty and to a sentimen-talized picture of family life. Gregers Werle's harping on the concept of "a true marriage," which shall not be based on lies and concealment, is certainly a mocking echo of the doctrines of *Ghosts* and *A Doll's House*. Moreover, Gregers Werle has been a radical before the opening of the play, and Ibsen, though he was a stock figure of respectability in private life, looked upon himself as a radical, even an anarchist, and throughout his plays, up to the very end, there is a doctrinal insistence on freedom and the necessity of self-realization that today has a some-what period and moralistic flavor, as though the notion of duty, reappearing in the guise of Duty to Oneself, had become, if anything, more puritan, more rigid, more sternly forbidding, than the notion of duty to God or family or bourgeois custom. If Gregers Werle is Ibsen in his tendentious and polemical aspect, then indeed he is a demon that Ibsen is trying to cast out through the exor-cism of this play—a grotesque and half-pathetic demon, in that he will never understand anything concrete, a demon, in fact, of abstraction who bursts into the play with his ugly face and ugly name like some parochial incorrupt-ible Robespierre whose activities are circumscribed by a sad fate to the reform of a single bohemian family. But if Gregers Werle represents the demand for truth in its ulti-mate, implacable form, then the message of the play is, as some critics have said, cynical and nihilistic, since the con-verse of Gregers is a Dr. Relling, a lodger downstairs who believes that lies and illusions are necessary to human survival.

A softer reading of Ibsen's intention suggests that Gregers represents only the eternal interfering busybody, but this reduces the play to a platitude—an object-lesson in what happens when an outsider tries to tell married people how to run their lives. Shaw's opinion was that Gregers is simply a particularly dangerous case of idealism and duty on the rampage, and according to Shaw's thesis Ibsen spent his life doing doughty battle against the joint forces of duty and idealism—the vested interests of the day. But Ibsen was a more divided nature than Shaw allowed for, and the battle was within.

Ibsen is not an attractive personality, and his work has, intermittently, a curious confessional closet-smell, as though he were using his play-writing as a form of psychotherapy. This is especially noticeable in *The Master Builder,* where the hero is Ibsen in a symbolic disguise. The master builder (read sound dramatic craftsman) has first built churches (the early poetic plays), then houses for people to live in (the social dramas), and is finally erecting houses with steeples (the late, symbolic plays). This hero, Master Solness, is very darkly motivated; there has been a fire, years ago, through which, indirectly, he and his wife lost their children, but which, at the same time, permitted him to start on his successful career as a builder and real-estate developer. Now he is obsessed with jealousy of younger men in his profession, and he is suffering from a failure of nerve, which is connected with the fire, perhaps, or with his wife's compulsive sense of duty and her invalidism or with his abandonment of church architecture. The play is strangely thin, more like a scenario with several writers contributing suggestions in a story conference than like a finished play, and throughout its jerky development, there is a sense of something elusive, as though Ibsen, again, like Gregers Werle, meant something else all the time and not what he said. There is the same odd feeling in *Rosmersholm,* which is full of disjointed references, like the talk of an insane person— what are those white horses, really, and what is the mill race, and what is that quest for total innocence, on which the play seems to turn and yet not to turn?

The idea of guilt for some sin of the past, a sin, even, of the fathers, plays a great part in Ibsen. Like many of his characters, he has a secret in his early life—a poor girl whom he got in trouble and left to fend for herself. Hereditary disease, illegitimacy, the death of children haunt the Ibsen world; they are all in *The Wild Duck.* In the early plays, the guilt or the sin is localized; we know what the protagonist has done, in the past, which will spring the trap on him. But in the later plays, starting with *Rosmersholm,* the guilt has become diffuse, and it is no longer clear what is the matter. A kind of corny symbolism replaces the specific fact in the mechanism of the plot—white horses, steeples, trolls, a sailor, a mermaid, and the sea and a ring. And these symbols, which are only vague portents, correspond to a vague ache or yearning in the breasts of the principal characters, who talk about themselves distractedly, as though they were relating their symptoms in a session of group analysis. *Hedda Gabler* is an exception; next to *The Wild Duck,* it is Ibsen's most successful play. Hedda does not discuss herself; the General's daughter is too haughty for that. Instead, she behaves, and the subject of the play is visibly present, as it was in *The Doll's House,* as it still is in *The Wild Duck.* Her suicide at the end is less convincing than her burning of the manuscript, and her burning of the manuscript is less convincing than the transfixing moment in the first act when she pretends to think that the aunt's new hat, lying on the sofa, is the servant's old bonnet. But Ibsen is not very good at making big events happen; he is better at the small shocking event, the psychopathology of everyday life: Hedda and her husband's aunt's hat, Nora, when she nonchalantly pushes off the sewing on her poor widowed friend, Christine, Hjalmar, when he talks himself into letting Hedwig with her half-blind eyes do his retouching for him so that he can go off and play hunter with his father in the attic, Hjalmar cutting his father at the Werle soirée, Hjalmar eating butter obliviously while his hungry daughter watches him. These are the things one knows oneself to be capable of. If the larger gestures are less credible in Ibsen, this is possibly because of his very success in the realistic convention, which implies a norm of behavior on the part of its guilty citizens within their box-like living rooms. The realistic convention requires credibility, that is, a statistical norm; the audience must believe that the people on the stage are more or less like themselves, no worse and no better, in short, that they are ordinary, restrained by cowardice or public opinion from stooping too low or rising too high. The faculty for determining likelihood or credibility becomes more and more highly developed—a sensitized measuring instrument—as a society becomes more homogeneous and parochial and less stratified in terms of class.

But this very ordinariness, this exaction of truth to life, is a limitation on an artist, especially on one with "titanic" ambitions, like Ibsen. And this is where symbolism enters, as a device to deepen or heighten the realistic drama while keeping it within the frame of the three-wall stage. Symbolic thinking was already natural to him, as *Peer Gynt* and *Brand* indicate. Here, however, it was used in the old-fashioned way, to sustain a philosophical argument, that is, to make abstractions concrete and visible, with the text of the play serving as a kind of libretto to the music of the thought behind it. But starting with *Pillars of Society*, Ibsen began to reverse the process —to make the concrete abstract, in the "coffin-ships," whose rotting hulls are supposed to symbolize the whole of Norwegian society. But the temptation of this new, allusive method (the method described by Hedwig in the passage quoted) was that it led to grandiosity and cunning or more precisely, to the kind of schematic thinking exemplified by Gregers Werle, this schematic thinking being really a form of God-identification, in which the symbolist imposes on the concrete, created world his own private design and lays open to question the most primary facts of existence, i.e., whether an attic is "really" an attic or is not in fact a swamp or something else. The allusive, hinting language employed by Gregers is the language of all messianic individuals and interfering, paranoid prophets. And like Hjalmar's sentimental flow of metaphor, it is the language of bad art, art that is really religion or edification. This type of symbolism is often found in sermons and in addresses by college presidents, who liken the institution to a ship, themselves to the pilot at the helm, etc.

Ibsen sees all this in Gregers, and he sees, furthermore, that Gregers is incurable. In his last speech of the play, Gregers has merely shifted metaphors: "GREGERS (*looking in front of him*). In that case, I am glad my destiny is what it is. RELLING. May I ask—what *is* your destiny? GREGERS (*on the point of going*). To be thirteenth at table." This cryptic and portentous remark means something more than it says, evidently—either that the speaker is going to commit suicide or that he sees himself from henceforth as the odd, unassimilable man, the bird of ill omen, and that he finds a mysterious satisfaction in the picture.

Odious, baneful creature. And yet one cannot throw off the feeling that Gregers is something more than a repudiation of an earlier stage in the author's development. As in

The Master Builder, where Solness is fond of likening himself fatly to a troll, there is a sense of confession here which lingers in that last remark and far from rounding off the play leaves it hanging, like an unanswered doubt. The fact is, in any case, that Ibsen, if he did unburden himself of a certain amount of self-dislike through the medium of Gregers, did not follow this up with any reforms. Quite the contrary. In the light of the later plays, this confession appears as a sort of indulgence bought for all future sins. The wild duck in the attic is revived as the carp in the pond of *The Lady from the Sea,* and here it is the *sympathetic* characters who hint that the carp is "really" a symbol of themselves in their brackish village. The pietistic talk of a "task" or a "purpose in life," which has already been heard in *A Doll's House,* is not silenced by the pistol shot in *The Wild Duck*; it breaks out again, irrepressibly, in *Rosmersholm,* in *The Lady from the Sea,* and even in *Hedda Gabler*; once more it is the sympathetic characters who voice the notions of Gregers and Hjalmar and who allegorize themselves as instruments of a hidden Will. The plays grow more grandiose as the symbolic content inflates them, and the scenery changes to cliffs and mountain tops that evoke the painted canvas settings of Hjalmar's photographic studio.

No doubt there is a good deal of bathetic "studio" art in all the great late nineteenth-century writers, with the exception of Tolstoy. It is in Dickens and George Eliot and Dostoevsky, certainly; they paid for being titans and for the power to move a mass audience by a kind of auto-intoxication or self-hypnosis that allowed them to manipulate their emotions like a stage hand cranking out a snowstorm from a machine containing bits of paper. This effect of false snow falling on a dramatic scene is more noticeable in Ibsen than in any of his great coevals, and he left it as his legacy to the American school of play-wrights, to O'Neill and now Tennessee Williams, Arthur Miller, and William Inge. (Shaw, who considered himself indebted to Ibsen, never learned anything from him, for he did not work in the realistic convention, though he may not always have been aware of the fact.) If Ibsen's followers are not better than they are, this may be partly because the master, compared to the great architect-novelists of his period, was only a master builder. The "Freudian" character of his symbols has often been re-marked upon, and perhaps his most important contribu-tion was clinical: he was the first to put a neurotic woman —Hedda, Ellida Wangel, Mrs. Solness, Nora—on the stage.

But his work, viewed as a whole, seems at once repeti-tive and inchoate. Twice, in *Hedda Gabler* and *The Wild Duck,* he created a near-masterpiece. The rest of his career appears as a series of false starts and reverses in an interior conversation that keeps lapsing into reverie. The goal of all Ibsen's heroes and heroines—self-realization—looms throughout his plays like one of his symbolic moun-tain peaks, which the toiling author himself could never reach.

SHEEP IN WOLVES' CLOTHING

THE GOVERNING IDEA of Graham Greene's *The Potting Shed* is satiric. What would happen, the playwright inquires, if a miracle were to occur in the family of a leading rationalist? The answer is easy: consternation. "A miracle in the family is worse than a murder case," says one of the characters gloomily, and that is exactly the predicament. A young boy, it seems, who had hanged himself in the gardener's shed was raised from the dead by prayer. This "proof" of the existence of a deity, naturally, has been an extreme embarrassment to the rationalist family, and every effort has been bent to cover up what occurred. The resurrected youth has been hurriedly sent away to school; the gardener who witnessed the miracle has been pensioned off. The next twenty years have been devoted to living down the divine intervention, as though it were a disgrace. The event is blotted out of the family annals, and the culprit himself, when we meet him—now approaching middle age, ostracized by his free-thinking parents, since the sight of him constitutes an intolerable reminder—has sunk to the bottom of society. That is, he has become a newspaperman, is divorced from his wife, lives in furnished rooms, with only a dog and a fellow newspaperman for companions; when the play opens, he is being treated by a psychiatrist. The treatment is not progressing because the traumatic event in the potting shed has been sheared out of his memory—censored by the rationalist super-ego. As the curtain rises, the old rationalist, now superannuated (his books no longer sell), is dying; the black sheep appears in the family living-room, carrying his faithful dog's leash; his mother fiercely bars him from the death-bed, while refusing to give a reason. Shortly after this, driven back to his rooms in Nottingham, he decides to attempt suicide.

It is a saturnine conception, based on a simple reversal. Something good—a miracle or seeming miracle—is treated as though it were something bad. The rationalist family expels belief from its midst, as a pious family would expel unbelief. The shoe is on the other foot, but it still pinches. Expediency is shown to have played its customary part. The old rationalist suppresses the miracle because he has a proprietary interest in non-belief, just as the Church he has spent his life exposing has a proprietary interest in belief. "Henry was a fraud," his widow admits, wearily, after his funeral.

This fraudulence is rendered poignant by the fact of failure. A shift in fashion has made God popular and Henry unpopular. "Bertrand Russell to lunch," says the visitors' book of twenty years back, and the audience chuckles, as if at a rusty joke. A visitor from another century might ask what was funny about Bertrand Russell, but today's audiences catch on without being told. Bertrand Russell is funny because he "went out" with the cloche hat. Henry Callifer's weakness was his inability to face the truth. In the Callifer home, Jesus was known under the euphemism of "the great Palestinian leader," and Christmas was re-christened "Children's Day." Yet this weakness, these evasions, are almost condoned by the playwright on account of their period quality. If crusading rationalism is "seen through" as a species of quackery, it nevertheless, for Graham Greene, as for Angus Wilson, has its lovable aspect, because it partakes of innocence, of a time before the Fall, which for these modern English writers seems to coincide with the literary discovery of evil (circa 1939). Those darling dodos, poor dears, were not hep to evil; this is the prevailing attitude.

That there were brave men among those old rationalists does not occur to Mr. Greene, all bravery being reserved for the present generation, and, in particular, for Catholics, who have dared to acknowledge God and His corollary, the devil. How much courage this took is debatable, but Mr. Greene is certain that it took a great deal, and his work, from beginning to end, is a parade of venturesomeness, to the accompaniment of a lugubrious prose-music, as of a death march. Nearly every one of Mr. Greene's works features a "daring" notion, verging on blasphemy but redeemed by a sententious piety that seems to leave it to God to judge whether Mr. Greene is not, after all, a better Catholic than the Pope. *The Potting Shed* is no exception. The satire on rationalism, after the first act, yields place to a somewhat maudlin "Catholic" drama, of faith lost and regained. The miracle about which the play centers proves to be no ordinary miracle, such as any saint might have performed, but an unsavory, dubious miracle that was just as well hushed up. The miracle-worker is revealed to be the familiar "bad" priest of Mr. Greene's work, the convert brother of the famous rationalist, in this instance—found drinking himself sodden in a rectory in East Anglia because he has lost God. It was he who raised the dead boy by prayer. "Take what I love best," he said to God, when he came upon the lifeless form in the potting shed, "and let him live." God obliged him, it seemed, by taking away his faith—the thing, of course, he loved best—and restoring the boy to life. (The boy, by the way, had been deprived of *his* faith by his rationalist father; that was why he hanged himself—in despair.)

It is a striking idea, this drastic bargain with God, and typical of Graham Greene's peculiar, sensational Catholicism. The truth is that this is the type of bargain ordinarily compacted with the devil. God does not have the power, at least in Catholic belief, to take faith away; faith can only be lost by the free will of the individual. The devil can take your faith away, if you consent to listen to him. But God would be shocked by the suggestion. If the priest's faith was lost, therefore, it must have been the devil who took it. But who, then, restored the boy's life? It must have been God, since the devil does not have the power to raise the dead. Or perhaps the boy was not dead at all, which was the rationalist view of the matter, and the *appearance* of death was one of the devil's counterfeits. But in that case there was no miracle. God's purpose, moreover, in working miracles, in so far as His purposes can be known to man, is to strengthen faith; a priest in real life who raised the dead by prayer would find his faith fortified. By this standard, the play's miracle is self-defeating; one believer, the priest, is lost from the fold, and no one is converted. Toward the end of the play, it is true, the priest regains his faith. "I left him praying," says the newspaperman, who has regained *his* faith also. But it is not specified how, through what agency, the priest got his faith back; it simply came.

This whole affair of the miracle will not stand any critical testing, including that of orthodoxy. As a Catholic, Graham Greene himself must know (or does he?) that the bargain he describes is diabolical—a version of the Faustian compact. Yet it is just this he trades on, as a playwright;

it is what the audiences eat up. Without the "daring" scene
of the drunken priest, living in peril of damnation, abandoned by God and berated by his housekeeper, the play
would be a failure. With it, the play is a mild success at
the box office and considered very chic, among people who
are not themselves religious but who recognize that religion is *à la mode,* together with psychiatry, while Bertrand Russell is "out."

Here, as in *The Cocktail Party,* another fashionable
success, there appears to be an unholy alliance between
religion and psychiatry. Like Sir Henry Harcourt-Reilly,
Dr. Kreutzer, the therapist of *The Potting Shed,* is presented as a stand-in for God. "I never give a patient up."
He repeats this three times, with an air of profound emphasis, in case the audience might have missed the significance; the analogy is, of course, the behavior of God
toward wayward man. God never gives up either, so long
as the patient is alive. The idea of the Hound of Heaven,
hunting down a soul like a retriever, is present, not only
in the figure of the psychiatrist ("Our Father, methadrine,
hallowed be thy name," says the newspaperman in a blasphemy that is really an inverted prayer), but in the actual
dog, who is heard howling offstage in the potting shed,
on the scent of the buried miracle. The rationalist mother
hates dogs and will not have one in the house; this means
that she hates God and will not have Him in the house
either. If God, like the mythical "George Spelvin," the
actor who doubles in a cast, appears as a psychiatrist and
a dog (the leash is symbolic too), He is also, I think, present
in the young girl who, by playing detective, clears up the
mystery at the center of the play. This mystery seems to
be original sin, as well, which is located in the potting
shed, i.e., the matrix of creation. The dismissed gardener
is called Potter, and perhaps he is God too, sent away by

the rationalists; the allusion seems to be both to the Garden of Eden and to the Potter's hand. In the final lines of the play, the young girl announces that she has had a dream in which she meets a lion on the path to the potting shed who licks her hand when she shows no fear of him—the Lion, presumably, would be Truth, and the young girl, then, the dauntless Sherlock, might be not God, but the Church, God's private eye, like the private agents of *The Cocktail Party.*

The audience, naturally, does not catch all these holy references on the fly—how many people have heard of the Hound of Heaven? But it is aware of a charge of meaning, something portentous in the atmosphere, something sly and suggestive. Religion, hinted at in this manner, becomes a form of obscenity; the same effect is achieved in *The Heart of the Matter,* where a broken rosary in Major Scobie's desk drawer drops into the story, lightly, like contraband, before the reader has been told that the police officer is, in fact, a Catholic. That praying for others can be a rather dangerous activity is intimated in *The Heart of the Matter* also. "Father," prays Major Scobie, injudiciously, at the bed of a sick child, "give her peace. Take my peace for ever but give her peace." God answers Scobie in the manner of a malicious fairy granting the wish of a mortal; He promptly takes the child's life (is this not giving her peace?), and contrives things so that Scobie will be driven to suicide. This God is a very doubtful customer to deal with; in *The End of the Affair,* another rash prayer is answered, to everyone's discomfiture, and God slides into the scene as the supposed illicit lover of a married woman. "I love you," she writes, and how could anyone be expected to guess that she meant Him and not a man?

Religion in Graham Greene has a monotonously bootleg

character; spirited into the plots, it is linked with crime (detectives, the police, murder) and with the vices of drunkenness and tedious adultery. The limp rhythms and flat similes of the writing ("Eternity going on and on, like a long litany on a wet day," "You were in love with Nothing, like a woman," "He's in my lungs like air," "Then God comes back like memory") enhance the sense of squalor, weariness, and self-pity, as if religion were a drug-addiction, a bad habit, to which a small coterie was condemned for life.

God is less like air in the lungs, in Graham Greene, than like a depressing smog that hangs over a modern industrial city. He permeates the novels and plays, with His unfailing presence, and in turn He soaks up the smells of His surroundings—bad cooking and mildew and dirty sheets and stale alcohol. You would not think that this was well calculated to make religion attractive to the general public. But the public is titillated by this deity, created in its own bored image. Religion, for non-believers (and almost everyone, at bottom, is a non-believer), has become the new pornography. If Graham Greene's works, in the aggregate, are tiresome, for all their gift for suspense, and "leave a bad taste in the mouth," this does not detract from their appeal, for pornography has always been tiresome, while catering to an appetite for novelty; it cannot escape this fate.

1956–1958: London

A NEW WORD

AT FIRST GLANCE, the main actors in *Look Back in Anger* appear to be three newspapers and an ironing-board. When the curtain goes up, on a cheap one-room flat, the audience sees a pair of Sunday papers, a cloud of pipe-smoke, and some men's feet and legs protruding; more papers are scattered on the floor, and, off to one side, a woman is silently ironing a shirt. "Why do I do this every Sunday?" exclaims Jimmy Porter, throwing his paper down. "Even the book reviews seem to be the same as last week's. Different books—same reviews." At the rise of the third-act curtain, months later, the two male figures are still enveloped in the Sunday papers, while a woman is silently ironing a shirt. Same scene—different girl. Nothing really changes; nothing can change. That is the horror of Sunday. Jimmy's wife, Alison, a colonel's daughter, has finally left him, but her girl-friend, Helena, has stepped into her shoes. Jimmy, a working-class intellectual, still has a hostage from the ruling class doing the washing and the cooking, and his friend, Cliff, an uneducated Welsh boy, who boards with them, is still looking on. There has been a swap of upper-class women, like the swap of posh newspapers: you put down *The Observer* and pick up *The Sunday Times*—same contents, different make-up. A blonde is replaced by a brunette, and there is a different set of make-up on the dressing-table. The two "class" newspapers, one Liberal, one Tory, are interchangeable, and the mass newspaper, *The News of the World,* is a weekly Psychopathia Sexualis. Other fixtures in the cast of characters are some church bells outside, the unseen landlady downstairs, and a storage-tank in the middle of the flat that represents Jimmy Porter's mother-in-law—in the third act, the new girl at the ironing-board, a home-maker, has put a slip-cover on "Mummy," which does not alter the fact that Mummy is still present, built in to the apartment, as she is built in to English life.

The stagnant boredom of Sundays in a provincial town, with the pubs closed and nothing to do but read the papers, is a travesty of the day of rest—the day which officially belongs to the private person, who is here seen as half an inert object and half a restless phantom staring through the bars of his prison. Nobody can deny that this feeling of being pent-up is characteristic of Sunday, per-haps for the majority of people in Anglo-Saxon countries. Jimmy Porter is still young enough to feel that something *ought* to happen, something a little different, to break the monotony. He believes that Sunday has a duty to be interesting. John Osborne's critics, on the contrary, be-lieve that Jimmy has a duty not to be bored or at least not to show it, not to keep talking about it. As Helena, who marches into the play waving the standard of criticism, tells her friend Alison, Jimmy will have to learn to be-have like everybody else.

"Why can't you be like other people?" This extreme demand, which always rises to the surface in quarrels between married couples, leaps from behind the footlights to confront Jimmy Porter; the play alerts a kind of in-timate antagonism in its audiences, as though audience and hero were a wedded pair, headed straight for the divorce court, recriminations, lawyers, ugly charges. Criticism has picked the play to pieces, as though it were a trumped-up story; imagined discrepancies or improbabilities are pounced on ("The play is not true to life; people do their ironing on Mondays," or "They would have finished reading the papers by four o'clock in the afternoon"). One critic, writing in *The New Republic,* thinks he knows why Jimmy Porter can't be like other people: homosexual tendencies. Nor would Jimmy Porter, if he could reply, change a single feature of his conduct to avoid the drawing of this inference. The play almost asks to be misunderstood, like an infuriated, wounded person; out of bravado, it coldly refuses to justify itself.

Jimmy Porter's boredom is a badge of freedom, and he will not be passive about it; for him, boredom is a positive activity, a proclamation. To be actively, angrily, militantly bored is one of the few forms of protest open to him that do not compromise his independence and honesty. At the same time it is one of the few forms of recreation he can afford; his boredom becomes an instrument on which he plays variations, as he does on his trumpet in the next room. But other people suffer, it is said. He ought not to make other people suffer because *he* is unhappy and out of sorts. No doubt, but this is unfortunately the way unhappy people are; they are driven to distribute the suffering.

For Jimmy Porter, moreover, there is a principle involved. He is determined to stay alive, which means that he must struggle against the soporific substitutes for real life that make up the Sunday program: the steady soft thud of the iron and the regular rustle of newsprint. His friend, Cliff, keeps telling him to shut up; his badgered wife, Alison, only wants peace, a little peace, but that is what Jimmy, or a part of Jimmy, his needling, cruel voice, has decided that she shall not have. He is fighting to keep her awake, to keep himself and his friend awake, as though all three were in the grip of a deathly coma or narcosis that had been spread over all of England by the gases emanating from the press, the clergy, the political parties, the B.B.C. Jimmy Porter's gibes are a therapeutic method designed to keep a few people alive, whether they like it or not, and patterned on the violent procedures used with patients who have taken an overdose of drugs and whose muttered plea, like Alison's, is always to be left alone.

This, at any rate, is what Jimmy thinks he is doing. His voice is a calculated irritant that prevents the other characters from lapsing into torpor. For his own part, he is tired of listening to himself and would be glad to tune in on another station, where something was really happening, where there was a little enthusiasm; he would like, some time, just once, to hear "a warm, thrilling voice cry out Hallelujah!" Instead, there is only the deadly static provided by the Sunday weeklies, the Bishop of Bromley blessing the hydrogen bomb, and the church bells ringing outside. He thinks he would like to listen to a concert of Vaughan Williams's music, but the ironing interferes with the reception, and he irritably shuts the radio off.

"Interference" is what Jimmy detests, whether it comes from the iron, his mother-in-law, his wife's girl-friend, or the church bells. He is morbidly suspicious in any case and morbidly sensitive to "foreign" noises. At the same time, he is unnerved by silence. The only sound he really trusts is the sound of his own voice, which he keeps turned on mechanically, almost absently, as other people keep a phonograph going. This voice is very droll and funny, which is how it placates censure; it is "as good as a show."

But the other characters sometimes plead with Jimmy to be quiet; they cannot "hear themselves think" or read the papers in peace or go on with the ironing because of that voice. And if it stops talking, it moves into the next room and starts blowing on a trumpet. It never runs down and when it seems to flag for a moment, it is only to gather fresh energy, like a phonograph that pauses to let the record turn over. Jimmy demands an undivided attention, even when he is absent, and he is quick to know when no one is listening. "I'm sorry; I wasn't listening properly," says Alison at the beginning of the play. "You bet you weren't listening," he retorts. "Old Porter talks and everyone turns over and goes to sleep. And Mrs. Porter gets 'em going with the first yawn."

Behind all this is more than egotism or a childish insistence on being the center of the stage. Jimmy Porter is a completely isolated person whose profoundest, quickest, most natural instinct is mistrust. This is the automatic, animal wariness of a creature that feels itself surrounded. Solidarity, a working-class virtue, is for him the only virtue that is real; he exacts complete allegiance and fealty from anyone who enters his life. His women appear, so to speak, wearing his colors; both girls, while they *are* his, are seen wearing one of his old shirts over their regular clothes. When Alison is found in a slip, dressing to go out, in the second act, this is proof that she is about to revert, away from him, back to her own kind. Jimmy would make his women into men if he could, *not* because he is a covert homosexual, but because, if they were men, he could trust them. Women do not have that natural quality of solidarity that exists between men, and they have always been suspected by men for precisely this reason; women live in the artificial realm of the social and are adepts at transferring allegiances ("making new friends") and at all the arts of deception and camouflage of which the dressing-table, stage left, is the visible sign. Alison lets Jimmy down at the crucial moment of the play—a thing he finds unthinkable, as does Alison's father, Colonel Redfern. This is followed, appropriately, by another betrayal: Alison's girlfriend, Helena, seizes Jimmy for herself.

The story of *Look Back in Anger* has, from this point of view, a great deal in common with *Hamlet*. Cliff, the working-class Welsh boy, is Jimmy Porter's Horatio, who sticks to him without understanding all the fine points of Jimmy's philosophy; and the scenes Jimmy makes with Alison have the same candid brutality that Hamlet showed to Ophelia. In both cases, the frenzied mockery springs from an expectation of betrayal. Ophelia is felt to be the ally of the corrupt Court with the murderer-king at its head, of her dull brother, Laertes, and her father, that ass Polonius. In *Look Back in Anger,* brother Nigel is Laertes and Alison's mother is cast in the role of Polonius, lurking behind the arras. The fact that Alison is secretly exchanging letters with her means that she is in communication with the enemy, like that other docile daughter, Ophelia. Women cannot be trusted because they do not understand that such an act is treachery; they do it "in all innocence." Apart from anything else, they do not take in the meaning of a declaration of war.

Both Hamlet and Jimmy Porter have declared war on a rotten society; both have been unfitted by a higher education from accepting their normal place in the world. They think too much and criticize too freely. Jimmy, like Hamlet, might have become a species of courtier or social sycophant; that is, he might have "got ahead." Critics complain that he ought to have found a job at a provincial university, instead of torturing himself and his nice wife by running a sweet stall. Hamlet, too, might have settled down to a soft berth in the Court of Denmark, married Ophelia, and waited for the succession. Hamlet's tirades and asides are plainly calculated to disturb and annoy the Court. He too cannot stop talking and, like Jimmy Porter, who practises vaudeville routines, he turns to the players for relief from the "real" world of craft, cunning, and stupidity. Both heroes are naturally histrionic, and in both cases the estrangement, marked by histrionics, is close at moments to insanity. Both have no fixed purpose beyond that of awakening the people around them from their trance of acceptance and obliging them to be conscious of the horror and baseness of the world. Both (though this is clearer in Hamlet's case) suffer from a horrible self-doubt that alternates with wild flashes of conviction, and neither wholly wills the events he himself is causing. Yet neither wants to repent whatever it is that is driving him to destroy everything in sight, and both repel pity. "He wouldn't *let* me pity him," said a young woman, sadly, coming out of *Look Back in Anger*. That is just the concession the play refuses to make; if the audience pitied Jimmy Porter, this would be interference.

The Entertainer is a softer play than *Look Back in Anger*. The enemy here is identified with the "men of Suez" and the right wing generally; this, being a political grievance, is easier for the audience to sympathize with. To be angry about politics is conventional. The Suez crisis is somewhat arbitrarily linked with a family of music-hall performers whose contact with the invasion is so remote, theatrically, that the fact that they have a son "out there," fighting, is only mentioned, like an afterthought, at the end of the third scene. On the surface, this play has far more plot than *Look Back in Anger*: Archie Rice, a down-and-out music-hall comedian, is pursued by bankruptcy and the figure of the Income Tax man; he wants to leave his old, sodden, moronic wife and marry a young girl; his daughter goes to the Trafalgar Square protest meeting against Suez and breaks her engagement; his father dies; his other son and probably his wife are going off to Canada to join some relations, while he is slated for jail. Yet much of this plot is clumsily messengered in, by telegrams, newspaper stories, straight narration, so that it seems a kind of dubious hearsay—the daughter's engagement to someone called "Graham"; the young girl they say Archie wants to marry; even the two deaths. The relations in Canada come to life, if life it can be called in the letter that is read from them describing their TV set and their new Chevrolet Bel-Air. This is enough to tell Archie that he would rather go to jail, and it is enough for the audience to get the picture in a flash. But, with this exception, nothing that occurs on the periphery carries much conviction; the center is Archie Rice, lit by a spot, standing before a curtain gamely doing his act, while beyond him, in the wings, there is only an empty blackness, a void of shadows. Somewhere in that void there is the Man with the Hook—death and taxes.

Jimmy Porter is "as good as a show," and Archie, with his tipped hat and bow tie and gloves and cane and blackened eyebrows, is the grisly show itself. He is the eternal performer who enters before the variety queens and who has to hold the audience or else be jerked off the stage. His function is to keep the show going, no matter what— if a fire breaks out or the bombs start falling or somebody dies. Like Jimmy, Archie cannot stop talking; this is his professional misfortune—the commitment he has made to the management. Silence, for this old pro, is the ultimate terror; he listens intently, head cocked, for the laugh or the patter of applause rising from the darkness of the pit, to assure him that he is still there, in the spotlight, in short that he still exists. If his own voice falters, if he dries up, he is done for; the orchestra will strike up to cover the silence, and the hook will come out to claim him. All the clichés of the stage, of the old trouper who "never missed a performance," take on in this play a quality of sheer horror.

The actor and the soldier have the same mythology; timing, co-ordination, a cool nerve, resourcefulness, are essential to the discipline. A vaudevillian like Archie Rice looks on the stage as a fort he is holding, until relief in the form of the next turn will appear. Before a performance every actor experiences a slight case of battle-nerves, and actors, like soldiers, are superstitious. In *The Entertainer* this equation between the actor and the soldier is instinctively caught and exploited for an effect of tragic pathos. The link with Suez seems strained in terms of stage-plotting, while the characters are merely talking and drinking gin, like other people. But when Archie, in costume, is revealed with a tall nude behind him, like a recruiting poster, who wears the helmet of Britannia and holds a bulldog and a trident, the grotesque relation becomes real. His fading personal fortunes are eerily identified with the fading of the Empire. His personal hollowness echoes the present hollowness of the Empire idea, and the proposed retreat to Canada signifies the shift of power. The old growling bulldog England is represented by Archie's father, an old trouper and veteran who went through the Dardanelles without a scratch and who re-enlists, as it were, when summoned by Archie to save the family's collective life; he dies at his post, performing, and his coffin is draped in the Union Jack. The old man's sacrifice, to save a "no-good, washed-up, tatty show," is a useless expenditure. The silence that Archie fears closes in at the end; it is the death of old England. The actor is finished, and it is the audience's turn to "have a go."

"Don't clap too hard, we're all in a very old building"— this grim antique vaudeville wheeze which is part of Archie's stock of gags evokes another play, written at another crisis of the declining Empire, during the First World War: Shaw's *Heartbreak House*. Shaw's draughty old country house, England, which is run by a mad, drunken sea-captain, has gone down still another step with John Osborne, and become a draughty old vaudeville house at a run-down coastal resort, with an alcoholic comedian introducing a girl-show. Shaw was a man of sixty when he wrote *Heartbreak House,* and Osborne was twenty-eight, last year, when *The Entertainer* was first produced. Both men had received a bitter education in the school of poverty that made the protected assumptions of well-to-do people appear to them as a kind of ludicrous insanity. Shaw's father was a drunkard; Osborne's mother was a barmaid. Shaw got his training for the stage as a speaker at street-corners and socialist meetings; Osborne got his as an actor, often unemployed. Bravado, impatience of cant, and a gift of gab are the product of these experiences. Shaw, to the day of his death, was obsessed with waking people up, rubbing their noses in the raw facts of life, of which they seemed so incredibly ignorant; Osborne is the same, though somewhat more savage, having come from lower down in the social scale. Shaw was, of course, an inveterate entertainer; that was his calamity, like Archie Rice's. And, like Jimmy Porter, he could never give his public a rest, leave them in peace to read the paper; he was always "at" them, telling them their faults, just as he did with his friends. The audience, toward the end, got a little tired of him, and he, no doubt, got a little tired of himself, coming on to do his turn, in his grizzled stage eyebrows and beard. More and more, as he grew older, he had the feeling that he was talking sense and no one was listening.

Throughout both John Osborne's plays there is a longing for a message, a "new word"—for purification, simplification. Personally, like Shaw, he is a vegetarian and does not drink alcohol. Shaw thought he had a message, if he could only get people to hear it. Osborne is in a more radical fix. Shaw could not sell him simplified spelling or an easy way to socialism. There is no new word, and, if there were, nobody would listen. One of Archie Rice's sons is a conscientious objector, but he has no hope of converting anyone and does not try; being a c.o. is his way of being an odd-ball, in a family of odd-balls, and he accepts it for that, as one accepts one's face. Archie Rice's daughter has been giving art lessons to a gang of tough kids in a London Youth Club; she does not expect any good to come of it. Yet she has been moved by the Trafalgar Square meeting to the point where she feels that something *might* happen, something in fact *must* happen, some change or redemption. Hence she comes home and starts trying to redeem Archie. But Archie is way ahead of her— a nice man, friendly, but far beyond recall, off in lunar space, where no new word could reach him. The transparent gauzes and dissolving walls of the stage set explain what has happened to the home the girl has come back to and which she takes for solid. It is a transparent deception; you can see straight through it, out into the blackness. This ectoplasm of a home is inhabited by monologists; nobody listens, as the girl and the old man protest; everyone tells the same story, airs the same objections, like a collection of tired phonographs. The voices are slurred and they forget what they started to say; there was a point to be made, long ago, but it has been forgotten.

Archie, the head of this dissolving household, has been dead a long time and floated off into filmy unreal distances, beyond the pull of gravity, with the spotlight still playing on him, picking him out, like some powerful telescope. Nothing can happen to Archie any more because he is a spook, dead, as he says, behind the eyes. Archie is in eternity, steadily doing his routine, grinding out his grinning patter, like the salt mill that fell into the sea ("You wouldn't think I was sexy to look at me, would you? No, honestly, would you, lady?"). He has heard something once (the "warm, thrilling voice"), an old Negress singing, but he was half-slewed at the time, so that his account of the message is garbled. Now he half-listens to his daughter, politely, warily, trying to get her point of view, that is, to fix the remote point in space where this new sound is coming from. Archie is not always certain when he is onstage and when he is at home; it is all a cover-up anyway. He may be dead, but he is not taken in. The last story he tells, in his final stage appearance, is a story about a little man who finds himself in eternity, in paradise, and when a saint on the welcoming committee asks him what he thinks of it, he looks around the upper regions and answers with a four-letter word. After a moment's consternation, the saint throws his arms around the little man and kisses him. He has been waiting to hear that word ever since he came there—that is, for all eternity.

What is that word, exactly? And what has John Osborne got against Heaven? The answer is very simple. The word is hell (h-e-l-l), and that is what John Osborne has to say about this other-Eden, demi-paradise, the Welfare State, where, as Archie observes ironically, "nobody wants, and nobody goes without, all are provided for." The anger of John Osborne, which has angered so many people, is total and uncompromising; these two plays are nothing more or less than lively descriptions of hell. Those who want to be told what is biting the playwright have only to look around them, at the general fatuity and emptiness which is so much taken for granted that it appears as normal and almost no one hopes or wishes for anything better. A good deal has been made of the fact that Osborne, in an essay published in a volume called *Declaration,* attacked the Queen and the Tories; but the Queen, as admirers of royalty are fond of pointing out, is only a symbol anyway, a symbol of the universal cover-up in which the Tories co-operate, but not the Tories alone. Osborne is no Labour-Party canvasser, offering false teeth and nationalized steel to the masses; the changes which might be effected, under present conditions, by a return of Labour to power would be minute, and Osborne knows this. To have Labour in power would make a tiny difference, a break in the monotony; a *little* reality might filter in. Osborne is a socialist who prefers working-class people to people who have never seen a flat with an outside toilet for the same reason that Shaw did: because, on the whole, they are more real; because, like Candida's father and Eliza Doolittle's father, they are shameless and unregenerate observers of what goes on around them. Sixty or seventy years ago, when Shaw began writing, such a preference appeared less shocking and mystifying than it does today, which itself is a proof that it was time someone spoke out again, plainly, and let the sound of a human voice, now evidently so unfamiliar, rattle the old building.

ODD MAN IN

A TOUCH OF THE POET. EUGENE O'NEILL. HELEN HAYES THEATER.
EPITAPH FOR GEORGE DILLON. JOHN OSBORNE AND ANTHONY CREIGHTON. JOHN GOLDEN THEATER.
DEATHWATCH. JEAN GENÊT. THEATER EAST.

A DRUNKARD, an unemployed actor, and a petty criminal are the non-heroes of these new plays, all written by men of real talent in a mode of defiant honesty that has come to be their professional signature. Each deals with a *mauvais sujet* who is also a painful subject, and each is tense with a lyrical rhetoric of confession and self-exposure that at times amounts to hysteria, embarrassing to the audience, which, not being trained as a priestly confessor, regards the stage revelations as an attack. More and more today, the theater at its most serious is becoming an arena of combat with the audience; arena theater or theater-in-the-round is not just a presentational gimmick but a style of writing that involves the spectator as an unwilling accessory and that works just as well when the proscenium arch is kept.

The non-hero as a disturbing central figure had already been discovered by Chekhov, in the early play, *Ivanov,* now running at the Renata Theatre. Nothing Chekhov did later is as radical as this study. Uncle Vanya is ineffectual and the novelist Trigorin is a middling sensual man, but their non-heroic qualities are seen in a softened and palliated light: "Well, it's only human nature," a neighbor might philosophize of their conduct. This is not true of Ivanov, a very strange man, sallow, nervous, good-looking, sensitive, fond of reading, without evident vices, who is ruining his property and the lives and characters of everyone around him by an inner demoralization. He is married to a tubercular Jewess, whom he once loved and who is now just such a febrile, melancholy invalid as a provincial doctor, like Chekhov, might see regularly on his rounds. Ivanov's family doctor has told him, repeatedly, that his course of conduct is literally killing his wife: the inability to settle down to anything, to stay home for a single evening or put any kind of order into his affairs. Ivanov feels compunction without being able to change. You would think, comments the spectator, that he could be nice to her for a few hours at least, under the circumstances. But no, he cannot. It is off to the town in a buggy —to a vulgar provincial salon that bores him. And yet he is not a villain—only not a hero; Chekhov, a realist, takes pains to show that it would require actual heroism for this restless person to spend a few hours with his ailing wife. Invalids are trying to be with. But just this allowance that Chekhov, as an experienced doctor, makes for Ivanov renders the character highly disturbing to the audience. Is he excusable or isn't he? Or, as the audience keeps arguing during the intermission, is he supposed to be "sympathetic"?

The audience, furthermore, could be reconciled to Ivanov if it were assured that he was the victim of a complex or a typical product of a social environment and hence "determined," an effect of a known cause. But no explanation is forthcoming; it really is not clear why this

man is falling to pieces. All that is plain is that Ivanov
cannot control his actions, that his actions are indeed the
reverse of what he would will them to be. His behavior is
a doom or tic to which he is subject without being altered
in his inner nature. A liberal of emancipated views, he
commits the unforgivable sin, at a climactic point of the
plot, of taunting his sick wife with being Jewish; this sin,
just because it is unforgivable, has been waiting for him all
along, as though it were endowed with consciousness and
had only to bide its time for him to commit it—at the most
unforgivable moment. "Why did you have to say that
then?" the audience, appalled, wants to shriek at him.
"You know the poor woman is dying." But the truth is
that the cry "Jewess!" had to leap out of him at the very
instant when he would least consent to utter it, when, in
other words, it could not be taken back. And having gone
this far, Ivanov goes still further in shamelessness; he lets
her know what the doctor had been keeping from her, the
facts of her condition.

After such knowledge, what forgiveness? Ivanov has
done the unpardonable and yet he is not even a villain.
This position is the very essence of the non-heroic. It is not
the immortal gods that have been offended but Ivanov's
conception of himself as an educated, civilized gentleman
who would not do precisely what he has just done. This
sensitive conception feels pain, and in that very idea there
is naturally something ludicrous. "Forgive me, Nora; that
was unpardonable," says Major Con Melody in *A Touch
of the Poet,* apologizing to his wife for an ugly statement
that "slipped out." Almost immediately, he does it again.
"Deeply moved," he kisses her and then suddenly pushes
her away. "For God's sake, why don't you wash your hair?
It turns my stomach with its stink of onions and stew."
And once more: "Forgive me, Nora." This is Jimmy

Porter, all over, in *Look Back in Anger:* "Darling, I'm sorry. . . . I'm sorry. . . . I mean it." Such jerky, inconsonant behavior, like the twitching of a nerve, is found in all the non-heroes of the modern stage, in James Tyrone of *Long Day's Journey into Night,* Jimmy, Archie Rice of *The Entertainer,* Lefranc, the petty thief of *Deathwatch,* as well as Ivanov, George Dillon, and Con Melody. They carry the unpardonable to its furthest limits, and yet in themselves they do not appear to be sufficient cause for what they do, even though, in fact, they may be directly responsible for the death or destruction of another person: Ivanov for the death of his wife, James Tyrone for the drug-addiction of *his* wife and the near-death of his son, Jimmy for the death of Alison's unborn child, Archie for the death of his father, Lefranc for the murder of Maurice, a harmless seventeen-year-old punk. Their actions do not make them great, even in a criminal sense, because their actions are somehow inexpressive of who they are, and many of these non-heroes require a forgiving woman who claims to "understand."

Of the three new plays, Jean Genêt's *Deathwatch* is the coldest examination of the non-hero, because the scene is laid, not in conventional society where "forgiveness" and "understanding" are readily accorded and have to be (otherwise, there would be no getting on), but in a prison cell, where an inflexible code prevails. The criminal code is one of strict rank: a killer rates highest and a pickpocket or housebreaker is lowest on the scale. Multiple crimes of immense daring (e.g., sensational d light holdups) may be matched against the beauty of a s gle exquisite killing, and other factors, such as the amou t of newspaper publicity, the length and breadth of the manhunt, and the demeanor of the accused when captured, are taken into consideration. These standards, at which the audience laughs, are taken very seriously by the prisoners and the guards, who are concerned with definitions of greatness: which is greater, the Negro called Snowball (never seen onstage), whose crimes include the hold-up of a gold train, or Green Eyes, who has killed a little girl? In reality, the atmosphere of Genêt's prison is remarkably like that of a big-city American high school, with its football and basketball heroes, secret societies, crushes, jealousies, favoritism, and interracial tension. "Snowball is exotic," boasts Lefranc at the beginning, excited because the big Negro has smiled at him in the corridor that morning. Nevertheless, those who laugh at all this are probably being philistines, from Genêt's point of view: they are people who laugh at a poem. "Snowball is black, but he dazzles," says Lefranc, and Green Eyes shines in the cell like a steady burning jewel, quickening in Lefranc, a small-time thief and liar, an impulse to rob him of his glory, that is, to become his equal by committing a murder of his own. He strangles Maurice, Green Eyes's lover, the third occupant of the cell. But he is not "big" enough for his action, which remains a mere inert byproduct of his petty will and thieving ambition. "What am I going to do? Green Eyes, help me," he cries out, and Green Eyes replies, "*I* help you? You disgust me. To rub out a boy who hadn't done a thing. For nothing. For glory. . . . You disgust me." Green Eyes, a natural being, had not wanted his own unnatural crime; it had chosen him, singled him out as he walked down the street with a sprig of lilac in his teeth. God or the devil had presented him with his "glory," a dubious gift, that had caused him much suffering to accept. In the words of society, he has paid for his crime. Lefranc's misunderstanding of all this is what keeps him from belonging, from being accepted in the prison, even by the guards. "You are right. I am really alone," says Lefranc as the curtain falls.

Lefranc, though not an artist in crime, is an artist in words; he has been writing Green Eyes's letters to his wife. "I am the postoffice," he says at one point, recalling Joyce's Shem the Postman. The word-artist is the permanent outsider; even the humblest criminals, like Maurice, will not accept him as one of them. For John Osborne in *Epitaph for George Dillon,* it is the shabby smallness of George Dillon that marks him straight off for an artist. You would know he was some sort of actor or writer (actually, he is both) because of his long rather greasy hair, with the forelock hanging down, hungry, ferret face, sleepy gait, selfishness, and mooching habits; added to this, he is a vegetarian, speaks in an educated voice, and tells lies. No ordinary person could be as awful as George, and he is half-persuaded of this himself. The very word, *actor,* which is what he is, strikes him as derisory and shameful. Toward ordinary people, among whom he is thrown by necessity, his attitude is one of mingled contempt and stark wonder. A brisk, sentimental, lower-middle-class woman, Mrs. Elliot, has brought him home from the office to live with her family because she "believes" in him and his future; to George, her belief is at once grotesque and wonderful. She identifies him, quite illusorily, with her son, who was killed in the war and whose room George moves into as a non-paying boarder. "You stupid-looking bastard," exclaims George violently, as soon as he is left alone with the cherished son's photo.

The saddest part about George—the source of confusion—is that he is not altogether a faker. The play he has been writing improbably gets produced, after it has been edited to suit the popular taste. He becomes, in the end, a success, which was what he and Mrs. Elliot wanted for him, but being a "success" is the ultimate absurd ignominy. "Turned out to be Bernard Shaw, after all, eh?"

says Mrs. Elliot's husband, Percy, contemplating the box office returns; George, in short, has compelled the admiration of "a small, mean little man" by the vulgarity of making good. He has moved, like a clown, from the cliché of failure to the platitude of success, and indeed he is trapped in clichés and platitudes, detected by his ear but beyond the power of his will to escape from, like the hideous furniture—the cocktail cabinet, the "contemporary" chair, the telly, and the painting of ducks in flight ("those blasted birds")—of the Elliot home. George had "hoped, thought he was that mysterious, ridiculous being called an artist"; instead, he finds himself written into a script of his own creation, which has him having to marry the younger Elliot daughter, whom, incredibly, he has got in the family way. "Incredibly," "improbably"—that is the way things happen to George; either he is real to himself and outside events are therefore incredible because they seem to have no connection with him, or vice versa: the events are real and he, amidst them, is the improbability.

It cannot be a coincidence that all three of the current non-heroes are fish out of water—educated men confined with illiterates or the nearest thing to it—and that all three, as if to emphasize their false position, are liars. To the Elliot family (Percy Elliot excepted), George is always a gentleman, that is, a superior order of person entitled to superior consideration. This is only another way of saying that George, to them, is an artist; seen from below, the two appear to be the same thing. In the prison world of *Deathwatch,* such illusions do not exist, and Lefranc's superior education makes him, if anything, suspicious to his cellmates. But in *A Touch of the Poet,* as the title indicates, you again find an artist-gentleman profiting with a bad conscience from the respect of the uncultured. Major Cornelius Melody, late of the Duke of Wellington's

service in the Peninsular War, now a derelict tavernkeeper
in New England, is worshipped and coddled as an aristocrat by his low-born, rheumatic drudge of a wife, who
wears herself out in the inn so that he can keep a thorough-
bred mare in the barn, spout passages of Lord Byron, and
once a year put on his fine red uniform to celebrate at a
drunken dinner the anniversary of the Battle of Talavera.
He and George are really museum-pieces kept in the house
by the lower orders and tenderly brushed and polished;
this is vividly symbolized by O'Neill in the red uniform
of the British Army officer that is brought down from the
trunk ceremonially every July 27 for the ruined Irish
major to posture inside of. But like so many home-pre-
served museum-pieces, the major is of doubtful authenticity. He is not an aristocrat but the son of a new-rich
peasant; his army career was genuine, like the bit of
anguished truth in George, but, by the time the play
opens, Con Melody is nothing but a seamy drunkard living
off the sweaty labor of others, whom he despises for their
smell. The major's excuse is that, again like George, he
has a finer consciousness—a touch of the poet. Moreover,
the protective museum-atmosphere that surrounds him is
a prison, allowing him no freedom to be what he actually
is; it is his wife and daughter who press him to go upstairs
and put on his uniform. The major and George are half-
unwilling actors performing at the request of the pit.
Their lies and semi-truths are bolstered by other lies—the
shock-absorbent cushions of the unlettered. "It was the
liquor talking," says Nora, explaining Con away, even
though everyone else in his establishment knows that Con
means what he says but did not mean to say it . . . exactly.

The notion of a gentleman, above all of a poet-gentle-
man, cuts two ways. If it implies ready, soothing forgive-

ness on the part of the lower orders, it also implies that there are certain things a gentleman cannot do and be forgiven—at any rate by himself. Education and sensitivity are supposed, by those who have them, to constitute some sort of guarantee or safeguard; that, in fact, they do not is the terrible and banal discovery of the non-hero. He cannot, as they say, live with himself afterwards. The shock of hearing himself transgress the limits of what he feels to be civilized conduct is almost too much for Ivanov: he cannot be the person he thought he was. This is what happens to Green Eyes, 22 years old, handsome, and analphabetic, when the lurid crime he commits fastens itself on him like another, strange identity with which he must become reconciled before he can become a god, one of "les grands, les durs." But for the educated semi-gentleman, no other identity, including that of a god, is socially possible. "Live with himself *socially*" is what is meant. Neither Ivanov nor George Dillon nor Con Melody can tolerate his own shameless company.

What recourse is left to them? Ivanov, who is about to be married to a young girl, shoots himself instead. The title of the Osborne play, *Epitaph for George Dillon,* suggests that Mr. Osborne has finally got rid of Dillon, a bad lot. In the last act of the O'Neill play, a shot is heard, and the audience, together with Con's wife and daughter, assumes that he has killed himself. No such luck for him; he has only shot his beautiful mare, the sign of his lying pretensions, and comes into the tavern announcing in a thick peasant brogue that the major is dead—"the late lamented auld liar and lunatic, Major Cornelius Melody, av his Majesty's Seventh Dragoons. . . . He didn't bother shooting himself, since it'd be a mad thing to waste a bullet on a corpse!" This is just theatrics; the part of the

leering peasant is as much of a masquerade as the part of
the major. But it allows the play to stop.

A play without hero or villain has a hard time stopping
or indeed going anywhere. The equivocal character of
the central figure makes the action necessarily repetitious
and irresolute, a seesaw of conflicting motives. Nothing
for these people is *final*. The only play of the current group
that definitively ends is *Deathwatch,* which is the only one
with an uncompromising moral standard: Green Eyes has
stayed aloof from the action, watching, like a *deus ab-
sconditus,* and then steps in to judge Lefranc as though he
were Justice itself. There is nothing more to be said.

The Osborne play, his first, written in collaboration
with Anthony Creighton, has already closed; public opinion did not like it. It was extraordinarily well acted, but
this passed almost unnoticed, and why not? No one can
tell the difference any more. Winsome Helen Hayes, that
brave little body, was "hailed" for a performance in the
O'Neill play that would have caused real uneasiness in a
high school play; bent back, nodding, quavering head,
tottering gait, copious winks, groans, and sly, rheumy
grimaces left the impression that here was a child—plucky
thing too—playing the part of a hobbling crone of forty or
forty-five. It would be better to read the play than to be
obliged to watch her, even though Eric Portman is sometimes very striking as Con Melody. The acting in the
Genêt, done by young people, is quite passable.

THE AMERICAN REALIST
PLAYWRIGHTS

As soon as this title is announced for a lecture or
an article, a question pops up: who are they? Is there, as is
assumed abroad, a school of realists in the American
theatre or is this notion a critical figment? The question
is legitimate and will remain, I hope, in the air long after
I have finished. Nevertheless, for purposes of discussion,
I am going to take for granted that there is such a group,
if not a school, and name its members: Arthur Miller,
Tennessee Williams, William Inge, Paddy Chayevsky, the
Elmer Rice of *Street Scene*. Behind them, casting them in
the shadow, stands the great figure of O'Neill, and opposite them, making them seem more homogeneous, are
writers like George Kelly, Wilder, Odets, Saroyan. Their
counterparts in the novel are Dreiser, Sherwood Anderson,
James T. Farrell, the early Thomas Wolfe—which illustrates, by the way, the backwardness of the theatre in
comparison with the novel. The theatre seems to be
chronically twenty years behind, regardless of realism, as
the relation of Beckett to Joyce, for example, shows. The
theatre feeds on the novel; never vice versa: think of the
hundreds of dramatizations of novels, and then try to
think of a book that was "novelized" from a play. There

is not even a word for it. The only actual case I can call
to mind is *The Other House* by Henry James—a minor
novel he salvaged from a play of his own that failed. To
return to the main subject, one characteristic of American
realism in the theatre is that none of its practitioners cur-
rently—except Chayevsky—wants to call himself a realist.
Tennessee Williams is known to his admirers as a "poetic
realist," while Arthur Miller declares that he is an ex-
ponent of the "social play" and identifies himself with the
Greek playwrights, whom he describes as social playwrights
also. This delusion was dramatized, if that is the word, in
A View from the Bridge.

The fact that hardly a one of these playwrights cares to
be regarded as a realist without some qualifying or mitigat-
ing adjective's being attached to the term invites a definition of realism. What does it mean in common parlance?
I have looked the word "realist" up in the Oxford English
Dictionary. Here is what they say. ". . . In reference to
art and literature, sometimes used as a term of commenda-
tion, when precision and vividness of detail are regarded
as a merit, and sometimes unfavorably contrasted with
idealized description or representation. In recent use it has
often been used with the implication that the details are
of an unpleasant or sordid character." This strikes me as
a very fair account of the historical fate of the notion of
realism, but I shall try to particularize a little, in the hope
of finding out why and how this happened. And I shall
not be condemning realism but only noting what people
seem to think it is.

When we say that a novel or a play is realistic, we
mean, certainly, that it gives a picture of ordinary life. Its
characters will be drawn from the middle class, the lower
middle class, occasionally the working class. You cannot
write realistic drama about upper-class life; at least, no

one ever has. Aristocracy does not lend itself to realistic treatment, but to one or another kind of stylization: romantic drama, romantic comedy, comedy of manners, satire, tragedy. This fact in itself is a realistic criticism of the aristocratic idea, which cannot afford, apparently, to live in the glass house of the realistic stage. Kings and noble men, said Aristotle, are the protagonists of tragedy— not women or slaves. The same is true of nobility of character or intellect. The exceptional man, whether he be Oedipus or King Lear or one of the romantic revolutionary heroes of Hugo or Musset, is fitted to be the protagonist of a tragedy, but just this tragic fitness disqualifies him from taking a leading role in a realist drama. Such figures as Othello or Hernani can never be the subject of realistic treatment, unless it is with the object of deflating them, showing how *ordinary*—petty or squalid— they are. But then the hero is no longer Othello but an impostor posing as Othello. Cut down to size, he is just like everybody else but worse, because he is a fraud into the bargain. This abrupt foreshortening is why realistic treatment of upper-class life always takes the harsh plunge into satire. No man is a hero to his valet, and Beaumarchais' Figaro is the spokesman of social satire—not of realism; his personal and private realism turns his master into a clown. Realism deals with ordinary men and women or, in extreme forms, with sub-ordinary men, men on the level of beasts or of blind conditioned reflexes (*La Bête Humaine, The Hairy Ape*). This tendency is usually identified with naturalism, but I am regarding naturalism as simply a variety of realism.

Realism, historically, is associated with two relatively modern inventions, i.e., with journalism and with photography. "Photographic realism" is a pejorative term, and enemies of realistic literature often dismissed it as "no

more than journalism," implying that journalism was a
sordid, seamy affair—a daily photographic close-up, as it
were, of the clogged pores of society. The author as sheer
observer likened himself to a camera (Dos Passos, Chris-
topher Isherwood, Wright Morris), and insofar as the
realistic novel was vowed to be a reflector of ordinary life,
the newspapers inevitably became a prime source of
material. Newspaper accounts impressed the nineteenth
century with their quality of "stark objectivity," and
newspapers, which appeared every day, seemed to be the
repositories of everydayness and to give a multiple image
of the little tragedies and vicissitudes of daily life. In
America, in the early part of this century, the realistic
novel was a partner of what was called "muck raking"
journalism, and both were linked with populism and
crusades for political reform.

Hence, perhaps, in part, the unsavory associations in
common speech of the word "realistic," even when applied
in nonliterary contexts. Take the phrase "a realistic decision." If someone tells you he is going to make "a realistic decision," you immediately understand that he has
resolved to do something bad. The same with "Realpoli-
tik." A "realistic politics" is a euphemism for a politics of
harsh opportunism; if you hear someone say that it is time
for a government to follow a realistic line, you can inter-
pret this as meaning that it is time for principles to be
abandoned. A politician or a political thinker who calls
himself a political realist is usually boasting that he sees
politics, so to speak, in the raw; he is generally a pro-
claimed cynic and pessimist who makes it his business to
look behind words and fine speeches for the motive. This
motive is always low.

Whatever the field, whenever you hear that a subject is
to be treated "realistically," you expect that its unpleasant

aspects are to be brought forward. So it is with the play and the novel. A delicate play like Turgenev's *A Month in the Country,* though perfectly truthful to life, seems deficient in realism in comparison with the stronger medicine of Gorki's *The Lower Depths.* This is true of Turgenev's novels as well and of such English writers as Mrs. Gaskell. And of the peaceful parts of *War and Peace.* Ordinary life treated in its uneventful aspects tends to turn into an idyl. We think of Turgenev and Mrs. Gaskell almost as pastoral writers, despite the fact that their faithful sketches have nothing in common with the artificial convention of the true pastoral. We suspect that there is something arcadian here—something "unrealistic."

If realism deals with the ordinary man embedded in ordinary life, which for the most part is uneventful, what then is the criterion that makes us forget Turgenev or Mrs. Gaskell when we name off the realists? I think it is this: what we call realism, and particularly dramatic realism, tends to single out the ordinary man at the moment he might get into the newspaper. The criterion, in other words, is drawn from journalism. The ordinary man must become "news" before he qualifies to be the protagonist of a realistic play or novel. The exceptional man is news at all times, but how can the ordinary man get into the paper? By committing a crime. Or, more rarely, by getting involved in a spectacular accident. Since accidents, in general, are barred from the drama, this leaves crime—murder or suicide or embezzlement. And we find that the protagonists of realistic drama, by and large, are the protagonists of newspaper stories—"little men" who have shot their wives or killed themselves in the garage or gone to jail for fraud or embezzlement. Now drama has always had an affinity for crime; long before realism was known, Oedipus and Clytemnestra and Macbeth and

Othello were famous for their deeds of blood. But the crimes of tragedy are the crimes of heroes, while the crimes of realistic drama are the crimes of the nondescript person, the crimes that are, in a sense, all alike. The individual in the realistic drama is regarded as a cog or a statistic; he commits the uniform crime that sociologically he might be expected to commit. That is, supposing that 1,031 bookkeepers in the state of New York are destined to tamper with the accounts, and 304 policemen are destined to shoot their wives, and 1,115 householders to do away with themselves in the garage, each individual bookkeeper, cop, and householder has been holding a ticket in this statistical lottery, like the fourteen Athenian youths and maidens sent off yearly to the Minotaur's labyrinth, and he acquires interest for the realist theatre only when his "number" comes up. To put it as simply as possible, the cop in *Street Scene* commits his crime—wife-murder— without having the moral freedom to choose to commit it, just as Willy Loman in *Death of a Salesman* commits suicide—under sociological pressure. The hero of tragedy, on the contrary, is a morally free being who identifies himself with his crime (i.e., elects it), and this is true even where he is fated, like Oedipus, to commit it and can be said to have no personal choice in the matter. Oedipus both rejects and accepts his deeds, embraces them in free will at last as *his*. It is the same with Othello or Hamlet. The distinction will be clear if you ask yourself what tragedy of Shakespeare is closest to the realistic theatre. The answer, surely, is *Macbeth*. And why? Because of Lady Macbeth. Macbeth really doesn't choose to murder the sleeping Duncan; Lady Macbeth chooses for him; he is like a middle-class husband, nagged on by his ambitious wife, the way the second vice-president of a bank is nagged on by his Mrs. Macbeth, who wants him to become first vice-president. The end of the tragedy, however, reverses all this; Macbeth becomes a hero only late in the drama, when he pushes Lady Macbeth aside and takes all his deeds on himself. Paradoxically, the conspicuous tragic hero is never free *not* to do his deed; he cannot escape it, as Hamlet found. But the mute hero or protagonist of a realistic play is always free, at least seemingly, not to emerge from obscurity and get his picture in the paper. There is always the chance that not he but some other nondescript bookkeeper or policeman will answer the statistical call.

The heroes of realistic plays are clerks, bookkeepers, policemen, housewives, salesmen, schoolteachers, small and middling businessmen. They commit crimes but they cannot be professional criminals (unlike the heroes of Genêt or the characters in *The Beggar's Opera*), for professional criminals, like kings and noble men, are a race apart. The settings of realistic plays are offices, drab dining rooms or living rooms, or the backyard, which might be defined as a place where some grass has once been planted and failed to grow. The backyard is a favorite locus for American realist plays, but no realist play takes place in a garden. Nature is excluded from the realist play, as it has been from the realistic novel. The presence of Nature in Turgenev (and in Chekhov) denotes, as I have suggested, a pastoral intrusion. If a realist play does not take place in the backyard, where Nature has been eroded by clothes-poles, garbage cans, bottled-gas tanks, and so on, it takes place indoors, where the only plant, generally, is a rubber plant. Even with Ibsen, the action is confined to a room or pair of rooms until the late plays like *A Lady from the Sea, The Master Builder, John Gabriel Borkman,* when the realistic style has been abandoned for symbolism and the doors are swung open to the garden, mountains, the sea. Ibsen, however, is an exception to the general rule that the indoor scene must be unattractive: his middle-class Scandinavians own some handsome furniture; Nora's house, like any doll's house, must have been charmingly appointed. But Ibsen is an exception to another rule that seems to govern realistic drama (and the novel too, for that matter)—the rule that it must not be well written. (Thanks to William Archer's wooden translations, his work now falls into line in English.) This rule in America has the force, almost, of a law, one of those iron laws that work from within necessity itself, apparently, and without conscious human aid. Our American realists do not *try* to write badly. Many, like Arthur Miller, strive to write "well," i.e., pretentiously, but like Dreiser in the novel they are cursed with inarticulateness. They "grope." They are, as O'Neill said of himself, "fogbound."

The heroes are petty or colorless; the settings are drab; the language is lame. Thus the ugliness of the form is complete. I am not saying this as a criticism, only observing that when a play or a novel fails to meet these norms, we cease to think of it as realistic. Flaubert, known to be a "stylist," ceases to count for us as a realist, and even in the last century, Matthew Arnold, hailing Tolstoy as a realist, was blinded by categorical thinking—with perhaps a little help from the translations—into calling his novels raw "slices of life," sprawling, formless, and so on. But it is these clichés, in the long run, that have won out. The realistic novel today is more like what Arnold thought Tolstoy was than it is like Tolstoy or any of the early realists. This question of the beauty of form also touches the actor. An actor formerly was supposed to be a good-looking man, with a handsome figure, beautiful movements, and a noble diction. These attributes are no longer necessary for a stage career; indeed, in America they are a positive handicap. A good-looking young man who moves well and speaks well is becoming almost unemployable in American "legit" theatre; his best hope today is to look for work in musical comedy. Or posing for advertisements. On the English stage, where realism until recently never got a foothold, the good-looking actor still rules the roost, but the English actor cannot play American realist parts, while the American actor cannot play Shakespeare or Shaw. A pretty girl in America may still hope to be an actress, though even here there are signs of a change: the heroine of O'Neill's late play, *A Moon for the Misbegotten,* was a freckled giantess five feet eleven inches tall and weighing 180 pounds.

Eisenstein and the Italian neo-realists used people off the street for actors—a logical inference from premises which, being egalitarian and documentary, are essentially hostile to professional élites, including Cossacks, Swiss Guards, and actors. The professional actor in his greasepaint is the antithesis of the pallid man on the street. But film and stage realism are not so democratic in their principles as may at first appear. To begin with, the director and a small corps of professionals—electricians and cameramen—assume absolute power over the masses, i.e., over the untrained actors picked from the crowd; no resistance is encountered, as it would be with professional actors, in molding the human material to the director-dictator's will. And even with stars and all-professional casts, the same tendency is found in the modern realist or neo-realist director. Hence the whispered stories of stars deliberately broken by a director: James Dean and Brigitte Bardot. Similiar stories of brainwashing are heard backstage. This is not surprising if realism, as we now know it, rejects as nonaverage whatever is noble, beautiful, or seemly, whatever is capable of "gesture," whatever in fact is free.

Everything I have been saying up till now can be summed up in a sentence. Realism is a depreciation of the real. It is a gloomy puritan doctrine that has flourished chiefly in puritan countries—America, Ireland, Scandinavia, northern France, nonconformist England—chilly, chilblained countries, where the daily world is ugly and everything is done to keep it so, as if as a punishment for sin. The doctrine is spreading with industrialization, the growth of ugly cities, and the erosion of Nature. It came late to the English stage, long after it had appeared in the novel, because those puritan elements with which it is naturally allied have, up until now, considered the theatre to be wicked.

At the same time, in defense of realism, it must be said that its great enemy has been just that puritan life whose gray color it has taken. The original realists—Ibsen in the theatre, Flaubert in the novel—regarded themselves as "pagans," in opposition to their puritan contemporaries, and adhered to a religion of Beauty or Nature; they dreamed of freedom and hedonistic license (Flaubert) and exalted (Ibsen) the autonomy of the individual will. Much of this "paganism" is still found in O'Casey and in the early O'Neill, a curdled puritan of Irish-American stock. The original realists were half Dionysian aesthetes ("The vine-leaves in his hair") and their heroes and heroines were usually rebels, protesting the drabness and meanness of the common life. Ibsen's characters complain that they are "stifling"; in the airless hypocrisy of the puritan middle-class parlor, people were being poisoned by the dead gas of lies. Hypocrisy is the cardinal sin of the middle class, and the exposure of a lie is at the center of all Ibsen's plots. The strength and passion of realism is its resolve to tell the whole truth; this explains why the realist in his indictment of society avoids the old method of satire with

its delighted exaggeration. The realist drama at its highest
is an implacable exposé. Ibsen rips off the curtain and
shows his audiences to themselves, and there is something
inescapable in the manner of the confrontation, like a case
slowly being built. The pillars of society who sit in the
best seats are, bit by bit, informed that they are rotten and
that the commerce they live on is a commerce of "coffin
ships." The action on the Ibsen stage is too close for comfort to the lives of the audience; only the invisible "fourth
wall" divides them. "This is the way we live now!" Moral
examination, self-examination are practical as a duty, a
protestant stock-taking, in the realist mission hall.

For this, it is essential that the audience accept the
picture as true; it cannot be permitted to feel that it is
watching something "made up" or embellished. Hence
the stripping down of the form and the elimination of
effects that might be recognized as literary. For the first
time too, in the realist drama, the accessories of the action
are described at length by the playwright. The details
must strike home and convince. The audience must be
able to place the furniture, the carpets, the ornaments, the
napery and glassware as "just what these people would
have." This accounts for the importance of the stage set.
Many critics who scornfully dismiss the "boxlike set" of
the realistic drama, with its careful disposition of furniture, do not understand its function. This box is the box
or "coffin" of average middle-class life opened at one end
to reveal the corpse within, looking, as all embalmed
corpses are said to do, "just as if it were alive." Inside the
realist drama, whenever it is genuine and serious, there is
a kind of double illusion, a false bottom: everything appears to be lifelike but this appearance of life is death.
The stage set remains a central element in all true realism;
it cannot be replaced by scrim or platforms. In *A Long*

Day's Journey into Night, surely the greatest realist drama since Ibsen, the family living room, with its central overhead lighting-fixture, is as solid and eternal as oak and as sad as wicker, and O'Neill in the text tells the stage-designer what books must be in the glassed-in bookcase on the left and what books in the other by the entrance. The tenement of Elmer Rice's *Street Scene* (in the opera version) was a magnificent piece of characterization; so was the Bronx living room of Odets' *Awake and Sing*—his sole (and successful) experiment with realism. I can still see the bowl of fruit on the table, slightly to the left of stage center, and hear the Jewish mother interrupting whoever happened to be talking, to say, "Have a piece of fruit." That bowl of fruit, which *was* the Jewish Bronx, remains more memorable as a character than many of the people in the drama. This gift of characterization through props and stage set is shared by Paddy Chayevsky in *Middle of the Night* and by William Inge in *Come Back, Little Sheba,* where an unseen prop or accessory, the housewife's terrible frowsty little dog, is a master-stroke of realist illusionism and, more than that, a kind of ghostly totem. All these plays, incidentally, are stories of death-in-life.

This urgent correspondence with a familiar reality, down to the last circumstantial detail, is what makes realism so gripping, like a trial in court. The dramatist is witnessing or testifying, on an oath never sworn before in a work of art, not to leave out anything and to tell the truth to the best of his ability. And yet the realistic dramatist, beginning with Ibsen, is aware of a missing element. The realist mode seems to generate a dissatisfaction with itself, even in the greatest masters: Tolstoy, for example, came to feel that his novels, up to *Resurrection,* were inconsequential trifling; the vital truth had been left

out. In short, as a novelist, he began to feel like a hypo-
crite. This dissatisfaction with realism was evidently suffered also by Ibsen; halfway through his realist period, you
see him start to look for another dimension. Hardly had
he discovered or invented the new dramatic mode than he
showed signs of being cramped by it; he experienced, if
his plays are an index, that same sense of confinement, of
being stifled, within the walls of realism that his characters
experience within the walls of middle-class life. Something
was missing: air. This is already plain in *The Wild Duck,*
a strange piece of auto-criticism and probably his finest
play; chafing, restless, mordant, he is searching for something else, for a poetic element, which he represents,
finally, in the wild duck itself, a dramatic symbol for that
cherished wild freedom that neither Ibsen nor his characters can maintain, without harming it, in a shut-in space.
But to resort to symbols to make good the missing element
becomes a kind of forcing, like trying to raise a wild bird
in an attic, and the strain of this is felt in *Rosmersholm,*
where symbols play a larger part and are charged with a
more oppressive weight of meaning. In *The Lady from
the Sea, The Master Builder,* and other late plays, the
symbols have broken through the thin fence or framework
of realism; poetry has spread its crippled wings, but the
price has been heavy.

The whole history of dramatic realism is encapsulated
in Ibsen. First, the renunciation of verse and of historical
and philosophical subjects in the interests of prose and the
present time; then the dissatisfaction and the attempt to
restore the lost element through a recourse to symbols;
then, or at the same time, a forcing of the action at the
climaxes to heighten the drama; finally, the renunciation
of realism in favor of a mixed mode or hodgepodge. The
reaching for tragedy at the climaxes is evident in *Hedda*

Gabler and still more so in *Rosmersholm,* where, to me at any rate, the climactic shriek "To the mill race!" is absurdly like a bad film. Many of Ibsen's big moments, even as early as *A Doll's House,* strike me as false and grandiose, that is, precisely, as stagey. Nor is it only in the context of realism that they appear so. It is not just that one objects that people do not act or talk like that—Tolstoy's criticism of King Lear on the heath. If you compare the mill-race scene in *Rosmersholm* with the climax of a Shakespearean tragedy, you will see that the Shakespearean heroes are far less histrionic, more natural and *ordinary;* there is always a stillness at the center of the Shakespearean storm. It is as if the realist, in reaching for tragedy, were punished for his *hubris* by a ludicrous fall into bathos. Tragedy is impossible by definition in the quotidian realist mode, since (quite aside from the question of the hero) tragedy is the exceptional action one of whose signs is beauty.

In America the desire to supply the missing element (usually identified as poetry or "beauty") seems to grow stronger and stronger exactly in proportion to the author's awkwardness with language. The less a playwright can write prose, the more he wishes to write poetry and to raise his plays by their bootstraps to a higher realm. You find these applications of "beauty" in Arthur Miller and Tennessee Williams; they stand out like rouge on a pitted complexion; it is as though the author first wrote the play naturalistically and then gave it a beauty-treatment or face-lift. Before them, O'Neill, who was too honest and too philosophically inclined to be satisfied by a surface solution, kept looking methodically for a way of representing the missing element in dramas that would still be realistic at the core. He experimented with masks (*The Great God Brown*), with the aside and the soliloquy (*Strange Interlude*), with a story and pattern borrowed from Greek classic drama (*Mourning Becomes Electra*). In other words, he imported into the American home or farm the machinery of tragedy. But his purpose was always a greater realism. His use of the aside, for example, was very different from the traditional use of the aside (a kind of nudge to the audience, usually on the part of the villain, to let them in on his true intent or motive); in *Strange Interlude* O'Neill was trying, through the aside, to make available to the realistic drama the discoveries of modern psychology, to represent on the stage the unconscious selves of his characters, at cross-purposes with their conscious selves but just as real if not realer, at least according to the psychoanalysts. He was trying, in short, to give a more complete picture of ordinary people in their daily lives. It was the same with his use of masks in *The Great God Brown;* he was appropriating the mask of Athenian drama, a ritual means of putting a distance between the human actor and the audience, to bring his own audience closer to the inner humanity of his character—the man behind the mask of conformity. The fact that these devices were clumsy is beside the point. O'Neill's sincerity usually involved him in clumsiness. In the end, he came back to the straight realism of his beginnings: *The Long Voyage Home,* the title of his young Caribbean series, could also be the title of the great play of his old age: *A Long Day's Journey into Night.* He has sailed beyond the horizon and back into port; the circle is complete. In this late play, the quest for the missing element, as such, is renounced; poetry is held to be finally unattainable by the author. "I couldn't touch what I tried to tell you just now," says the character who is supposed to be the young O'Neill. "I just stammered. That's the best I'll ever do. I mean, if I live. Well, it will be faithful realism, at least. Stammering is the native eloquence of us fog people." In this brave acknowledgment or advance acceptance of failure, there is something very moving. Moreover, the acceptance of defeat was in fact the signal of a victory. *A Long Day's Journey into Night,* sheer dogged prose from beginning to end, achieves in fact a peculiar poetry, and the relentless amassing of particulars takes on, eventually, some of the crushing force of inexorable logic that we find in Racine or in a Greek play. The weight of circumstance itself becomes a fate or nemesis. This is the closest, probably, that realism can get to tragedy.

The "stammering" of O'Neill was what made his later plays so long, and the stammering, which irritated some audiences, impatient for the next syllable to fall, was a sign of the author's agonized determination to be truthful. If O'Neill succeeded, at last, in deepening the character of his realism, it was because the missing element he strove to represent was not, in the end, "poetry" or "beauty" or "philosophy" (though he sometimes seems to have felt that it was) but simply meaning—the total significance of an action. What he came to conclude, rather wearily, in his last plays was that the total significance of an action lay in the accumulated minutiae of that action and could not be abstracted from it, at least not by him. There was no truth or meaning beyond the event itself; anything more (or less) would be a lie. This pun or tautology, this conundrum, committed him to a cycle of repetition, and memory, the mother of the Muses, became his only muse.

The younger American playwrights—Miller, Williams, Inge, Chayevsky—now all middle-aged, are pledged, like O'Neill, to verisimilitude. They purport to offer a "slice of life," in Tennessee Williams' case a rich, spicy slab of Southern fruitcake, but still a slice of life. The locus of their plays is the American porch or backyard or living room or parlor or bus station, presented as typical, authen-

tic as home-fried potatoes or "real Vermont maple syrup."
This authenticity may be regional, as with Williams and
Paddy Chayevsky (the Jewish upper West side; a Brooklyn
synagogue) or it may claim to be as broad as the nation, as
with Arthur Miller, or somewhere rather central, in between the two, as with William Inge. But in any case, the
promise of these playwrights is to show an ordinary home,
an ordinary group of bus passengers, a typical manufacturer, and so on, and the dramatis personae tend to resemble a small-town, non-blue-ribbon jury: housewife,
lawyer, salesman, chiropractor, working-man, schoolteacher. . . . Though Tennessee Williams' characters are
more exotic, they too are offered as samples to the audience's somewhat voyeuristic eye; when Williams' film,
Baby Doll, was attacked by Cardinal Spellman, the director
(Elia Kazan) defended it on the grounds that it was true to
life that he and Williams had observed, on location, in
Mississippi. If the people in Tennessee Williams were
regarded as products of the author's imagination, his plays
would lose all their interest. There is always a point in
any one of Williams' dramas where recognition gives way
to a feeling of shocked incredulity; this shock technique is
the source of his sensational popularity. But the audience
would not be electrified if it had not been persuaded
earlier that it was witnessing something the author vouched
for as a common, ordinary occurrence in the Deep South.

Unlike the other playwrights, who make a journalistic
claim to neutral recording, Arthur Miller admittedly has
a message. His first-produced play, *All My Sons,* was a
social indictment taken, almost directly, from Ibsen's
Pillars of Society. The coffin ships, rotten, unseaworthy
vessels caulked over to give an appearance of soundness,
become defective airplanes sold to the government by a
corner-cutting manufacturer during the Second World

War; like the coffin ships, the airplanes are a symbol of the inner rottenness of bourgeois society, and the sins of the father, as *almost* in Ibsen, are visited on the son, a pilot who cracks up in the Pacific theatre (in Ibsen, the ship-owner's boy is saved at the last minute from sailing on *The Indian Girl*). The insistence of this symbol and the vagueness or absence of concrete detail express Miller's impatience with the particular and his feeling that his play ought to say "more" than it appears to be saying. Ibsen, even in his later, symbolic works, was always specific about the where, when, and how of his histories (the biographies of his central characters are related with al-most too much circumstantiality), but Miller has always regarded the specific as trivial and has sought, from the very outset, a hollow, reverberant universality. The re-luctance to awaken a specific recognition, for fear that a larger meaning might go unrecognized by the public, grew on Miller with *Death of a Salesman*—a strong and original conception that was enfeebled by its creator's in-sistence on universality and by a too-hortatory excitement, i.e., an eagerness to preach, which is really another form of the same thing. Miller was bent on making his Salesman (as he calls him) a parable of Everyman, exactly as in a clergyman's sermon, so that the drama has only the quality—and something of the canting tone—of an illustra-tive moral example. The thirst for universality becomes even more imperious in *A View from the Bridge,* where the account of a waterfront killing that Miller read in a newspaper is accessorized with Greek architecture, "arche-types," and, from time to time, intoned passages of verse, and Miller announces in a preface that he is not interested in his hero's "psychology." Miller does not understand that you cannot turn a newspaper item about Italian long-shoremen and illegal immigration into a Greek play by adding a chorus and the pediment of a temple. Throughout Miller's long practice as a realist, there is not only a naïve searching for another dimension but an evident hatred of and contempt for reality—as not good enough to make plays out of.

It is natural, therefore, that he should never have any interest in how people talk; his characters all talk the same way—somewhat funereally, through their noses. A live sense of speech differences (think of Shaw's *Pygmalion*) is rare in American playwrights; O'Neill tried to cultivate it ("dat ol davil sea"), but he could never do more than write perfunctory dialect, rather like that of somebody telling a Pat and Mike story or a mountaineer joke. The only American realist with an ear for speech, aside from Chayevsky, whose range is narrow, is Tennessee Williams. He does really hear his characters, especially his female characters; he has studied their speech patterns and, like Professor Higgins, he can tell where they come from; Williams too is the only realist who places his characters in social history. Of all the realists, after O'Neill, he has probably the greatest native gift for the theatre; he is a natural performer and comedian, and it is too bad that he suffers from the inferiority complex that is the curse of the recent American realists—the sense that a play must be bigger than its characters. This is really a social disease— a fear of being underrated—rather than the claustrophobia of the medium itself, which tormented Ibsen and O'Neill. But it goes back to the same source: the depreciation of the real. Real speech, for example, is not good enough for Williams and from time to time he silences his characters to put on a phonograph record of his special poetic long-play prose.

All dramatic realism is somewhat sadistic; an audience is persuaded to watch something that makes it uncomfortable and from which no relief is offered—no laughter, no tears, no purgation. This sadism had a moral justification, so long as there was the question of the exposure of a lie. But Williams is fascinated by the refinements of cruelty, which with him becomes a form of aestheticism, and his plays, far from baring a lie that society is trying to cover up, titillate society like a peepshow. The curtain is ripped off, to disclose, not a drab scene of ordinary life, but a sadistic exhibition of the kind certain rather specialized tourists pay to see in big cities like New Orleans. With Williams, it is always a case of watching some mangy cat on a hot tin roof. The ungratified sexual organ of an old maid, a young wife married to a homosexual, a subnormal poor white farmer is proffered to the audience as a curiosity. The withholding of sexual gratification from a creature or "critter" in heat for three long acts is Williams' central device; other forms of torture to which these poor critters are subjected are hysterectomy and castration. Nobody, not even the SPCA, would argue that it was a good thing to show the prolonged torture of a dumb animal on the stage, even though the torture were only simulated and animals, in the end, would profit from such cases being brought to light. Yet this, on a human level, is Tennessee Williams' realism—a cat, to repeat, on a hot tin roof. And, in a milder version, it is found again in William Inge's *Picnic*. No one could have prophesied, a hundred years ago, that the moral doctrine of realism would narrow to the point of becoming pornography, yet something like that seems to be happening with such realistic novels as *Peyton Place* and the later John O'Hara and with one branch of the realist theatre. Realism seems to be a highly unstable mode, attracted on the one hand to the higher, on the other to the lower elements in the human scale, tending always to proceed toward its opposite, that is, to irreality, tracing a vicious circle from which it can escape only by repudiating itself. Realism, in short, is forever begging the question—the question of reality. To find the ideal realist, you would first have to find reality. And if no dramatist today, except O'Neill, can accept being a realist in its full implications, this is perhaps because of lack of courage. Ibsen and O'Neill, with all their dissatisfaction, produce major works in the full realist vein; the recent realists get discouraged after a single effort. *Street Scene; All My Sons; The Glass Menagerie; Come Back, Little Sheba; Middle of the Night,* perhaps *Awake and Sing* are the only convincing evidence that exists of an American realist school—not counting O'Neill. If I add *Death of a Salesman* and *A Streetcar Named Desire,* it is only because I do not know where else to put them.

DRAPES

CURTAINS. KENNETH TYNAN. ATHENEUM. $7.95.

Is THE title of this collection a pun ("It's curtains for me, pal")? Certainly, Tynan belongs to the school of wits who have been indentured to dramatic criticism: Beerbohm, Benchley, George Jean Nathan, Wolcott Gibbs. A turn-of-the-century example was the American humorist Eugene Field who said of a Claudius in *Hamlet,* "He plays the king as though somebody else were about to play the ace." Compare Tynan on Sir Ralph Richardson in *Macbeth:* ". . . a man long past feeling who had been stumping across the broad stage as if in need of a compass to find the exit." Or of an American "method" actor: ". . . he conforms to that modish acting technique, mistakenly associated with the teachings of Stanislavsky, whereby gesture precedes utterance by at least five seconds." Or—less drawling and japish—on Gielgud in modern dress: "The general aspect of a tight, smart, walking umbrella." The gift of characterizing a performance within a line or two is related to the gift of caricature; it is visual, like a cartoon. The written equivalent of caricature is surely parody, and Tynan, like Beerbohm, like Benchley, like Gibbs, is a facile parodist. He has very funny take-offs

---

This review also appeared in *The Observer* of London.

of Graham Greene, of Beckett, of Teutonic dialogue, of love scenes from English country-house comedy; the best is his parody of Faulkner's *Requiem for a Nun,* done in the style of the stage manager of Wilder's *Our Town:*

"Well, folks, reckon that's about it. End of another day in the city of Jefferson, Yoknapatawpha County, Mississippi. Nothin' much happened. Couple of people got raped, couple more got their teeth kicked in, but way up there these faraway old stars are still doing their old cosmic criss-cross, and there ain't a thing we can do about it. Folks hereabouts get to bed early, those that can still walk. Down behind the morgue a few of the young people are roastin' a nigger over an open fire, but I guess every town has its night owls. . . . Movin' along toward dawn in our town. Pretty soon folks'll start up on that old diurnal round of sufferin' and expiatin' and spoutin' sentences two pages long. . . ."

This double play (the allusion is to baseball) catches two runners on base.

Parody in certain cases (like this one) may be the best criticism, as leaving the room may be the best means of ending an argument. But it is not criticism; it is a kind of quoting. No author can be parodied successfully who has not already committed self-parody. Parody begins where words, in the sense of rational discourse, fail the critic. Rational discourse is not Tynan's strong point. When, for example, he tries to make an intellectual demonstration of the weaknesses of MacLeish's *J. B.* and decides that these are due to the author's failure to take account of "Oriental philosophy," the reader would settle gladly for a simple parody: a Zen *J. B.* by MacLeish is too horribly easy to imagine—that is just the trouble. Like most of the humorists who have written about the theatre, Tynan is less a critic than a performer and mime in his own right; his reviews are excited performances. He can make you see and hear an actor, sometimes a whole play or rather its production; he can spot a defect or a virtue, but he cannot reason or analyze. It is interesting that in a long "probing" piece on Shaw he fails to mention his intelligence. Instead he discovers what he takes to be a telling fact about Shaw, a give-away: "as a public playwright he could not create an artist; Dubedat is a parasite, and Marchbanks is a hollow fraud. . . ." This evidently expects the reader-response "How terrible!" But what public playwright could "create an artist?" Sophocles, Shakespeare, Congreve, Moliere, Wilde, John Osborne??? He suggests, sententiously, that Shaw was "scared to feel," yet there was a generous passion in Shaw that is absent from Tynan, who is most unconvincing when he is most in earnest, when he is writing valentines to Tennessee Williams, worshipping the Berliner Ensemble, exposing Ionesco ("as a serious thinker he is banal").

On his "positive" side, Tynan tends to write advertising copy. "This is an honest performance, true and watchful and ruthless." "The imposture is total and terrifying." "Peter Brook plants us firmly in Mexico." ". . . an artistic credo as stimulating as any in our time"—this of Arthur Miller's preface to *A View from the Bridge*. And of Miller and Tennessee Williams: "the finest two playwrights at present writing in English." "The exciting thing about Mr. Lawler is that he can also construct." This "quotable" manner of praising is sometimes like *Time* magazine, sometimes like *Mademoiselle:* "a select gaggle of alumni that includes Marlon Brando, Julie Harris, Eli Wallach, Marilyn Monroe . . ." He talks of "meaty" dialogue and refers to King Lear as "this huge flawed pyramid of a play." A "punchy" style of writing, packing in the metaphors, to advertise to the customers that it *is* writing.

At his best—on Sir Laurence Olivier, on Vivien Leigh— he is far, far better than these samples, but it is not a case of Homer nodding. In comparison with the average dramatic critic, he is a Angel, as Magwitch might say, but he will not bear comparison with Shaw, with Stark Young, with, today, Nicola Chiaromonte in Italy or Francis Fergusson in America, though it is not fair, probably, to compare him with Fergusson, who is neither a journalist nor a wit—it is like comparing pears to green. The worst I can say of Tynan is that I thought better of him when I began this book than when I finished it. There is too much common coin here or protective coloration; you cannot tell the butterfly from the log. The profiles of and interviews with stars and celebrities—Bea Lillie, Gordon Craig, Tennessee Williams, Cagney, W. C. Fields— are like *New Yorker* profiles or Sunday feature stories: "cute" personality pieces, biography and physical impressions factory-woven with anecdotes. Taken at random from the Bea Lillie piece: "Offstage she leads a fairly intense social life and has arguably slept through more hours of daylight than of dark." The "fairly" and "arguably" are unarguable *New Yorker* profile. We learn in the same paragraph that her "last Christmas present to Noel Coward was a baby alligator." Cute? Such journalism can be produced by automation, with the reader's chuckles built in.

On the opposite façade of Tynan is a somewhat adenoidal spokesman-for-those-under-thirty—didactic and moralizing. His general ideas comprehend a preference for prose theatre over verse theatre, a preference, until recently, for foreign writers over English writers, a belief that the drama should show "respect for ordinary people," and a definition of drama (it shows human beings reduced by ineluctable process to a state of desperation). But these reiterated thoughts (and I cannot find any others except for the insistence that the theatre is a public place) are not so much ideas as crochets, like the crochets of an old person. His wit and humor, moreover, have the middle-aged quality of long-suffering—the classic henpecked humor of the drama reviewer wedded to a seat on the aisle. The drama reviewer in fact is an archetype of the human being reduced by ineluctable process to a state of desperation: a state well defined by Tynan in his remark about *Requiem for a Nun,* which he was seeing for the fourth time. "I begin to understand how Francis Thompson felt when the Hound of Heaven picked up his spoor." Very good.

GENERAL MACBETH

A brilliantly unconventional critic takes a
fresh look at Shakespeare's most "modern"
play—and shows how its hero is the
very model for one kind of organization man.

HE IS a general and has just won a battle; he enters
the scene making a remark about the weather. "So fair
and foul a day I have not seen." On this flat note Macbeth's character tone is set. "Terrible weather we're
having." "The sun can't seem to make up its mind." "Is
it hot/cold/wet enough for you?" A commonplace man
who talks in commonplaces, a golfer, one might guess,
on the Scottish fairways, Macbeth is the only Shakespeare
hero who corresponds to a bourgeois type: a murderous
Babbitt, let us say.

You might argue just the opposite, that Macbeth is over-
imaginative, the prey of visions. It is true that he is im-
pressionable. Banquo, when they come upon the witches,
amuses himself at their expense, like a man of parts idly
chaffing a fortune-teller. Macbeth, though, is deeply impressed. "Thane of Cawdor and King." He thinks this
over aloud. "How can I be Thane of Cawdor when the
Thane of Cawdor is alive?" When this mental stumbling-
block has been cleared away for him (the Thane of Cawdor

has received a death sentence), he turns his thoughts *sotto voce* to the next question. "How can I be king when Duncan is alive?" The answer comes back, "Kill him." It does fleetingly occur to Macbeth, as it would to most people, to leave matters alone and let destiny work it out. "If chance will have me king, why, chance may crown me, without my stir." But this goes against his grain. A reflective man might wonder how fate would spin her plot, as the Virgin Mary wondered after the Angel Gabriel's visit. But Macbeth does not trust to fate, that is, to the unknown, the mystery of things; he trusts only to a known quantity—himself—to put the prophecy into action. In short, he has no faith, which requires imagination. He is literal-minded; that, in a word, is his "tragedy" and his tragedy.

It was not *his* idea, he could plead in self-defense, but the witches', that he should have the throne. *They* said it first. But the witches only voiced a thought that was already in his mind; after all, he was Duncan's cousin and close to the crown. And once the thought has been put into *words,* he is in a scrambling hurry. He cannot wait to get home to tell his wife about the promise; in his excitement, he puts it in a letter, which he sends on ahead, like a businessman briefing an associate on a piece of good news for the firm.

Lady Macbeth—has this been noted?—takes very little stock in the witches. She never pesters her husband, as most wives would, with questions about the Weird Sisters: "What did they say, exactly?" "How did they look?" "Are you sure?" She is less interested in "fate and metaphysical aid" than in the business at hand—how to nerve her husband to do what he wants to do. And later, when Macbeth announces that he is going out to consult the Weird Sisters again, she refrains from comment. As though she were

keeping her opinion—"O proper stuff!"—to herself. Lady
Macbeth is not superstitious. Macbeth is. This makes her
repeatedly impatient with him, for Macbeth, like many
men of his sort, is an old story to his wife. A tale full of
sound and fury signifying nothing. Her contempt for him
perhaps extends even to his ambition. "Wouldst not play
false, And yet wouldst wrongly win." As though to say,
"All right, if that's what you want, have the courage to
get it." Lady Macbeth does not so much give the impression of coveting the crown herself as of being weary of
watching Macbeth covet it. Macbeth, by the way, is surely
her second husband (she has "given suck" and Macbeth
"has no children"), and either her first husband was a
better man than he, which galls her, or he was just another
general, another superstitious golfer, which would gall
her too.

Superstition here is the opposite of reason on the one
hand and of imagination on the other. Macbeth is credu-
lous, in contrast to Lady Macbeth, to Banquo, and, later, to
Malcolm, who sets the audience an example of the right
way by mistrusting Macduff until he has submitted him to
an empirical test. Believing and knowing are paired in
Malcolm's mind; what he *knows* he believes. Macbeth's
eagerness to believe is the companion of his lack of faith.
If all works out right for him in this world, Macbeth says,
he can skip the next ("We'ld jump the life to come").
Superstition whispers when true religion has been silenced,
and Macbeth becomes the butt of his own know-nothing
materialism incarnate in the jeering witches on the heath.

As in his first interview with them he is too quick to act
literally on a dark saying, in the second he is too easily
reassured. He will not be conquered till "Great Birnam
Wood to High Dunsinane shall come against him."

"Why, that can never happen!" he cries out in immediate relief, his brow clearing.

It never enters his mind to examine the saying more closely, test it, so to speak, for a double bottom, as was common in those days (Banquo even points this out to him) with prophetic utterances, which were known to be ambiguous and tricky. Any child knew that a prophecy often meant the reverse of what it seemed to say, and any man of imagination would ask himself how Birnam Wood *might* come to Dunsinane and take measures to prevent it, as King Laius took measures to prevent his own death by arranging to have the baby Oedipus killed. If Macbeth had thought it out, he could have had Birnam Wood chopped down and burned on the spot and the ashes dumped into the sea. True, the prophecy might still have turned against him (since destiny cannot be avoided and the appointment will be kept at Samarra), but that would have been another story, another tragedy, the tragedy of a clever man not clever enough to circumvent fate. Macbeth is not clever; he is taken in by surfaces, by appearance. He cannot think beyond the usual course of things. As with "No man of woman born." All men, he says to himself, sagely, are born of women; Malcolm and Macduff are men; therefore I am safe. This logic leaves out of account the extraordinary: the man brought into the world by Caesarean section. In the same way, it leaves out of account the supernatural—the very forces he is trafficking with. He might be overcome by an angel or a demon, as well as by Macduff.

Who Knows Remorse?

Yet this pedestrian general sees ghosts and imaginary daggers in the air. Lady Macbeth does not, and this tendency in her husband grates on her nerves; she is sick of his terrors and fancies. A practical woman, Lady Macbeth, more a partner than a wife, though Macbeth treats her with a trite domestic fondness—"Love," "Dearest love," "Dearest chuck," "Sweet remembrancer." These endearments, this middle-aged, middle-class cuddliness, as though he called her "Honey-bunch" or "Sweetheart," as well as the obligatory "Dear," are a master stroke of Shakespeare's and perfectly in keeping with the prosing about the weather, the heavy credulousness.

Naturally Macbeth is dominated by his wife. He is old Iron Pants in the field (as she bitterly reminds him), but at home she has to wear the pants; she has to unsex herself. No "chucks" or "dearests" escape her tightened lips, and yet she is more feeling, more human at bottom than Macbeth. She thinks of her father when she sees the old King asleep, and this natural thought will not let her kill him. Macbeth has to do it, just as the quailing husband of any modern virago is sent down to the basement to kill a rat or drown a set of kittens. An image of her father, irrelevant to her purpose, softens this monster woman; sleepwalking, she thinks of Lady Macduff. "The Thane of Fife had a wife. Where is she now?" Stronger than Macbeth, less suggestible, she is nevertheless imaginative, where he is not. She does not see ghosts and daggers; when she sleepwalks, it is simple reality that haunts her—the crime relived. "Who would have thought the old man to have had so much blood in him?" Over and over, the details of the crime repeat themselves on the screen of her consciousness. This nightly reliving is not penitence but more terrible—remorse, the agenbite of the restless deed. Lady Macbeth's uncontrollable imagination drives her to put herself in the place of others—the wife of the Thane of Fife—and to recognize a kinship between all human kind: the pathos of old age in Duncan makes her think, "Why, he might be my father!" This sense of a natural bond among men opens her to contrition—sorrowing with. To ask whether, waking, she is "sorry" for what she has done is impertinent. She lives with it and it kills her.

Macbeth has absolutely no feeling for others, except envy, a common middle-class trait. He *envies* the murdered Duncan his rest, which is a strange way of looking at your victim. What he suffers on his own account after the crimes is simple panic. He is never contrite or remorseful; it is not the deed but a shadow of it, Banquo's spook, that appears to him. The "scruples" that agitate him before Duncan's murder are mere echoes of conventional opinion, of what might be *said* about his deed: that Duncan was his king, his cousin, and a guest under his roof. "I have bought golden opinions," he says to himself (note the verb), "from all sorts of people"; now these people may ask for their opinions back if they suspect him of the murder. It is like a business firm's being reluctant to part with its "good will"—an asset. The fact that Duncan was such a good king bothers him, and why? Because there will be universal grief at his death. But his chief "scruple" is even simpler. "If we should fail?" he says timidly to Lady Macbeth. Sweet chuck tells him that they will not. Yet once she has ceased to be effectual as a partner, Dearest love is an embarrassment. He has no time for her; she should have died hereafter. That is, when he was not so busy. Again the general is speaking.

The idea of Macbeth as a conscience-tormented man is a platitude as false as Macbeth himself. Macbeth has no conscience. His main concern throughout the play is that most selfish of all concerns: to get a good night's sleep. His invocation to sleep, while heartfelt, is perfectly conventional; sleep builds you up, enables you to start the day fresh. Thus the virtue of having a good conscience is seen by him in terms of bodily hygiene, as if it were a Simmons mattress or an electric blanket. Lady Macbeth shares these preoccupations. When he tells her he is going to see the witches, she remarks that he needs sleep.

A Woman Unsexed

Her wifely concern is mechanical and far from real solicitude. She is aware of Macbeth; she *knows* him (he does not know her at all, apparently), but she regards him coldly as a thing, a tool that must be oiled and polished. His soul-states do not interest her; her attention is narrowed on his morale, his public conduct, the shifting expressions of his face. But in a sense she is right, for there is nothing to Macbeth but fear and ambition, both of which he tries to hide, except from her. This naturally gives her a poor opinion of the inner man.

Why is it, though, that Lady Macbeth seems to us a monster while Macbeth does not? Partly because she is a woman and has "unsexed" herself, which makes her a monster by definition. Also because the very prospect of murder quickens an hysterical excitement in her, like the discovery of some object in a shop—a set of emeralds or a sable stole—which Macbeth can give her and which will be an "outlet" for all the repressed desires he cannot satisfy. She behaves as though Macbeth, through his weakness, will deprive her of self-realization; the unimpeded exercise of her will is the voluptuous end she seeks. That is why she makes naught of scruples, as inner brakes on her throbbing engines. Unlike Macbeth, she does not pretend to harbor a conscience, though this, on her part, by a curious turn, *is* a pretense, as the sleepwalking scene reveals. After the first crime, her will subsides, spent; the devil has brought her to climax and left her.

Macbeth is not a monster, like Richard III or Iago or

Iachimo, though in the catalogue he might go for one because of the blackness of his deeds. But his deeds are only the wishes and fears of the average, undistinguished man translated halfheartedly into action. Pure evil is a kind of transcendence that he does not aspire to. He only wants to be king and sleep the sleep of the just, undisturbed. He could never have been a good man, even if he had not met the witches; hence we cannot see him as a devil incarnate, for the devil is a fallen angel. Macbeth does not fall; if anything, he somewhat improves as the result of his career of crime. He throws off his dependency and thus achieves the "greatness" he mistakenly sought in worldly symbols.

The isolation of Macbeth, which is at once a punishment and a tragic dignity or honor, takes place by stages and by deliberate choice; it begins when he does not tell Lady Macbeth that he has decided to kill Banquo and reaches its height in the final action. Up to this time, though he has cut himself off from all human contacts, he is relying on the witches as a substitute. When he first hears the news that Macduff is not "of woman born," he is unmanned; everything he trusted (the literal word) has betrayed him, and he screams in terror, "I'll not fight with thee!" But Macduff's taunts make a man of him; he cannot die like this, shamed. His death is his first act of courage, though even here he has had to be pricked to it by mockery, Lady Macbeth's old spur. Nevertheless, weaned by his very crimes from dependency, nursed in a tyrant's solitude, he meets death on his own, without metaphysical aid. "Lay on, Macduff."

The Trepidant Executive

What is modern and bourgeois in Macbeth's character is his wholly *social* outlook. He has no feeling for others, and yet until the end he is a vicarious creature, existing in his own eyes through others, through what they may say of him, through what they tell him or promise him. This paradox is typical of the social being—at once a wolf out for himself and a sheep. Macbeth, moreover, is an expert buck-passer; he sees how others can be used. It is he, not Lady Macbeth, who thinks of smearing the drunken chamberlains with blood, so that they shall be caught "red-handed" the next morning when Duncan's murder is discovered. At this idea he brightens; suddenly, he sees his way clear. It is the moment when at last he decides. The eternal executive, ready to fix responsibility on a subordinate, has seen the deed finally take a *recognizable* form. Now he can do it. And the crackerjack thought of killing the grooms afterwards (dead men tell no tales—old adage) is again purely his own on-the-spot inspiration; no credit to Lady Macbeth.

It is the sort of thought that would have come to Claudius in *Hamlet,* another trepidant executive. Indeed, Macbeth is more like Claudius than like any other character in Shakespeare. Both are doting husbands; both rose to power by betraying their superior's trust; both are easily frightened and have difficulty saying their prayers. Macbeth's "Amen" sticks in his throat, he complains, and Claudius, on his knees, sighs that he cannot make what priests call a "good act of contrition." The desire to say his prayers like any pew-holder, quite regardless of his horrible crime, is merely a longing for respectability. Macbeth "repents" killing the grooms, but this is strictly for public consumption. "O, yet I do repent me of my fury, That I did kill them." In fact, it is the one deed he does *not* repent (*i.e.,* doubt the wisdom of) either before or after. This hypocritical self-accusation, which is his sidelong way of announcing the embarrassing fact that he has just done away with the grooms, and his simulated grief at Duncan's murder ("All is but toys; renown and grace is dead; The wine of life is drawn," etc.) are his basest moments in the play, as well as his boldest; here is nearly a magnificent monster.

The dramatic effect, too, is one of great boldness on Shakespeare's part. Macbeth is speaking pure Shakespearean poetry, but in his mouth, since we know he is lying, it turns into facile verse, Shakespearean poetry parodied. The same with "Here lay Duncan, his silver skin lac'd with his golden blood. . . ." If the image were given to Macduff, it would be uncontaminated poetry; from Macbeth it is "proper stuff"—fustian. This opens the perilous question of sincerity in the arts: is a line of verse altered for us by the sincerity of the poet (or speaker)? In short, is poetry relative to the circumstances or absolute? Or, more particularly, are Macbeth's soliloquies poetry, which they sound like, or something else? Did Shakespeare intend to make Macbeth a poet, like Hamlet, Lear, and Othello? In that case, how can Macbeth be an unimaginative mediocrity? My opinion is that Macbeth's soliloquies are not poetry but rhetoric. They are tirades. That is, they do not trace any pensive motion of the soul or heart but are a volley of words discharged. Macbeth is neither thinking nor feeling aloud; he is declaiming. Like so many unfeeling men, he has a facile emotionalism, which he turns on and off. Not that his fear is insincere, but his loss of control provides him with an excuse for histrionics.

These gibberings exasperate Lady Macbeth. "What do you mean?" she says coldly after she has listened to a short harangue on "Methought I heard a voice cry 'Sleep no more.'" It is an allowable question—what *does* he mean? And his funeral oration on *her,* if she could have heard it, would have brought her back to life to protest. "She should have died hereafter"—fine, that was the real Mac-

beth. But then, as if conscious of the proprieties, he at
once begins on a series of bromides ("Tomorrow and
tomorrow . . .") that he seems to have had ready to hand
for the occasion like a black mourning suit. All Macbeth's
soliloquies have that ready-to-hand, if not hand-me-down,
air, which is perhaps why they are given to school children
to memorize, often with the result of making them hate
Shakespeare. What children resent in these soliloquies is
precisely their sententiousness—the sound they have of
being already memorized from a copybook.

Macbeth's speeches often recall the Player's speech in
Hamlet—Shakespeare's example of how-not-to-do-it. He
tears a passion to tatters. He has a rather Senecan rhetoric,
the fustian of the time; in the dagger speech, for example,
he works in Hecate, Tarquin, and the wolf—recherché
embellishment for a man who is about to commit a real
murder. His taste for hyperbole goes with a habit of
euphuism, as when he calls the sea "the green one." And
what of the remarkable line just preceding, "The multitudinous seas incarnadine," with its onomatopoeia of the
crested waves rising in the t's and d's of "multitudinous"
and subsiding in the long swell of the verb? This is sometimes cited as an example of pure poetry, which it would
be in an anthology of isolated lines, but in the context,
dramatically, it is bombast, a kind of stuffing or padding.

The play between poetry and rhetoric, the *conversion*
of poetry to rhetoric, is subtle and horrible in *Macbeth,*
being itself a subversive process or treasonous manipulation. The suggestion seems to be that poetry used for an
ulterior purpose (as Macbeth uses it) turns into rhetoric.
Macbeth is the perfect utilitarian. If an explanation is
needed, you might say he learned to *use* words through
long practice in haranguing his troops, whipping them and

himself into battle frenzy. Up to recent times a fighting general, like a football coach, was an orator.

But it must be noted that it is not only Macbeth who rants. Nor is it only Macbeth who talks about the weather. The play is stormy with atmosphere—the screaming and shrieking of owls, the howling of winds. Nature herself is ranting, like the witches, and Night, black Hecate, is queen of the scene. Bats are flitting about; ravens and crows are hoarse; the house-martin's nests on the battlements of Macbeth's castle give a misleading promise of peace and gentle domesticity. "It will be rain tonight," say Banquo simply, looking at the sky (note the difference between this and Macbeth's pompous generality), and the First Murderer growls at him, striking, "Let it come down." The disorder of Nature, as so often in Shakespeare, presages and reflects the disorder of the body politic. Guilty Macbeth cannot sleep, but the night of Duncan's murder, the whole house, as if guilty too, is restless; Malcolm and Donalbain talk and laugh in their sleep; the drunken porter, roused, plays that he is gatekeeper of hell.

Nature Two-Sided

Indeed, the whole action takes place in a kind of hell and is pitched to the demons' shriek of hyperbole. This would appear to be a peculiar setting for a study of the commonplace. But only at first sight. The fact that an ordinary philistine like Macbeth goes on the rampage and commits a series of murders is a sign that human nature, like Nature, is capable of any mischief if left to its "natural" self. The witches, unnatural beings, are Nature spirits, stirring their snake-filet and owl's wing, newt's eye and frog toe in a camp stew: earthy ingredients boil down to an unearthly broth. It is the same with the man Macbeth. Ordinary ambition, fear, and a kind of stupidity make a deadly combination. Macbeth, a self-made king, is not kingly, but simply the original Adam, the social animal, and Lady Macbeth is Mother Eve.

There is no play of Shakespeare's (I think) that contains the words *Nature* and *natural* so many times, and the word *Nature* within the same speech can mean first something good and then something evil, as though it were a pun. Nature is two-sided, double-talking, like the witches. "Fair is foul and foul is fair," they cry, and Macbeth enters the play unconsciously echoing them, for he is never original but chock-full of the "milk of human kindness," which does not mean kindness in the modern sense but simply human "nature," human kind. The play is about Nature, and its blind echo, human nature.

Macbeth, in short, shows life in the cave. Without religion, animism rules the outer world, and without faith, the human soul is beset by hobgoblins. This at any rate was Shakespeare's opinion, to which modern history, with the return of the irrational in the Fascist nightmare and its new specters of Communism, Socialism, etc., lends support. It is a troubling thought that Macbeth, of all Shakespeare's characters, should seem the most "modern," the only one you could transpose into contemporary battle dress or a sport shirt and slacks.

The contemporary Macbeth, a churchgoer, is indifferent to religion, to the categorical imperative or any group of principles that may be held to stand above and govern human behavior. Like the old Macbeth, he'd gladly skip the future life, not only for himself but for the rest of humanity. He listens to soothsayers and prophets and has been out on the heath and in the desert, interfering with Nature on a grand scale, lest his rivals for power get ahead of him and Banquo's stock, instead of his, inherit the earth—why this should have seemed such a catastrophe to the real Macbeth, who had no children, is a mystery the scholars never mention. Unloosing the potential destructiveness that was always there in Nature, as Shakespeare understood, the contemporary Macbeth, like the old one, is not even a monster, though he may breed monsters, thanks to his activities on the heath; he is timorous, unimaginative, and the prayer he would like to say most fervently is simply "Amen."